_A.J._

A.J.

By A. J. Foyt

With William Neely

Times
BOOKS

Published by TIMES BOOKS, a division of
The New York Times Book Co., Inc.
Three Park Avenue, New York, N.Y. 10016

Published simultaneously in Canada by
Fitzhenry & Whiteside, Ltd., Toronto

Library of Congress Cataloging in Publication Data

Foyt, A. J., 1935-
  A.J.

    1. Foyt, A. J., 1935-   2. Automobile racing
drivers—United States—Biography.   I. Neely, William.
II. Title.   III. Title: AJ.
GV1032.F66A33   1983   796.7'2'0924 [B]   83-45036
ISBN 0-8129-1077-X

Book designed by Doris Borowsky

Manufactured in the United States of America
83 84 85 86 87 5 4 3 2 1

To Mother and Daddy,
who will always
be with me

—A. J. Foyt

Contents

Illustrations follow page 116.

Foreword

I met A. J. Foyt in 1963, and, over the years, I've watched him methodically break every automobile-racing record in the books. I mean, he has actually done everything he set out to do. And he's done it with the flair of a Manolete and a Dr. J. and a Babe Ruth all wrapped in one. Along the way, we wrecked a few motel rooms and rental cars. Just to keep things in their proper perspective.

The day I first met A.J., I was in the garage area at the Indianapolis Motor Speedway. It was raining, and a bunch of us were sitting in a tiny frame garage looking at his pearl-white Offenhauser Indy race car and swapping race stories. I handled racing public relations for the Goodyear Tire & Rubber Company—that's the way they like to see it written, with the ampersand and spelled out.

Over a millennium or two, Firestone—I've never been sure how they like to see it written; all I know is that they were the enemy in those days—had built up a dynasty that everybody considered invulnerable. They had supplied racing tires for each Indianapolis winner since 1920. It had never been written in the rules that Firestone *had* to supply all the tires for the Indianapolis 500; it was just taken for granted. Norman Rockwell and Steven Donahos did covers for *The Saturday Evening Post*. Firestone supplied race tires for the Indiananapolis 500. Simple.

Wrong.

A.J. got mad at Firestone because they had given a certain tire to Smokey Yunick to use on his lightweight roadster and they wouldn't give the same tire to A.J. His car, he claimed, was as light as if not lighter than Smokey's, so he, too, should have the new tires. But they wouldn't budge. So A.J. went to the nearest phone and called Goodyear in Akron.

"Listen," he said, "these sumbitches have been building these skinny, cast-iron racing tires for so long that they don't know a goddamn thing anymore. I want y'all to come on down here and talk to me and some of the other guys. And, oh, yeah, bring some of those wide race tires with you."

A big order. But I'll be damned if it didn't get Goodyear into Indianapolis racing, and within ten years Firestone was gone. Lock, stock and barrel gone. It would be roughly like taking Cathy Rigby away from the Stayfree maxi-pad commercials, or broken-down athletes from Lite beer.

There has never been a question in my mind that A. J. Foyt didn't single-handedly put Goodyear into Indy racing—and put them there so firmly that nobody could have competed against them. Oh, they had the product; nobody could argue that, least of all Firestone. But Foyt's very name was magic. You talk about people listening when somebody talked! Well, all A.J. had to do was stop in the pits and there was a crowd around him, hanging on his every word.

He walked into the garage that rainy morning wearing his most

charming manner, and he didn't say a word. Not "Good morning" or "Shitty weather." Nothing. He just flashed the smile that
has been known to paralyze full-grown women at ten paces. He
walked to the back of the garage and leaned against the workbench. "Where do we start?" he said.

Where do you start to move mountains? Well, first of all, you
listen to the guy who brought the only shovel. Foyt proceeded to
tell us tire experts what it was all about, what Firestone had done
wrong and how we could correct it. Well—without stealing any
of A.J.'s thunder—we tried it, and it worked. I'll let him tell you
how.

A. J. Foyt didn't seem that much bigger than life to me in
1963. Over the years, I've learned that I was wrong. I've spent a
large portion of my life around a racetrack somewhere or another, and I can tell you right now: There's never been a race
driver like A. J. Foyt. Ever. Anyplace. For one thing, there has
never been a driver who has won in every kind of race car—Indy
cars, NASCAR stock cars, sports cars, sprints, midgets. You
name it. Not only has he won in those cars; he has won four
Indianapolis 500s, the Daytona 500, Le Mans, and every other
race of importance he has chosen to run. He has won on road
courses and superspeedways and dog-assed dirt tracks, and if they
still had board tracks when he came along, he would have won
on those, too.

And he has done it with a pugnacious style, the likes of which
automobile racing has never seen. ("Motor sports," they like to
call it in Europe, but A.J. doesn't trust people who eat fish with
the head still on, so it's "automobile racing" to him.) A.J. says
and does pretty much what he wants. In fact, it became painfully
evident when he was starting to race the small dirt tracks around
his hometown of Houston, Texas, that he was going to be a winner. And, if not, he would be the damnedest light heavyweight
ever to come out of the Southwest.

He immediately projected this super-tough image to anybody
who dared to cross him. But his wife, Lucy, says that he's really

insecure, and the tough image is just a cover-up. She's probably right—there are a lot of psychologists around to back her up—but there are a lot of bruised heads along the way to the top that don't really care *why* he decked them; they just learned to stay out of his way. On or off the track.

Through the years, a couple dozen qualified authors have wanted to write the A. J. Foyt book. I'm glad that I was around in the early days and got to know him well enough for him to ask me to write it. We talked about it ten years ago, but he wasn't ready. Then, one morning—six-thirty in the morning, to be exact—the phone rang. As my wife, Martina, handed it to me she said, "It's A.J." "Sure," I said. "A.J." Well, it *was* A.J.

"When you gonna write that book about me?" he asked. It was the morning after a network-TV special had aired about Rocky Bleier, the former Pittsburgh Steeler football player and war hero. "Hell, I don't know, A.J.," I said. "You ready?"

"Yep. My life's a hell of a lot more interestin' than that god-damn football player I saw on TV last night."

And he's right.

WILLIAM NEELY

A.J.

Prologue

I've never told this to anybody before, but when I was a kid, growing up around dirt racetracks in Texas, every adult I knew teased me about my Daddy's race cars. If I heard "Whatsamatter, kid, can't your Daddy build race cars?" once, I heard it a thousand times. If I had to pick one thing that made me a winner, that would be it.

I wonder how many kids have made it in life—I mean, really got to the top—because some son of a bitch made fun of their daddy? I know one thing: If I had been big enough, I would have punched out every one of them right there on the spot. But all I could do was grin and bear it. And vow right then that someday I would get behind the wheel of a race car and show every single one of them. I was going to be Number One. I didn't care what it took.

Well, I made it to the top, and I'd like to thank every one of them. I'd still like to punch them out, but I'd also like to thank them.

And, you know, now that I look back at those years, Daddy's race cars weren't all *that* bad. They were pretty good, in fact, once we got an Offenhauser engine. It's just that it took a while, because Offy engines were expensive and we were a tad on the poor side. And Daddy's driver wasn't bad. Dale Burt was his name, and he had nearly everything it took to be a winner. He was smart enough and brave enough, and he didn't mind being greasy and hot and tired and a little hungry most of the time. Those actually were the things it took to be a *racer*. What it took to be a *winner* was a hunger for the checkered flag that was stronger than anything else. *Anything*. And that he didn't have. Maybe nobody made fun of *his* daddy's cars. It seemed to me that Daddy and Dale didn't care if they won or not. I was only ten, but I sure as hell cared.

I think what it was was this: Dale was a front-place runner if everything was perfect; otherwise he was a second- or third-place runner. Everything seldom was perfect, so we didn't win many races.

But that's how it all started. And if you expected an "A. J. Foyt was born in Houston and raced cars and loved his family" sort of biography, you're going to be disappointed. Oh, there will be some of that, too; it makes the story clearer. But what I really want to get to is just how it was in those tough days, when you couldn't *buy* a ride at Indy; back when you had to work your ass off to *earn* one. And, you know, they really *don't* make drivers like they used to. That's a fact.

One thing: I'm not insecure, as Lucy says I am. Let's set that straight right now. You don't win Indy four times by being insecure. Or the USAC championship seven times. Or Le Mans or the Daytona 500. I'm very competitive; that's what it is. And it's this competitiveness that has made me successful. I have a determination that just won't quit. That's what it takes to get to the top in anything. Even today, there are times when I have a car that's not very competitive, but I never give up. Anytime I strap myself in a race car, I feel like I can win. Otherwise I wouldn't be driving it. There are times when I know it's going to be tough, but there has never been a time when I really didn't think I *could* win, one way or another.

There have been many times, late in a race, when I felt I was beat, but I never fully accepted it until it was over, until the checkered flag dropped. I always have it on my mind that something might happen, some miracle, anything to get me to the winner's circle. Somehow, I might win that race. And there have been times when that something did happen and I won the race nobody gave me a chance in hell of winning.

Race drivers have gotten as lazy as the rest of the world. There's only a handful of drivers out there today who would be willing to work as hard as I did to get to the top. And fewer who actually did. I seriously doubt if there are that many who *could* come up the route I did. For one thing, most of them don't really know how to drive a race car. Oh, they go well enough on a superspeedway, but you really don't get the *feel* of a race car today. It's not at all like it was years ago when everybody was driving front-engine Offys, and all the cars were about the same. Then it was the driver that made the difference. Oh, a really good mechanic could find you a few extra horses here and there, but in the end it was the guy behind the steering wheel who won the races.

Man, in those days you could *feel* a race car. You could tell how it was handling and what it would take to go faster than the other guy. Today the cars have almost no feel to them at all. Nearly anybody could drive one of today's Indy cars. With the ground effects and the wings and the wide, super-sticky tires, the car almost drives itself. But I'll tell you, it gives you a false sense of security. With these new drivers, there is a potential hazard every time a race starts. It's a disaster looking for someplace to happen, because not only don't the cars have any feel to them but the drivers wouldn't know what to feel if they had it. It's why they crash so much; which would be bad enough, but they usually take somebody else with them. A lot of the time recently the somebody else has been me. And if you think that doesn't piss me off, you're wrong.

The new, easy-handling cars have taken most of the ability out of driving a race car. Today you have to have more brave than brains, and that's a bad thing. It would be bad in any sport if you took the thinking out of it. But that's what has happened to auto racing. If you get it all dialed in with the wings and tires and ground effects, all you have to do is punch the button.

This is why you see guys sitting on the pole at a race that don't have any business *in* a race car, let alone being the fastest qualifier, and out there in front of the pack. Racing is more dangerous today than it was when I started back in the '50s. In those days, you had to do a lot of things on your own. If a car didn't handle, you *made* it handle. And the only way you got the know-how was to make enough mistakes until you learned. You got there by trial and error. Now it's all built in for you.

That sounds easy for me to say—I mean, after I've won so many races and been around for so long—but I know what I'm talking about. I made mistakes. It's just that I didn't make as many as, say, Kevin Cogan or Hector Rebaque or some of these other young drivers today. I didn't make as many because I didn't drive over my head the way they do. Hell, there are some drivers who have been around for a long time who are driving over their heads most of the time, so the new guys don't have a franchise on it.

I found out early in the game that if I drove over my head, I got in trouble, which is spelled C-R-A-S-H, so there wasn't much point in doing something that was going to come back and bite me in the ass. It's common sense. You've always seen drivers out there going like the hammers of hell, with the car all hung out, taking chances. And the crowd always loves it. But you've got to remember that this is the same crowd that likes to see you bust your ass. It's why most of them come to the track in the first place. They cheer like mad while this guy is out there showboating and taking all these chances. And then a lap or two later, when he crashes, they say, "Well, hell, he was driving over his head. I could have told you that hoopie was going to crash."

Instead of winding up second, which is probably more than he deserved, he finished way back and wiped out the car. Don't get me wrong; I don't mean you shouldn't run hard. I run as hard as I can right from the start, but I have the *ability* to run that hard. I don't stretch that many times to the point where I'm out of control. And that's another point that most of these kids don't understand: What's complete control for one driver may be out of control for another. It differs from one driver to another and from one track to another. Even from one day to the next. I mean, one of these new kids might be out of control—totally *out* of control—at 150 miles an hour, where Mario Andretti or I might be *in* control at 200. You have to know what your limit is, and a lot don't.

I can make mistakes, like everyone else, and I have made them, but most of the time lately when I've been hurt or I've crashed bad, it's been somebody else's fault. And, I'll tell you, I'm getting pretty damned tired of it. I'm tired of getting hurt and I'm tired of losing and I'm tired of busting up my race cars.

$\textcircled{1}$
The Heights

Every town has one: a section that is so tough that people lock their car doors when they drive through it. Well, the Heights was it in Houston. The Heights is where I was born on January 16, 1935.

There wasn't all that much *crime* in the section, which is north of downtown Houston. Houston itself wasn't much more than a cow town itself in those days. It's just that the people were tough there. Super tough. You either learned to take care of yourself or you got the shit beat out of you. I heard somebody say one time—I was real little, but it made an impression on me— "You come out of the Heights in one of three ways: a millionaire, a convict, or dead."

I didn't know anybody that was a millionaire. None of our friends had any money. We didn't. We had a frame two-bed-

room bungalow—that's what they called them in those days—
and plenty of food and clean clothes to wear that were mostly
new. And I knew by the time I was three years old that I wouldn't
be a convict or dead, so I planned on being a millionaire. Some
kids plan early.

The Heights was made up of small, mostly neat homes like
ours, where middle-class people lived. They fenced in their back-
yards with hurricane fence and planted zoysia grass, and most of
them had big plaster pedestals in their front yards with mirrored
balls resting on them.

We lived on 25th Street, not far from the park on 19th. It was a
quiet sort of time, when people actually went to parks. They
packed up cane baskets with fried chicken and sandwiches and
potato salad—you had to have potato salad—and iced tea, and
they went to the park. They sat there without saying much of
anything and they ate their food. At dusk they went home. By
then it was cooler because the electric fans and the window-unit
air conditioners—if you were lucky enough to have one—finally
made the houses fit to live in again.

We spent a lot of time in the park.

Around the corner on Ashland and 19th was the Heights The-
atre, where we spent Saturday afternoons. The show cost a dime.
Most of the time it was a Gene Autry or Roy Rogers cowboy
movie—you see, kids in Texas watched cowboy movies, too.
After the show, we'd go across the street to Miz Bender's Ham-
burgers. For a nickel you could get this big—I mean really big—
hamburger. Today they'd call it "super colossal" or something
like that and they'd do television commercials and newspaper ads
and everything. For a dime you could get a hamburger that was
so big you couldn't eat it all. For twenty cents we could entertain
ourselves all day Saturday.

It was a good childhood. Very American. And, as cornball as
it's come to sound, I've got to say it: There was no drugs or booze
or stealing. You wouldn't have dared do any of those things anyway, for the simplest reason any of us knew: Our fathers would

have beat the hell out of us. I mean, *hurt* us. There weren't any psychologists around to tell our daddies they shouldn't beat on kids. We were *afraid* to do anything wrong.

And everybody was employed. Everybody. It was a long time before anybody knew about workmen's compensation and unemployment benefits. These were terms that came much later. I guess you could have called our section a blue-collar suburb, if you had to put a label on it.

Daddy was a mechanic. My grandfather had been a mechanic. I would be a mechanic. Simple. The nice part was that I actually *wanted* to be a mechanic. But I had a very good reason: race drivers. I had to know how to work on race cars. And, as far back as I can remember—I mean way back to where things are fuzzy and you only remember playing in dirt with a white metal car or Aunt Florence's visit when she brought a box of pecan brittle— well, way back to there, I can remember wanting to be a race driver.

Daddy and Dale Burt had a garage. And a race car. I can remember Daddy taking me over there. I was so little that he sat me up on the workbench and told me, "Just stay up there out of the way, boy," and then he went about working on a car. The workbench was covered with galvanized metal. I can remember that. And I can still remember how cold the metal was on my stomach when I slid down off the workbench. He should have put me in the race car in the first place, because it's where I always ended up. I guess he must have figured that getting off the workbench would give me something to do. It wasn't easy for a three-year-old kid to get down off a workbench. It took time.

Then there was a period when he didn't take me to the garage with him. A kid can't stand changes like that. I thought my world had ended, until I found out why: He was building me my own race car.

It was an open-wheel racer and was powered by a Briggs and Stratton gasoline engine, the kind that had a foot lever you could push on to start. I spent hour after hour running around the outside of the house in that race car. I was the best three-year-old racer in Houston. Maybe the *only* three-year-old racer in Houston. I learned that if I started it into a slide just at the swing set and drove it close to the corner of the house, I could go a lot faster down my straightaway at the side of the house. I do about the same thing today.

By the time I was five, I had the little red race car about worn out. So Daddy built me a real race car. Well, it was closer to real than the first one, if you must know. It was a blue and white midget-type race car, with a number 8 painted on it. It would go maybe 50 miles an hour. And it scared the shit out of me. At first.

They took me and that race car out to the Houston Speed Bowl along with their midget one night. I was supposed to drive the midget around the track, sort of a prerace show for the fans. "Here he is, ladies and gentlemen, A. J. Foyt, Jr., America's youngest race driver. He's five years old, and little A.J. will show these big guys how to race."

Well, five years old or not, I was smart enough to know there wasn't a race unless you had *two* race cars. There weren't any other kids around with race cars, so I decided to challenge one of those "big guys." Why not? I picked Doc Cossey, one of the top drivers. If you're going to do something, do it big. It was my motto even then.

I walked right up to him in the pits and said, "Doc, I can outrun that midget of yours."

"Sure, kid," Doc said, and went right back to the story he was telling to a couple other race drivers.

"I mean it, Doc. I can *beat* you." I wasn't going to give up.

"Are you serious, kid?" he said, knowing damn well I was. "Just hold on." He finished his story and went over to Daddy. "Tony, is this kid serious? Do you want to let him race me?"

Racers can't stand to be challenged; not even by a kid.

Daddy didn't know a thing about it, but I can remember him laughing like hell. "What'd he say?" he asked Doc.

"He said he could *outrun* me," Doc said.

"Well, he probably can," Daddy said. That's all it took.

Doc's midget was powered by an Elto outboard engine. Mine was a 3-horsepower lawn-mower motor. But my car was smaller and lighter and I had about a million miles of around-the-house racing experience. There was no question in my mind that I could beat Doc.

The public-address announcer went straight to the "kid and the big guy" pitch. The crowd loved it. I can remember sitting there at the starting line, as serious as I could be, and looking at Doc grinning the "I'll take it easy on you, kid" kind of smile that little kids get a lot.

Doc was still grinning when the man dropped the green flag. Good-bye, Doc. I got the jump on him and beat him into the first corner of the quarter-mile dirt track. I threw the midget sideways and I could hear the crowd cheering. If ever a kid knew that he had chosen the right profession for himself, I knew it at that moment. The feeling of that car sliding—the sort of bubble-in-your-stomach feeling—was one I'll never forget. That, and knowing that I could stop the slide anytime I wanted—the power that I had to control the car—beat anything I had ever felt. Keep in mind I was only five.

It was only a three-lap race, so I didn't see Doc's face again until after the race. The grin was gone. Doc said, in this typical, big-guy way, "You really did well, there, kid." It's a thing adults do to kids when they know they just got it in the ear. It doesn't make any difference if it's Monopoly or marbles; it's the impression that they *let* you win. Well, Doc and I knew damn well that he didn't let me win. And Daddy knew it.

It was my first taste of victory. That was more than forty years ago, and I've never lost my appetite for that taste yet. All the races and all the money and all the fame haven't dulled that desire to win one bit. It still feels good.

From that moment on, my only thoughts were of race cars. I talked race cars. I dreamed race cars. I lived and breathed race cars. I was driving everybody crazy, and you're talking about a family that was *used* to race cars. It's just that they weren't used to hearing about them every waking moment. My fifth-grade teacher sent a note home from school that said, "I don't know what to do with A.J. Every paper I pick up has a picture of a race car on it—no answers, just a race car."

I spent every day after school and weekends and every day in the summer at the B & F Garage—Burt and Foyt. When I wasn't at the business end of a broom, or running errands, I had my head under the hood of a car, asking, "What's that, Daddy?"

Daddy looked at the ceiling a lot. I was storing away all the knowledge I could. I must have asked a hundred questions about every repair job they worked on: what was wrong, how it broke, what it would take to fix it, how you tell if that particular thing was happening. It's not easy being a four-foot mechanic.

But it was race cars I really wanted to know about. You see, Daddy was one of the most respected race-car mechanics in Houston, and a lot of people brought their race cars there. Others came there to *talk* racing. I hung on every question and every answer.

On weekends we went racing—every Friday or Saturday and every holiday. It was the kind of life I would have *picked* for myself. It would have been a better life if we had won more races. For some reason, even then, winning meant everything to me, and I couldn't understand why everybody was so casual about it. It seemed to me that the guys who lost the most were the ones who cared the least. I was too young to figure out the connection, but I had this feeling that there must be one there somewhere.

Everywhere I went I heard "Why don't you come over and work for our team, kid? See what it feels like to work for a winner." Then the laughing and thigh-slapping. Damn, I hated that part. The teasing wasn't as bad as the laughing, or the thigh-slapping. I used to lie in bed at night and try to think up things to say to them that would knock them right on their ass. I had a bunch of good replies, but somehow I could never remember any of them when the time came. I always got so damn mad I'd just give them the finger and walk away. I guess if I hadn't reacted so much, they would have left me alone. I couldn't help it. They were right: I did want to be on a winning team.

I figured it was up to me. The time had come to do something about it. I mean, I had the little midget. Fine. But I needed something faster. After all, I couldn't play with toys all my life. I was eleven years old!

It took a week for me to get my chance. It came one night when Mother and Daddy had gone to Dallas and had left me at home to take care of my little sister, Marlene. It suited me fine because I had a career that was sorely in need of some attention.

They were hardly out of sight when I called three buddies to come over and help me get Daddy's midget car off the trailer. A race driver has to have a pit crew, doesn't he? The next thing I did was send Marlene over to play at the neighbors'.

Then my buddies and I opened up the garage and pushed that midget off the trailer. There sat my mount. We pushed it around the house enough times to win your average race. Well, actually, *they* pushed. I steered. After all, I was the race driver.

You would be surprised how hard it is to start a midget race car by pushing it, even one with a Ford V-8 60 engine in it. Maybe you wouldn't. But we finally got it fired up and I roared off around the corner of the house.

Hot damn!

The only thing I had to compare the midget to was my lawn-mower-powered car, but, man, that thing was powerful. I couldn't understand how anybody could lose in a car like that. I ran lap after lap, getting faster with each one. I'll never forget the awesome feeling of power. I particularly liked the way it felt when I slid around the corner of the house nearest the shop Daddy had built out back. I got a better bite there for some reason, and when I got back on the throttle, dust and dirt and zoysia grass flew up behind the car like a rooster tail of wake from a fast boat. They plant zoysia grass in places like Houston because it will stand heat, even if it won't stand race cars. My buddies cheered me on, and even though it was only an audience of three, it made me feel good. I mean, here I was, leading a one-car race around my house, with three kids cheering. They would have cheered ants screwing, but I didn't care. I loved it.

But the bubble burst. The engine backfired through the carburetor, which scared the hell out of me. What happened after that scared me even more. I was still on the throttle and the kids seemed to be yelling louder than ever. Why? Because the car was on fire, that's why. I slid it sideways to a stop and leaped from the car, throwing dirt and sand and grass—anything I could find—on the fire. I ripped off my shirt and tried to smother it. My hands were burned, but I knew I had to get that fire out. With the help of my buddies, we got it out before it did little more than bubble the paint on the hood and blacken everything else. Still, it looked like hell.

Man, I knew I was in trouble. I stood there for a long time, with my hands out in front of me, palms up and fingers outstretched. They hurt like hell, but I knew my ass was going to hurt worse than my hands when Daddy got home. As much as my hands hurt, we pushed the car into the garage, wiped off all the black that would come off, and I started to put together my story. Story: "Well, Daddy, I was gonna help you, see. I knew how busy you've been, so I decided if I washed the midget for you, it would save all this time, see. Man, that was nice of me, wasn't it?" Don't wait for an answer, A.J. Get to the good part. "Well, now, just as we were pushing that rascal off the trailer, my foot slipped off the clutch and—would you believe it?—that son of a . . . I mean, that rascal started and it backfired and next thing you know it was on fire."

Good story.

I was so pleased that I told it to my buddies. "How ya like it?" I asked.

"Fine, A.J.," one of them said. "But what about the yard?"

Jesus, the yard.

Well, I turned around slowly, hoping, I guess, that maybe the grass would all grow back if I took long enough. It didn't. The whole damn yard was torn up. The swing set was knocked over, and one corner of the house—the one closest to the shop—was all chopped up. I had gotten a little close to it a few times. Still, it was my best corner.

Marlene came home from the neighbors' about this time. "What happened to the yard, A.J.?" she asked.

"Gophers," I said. "Now get in the house and get ready for bed."

"Bed?" she asked. "Bed? We never go to bed this early."

"Well, we are tonight," I said. "Gotta get our rest. We're growing kids, you know." She was confused.

I thought bed was the safest place. Marlene and I shared a bedroom, and I figured Daddy wouldn't beat on me too bad if we both were asleep in that room. I waited and I waited, going over story after story. There wasn't one good enough. I mean, out there in the garage was a race car that obviously had been on fire. And the yard was all torn up. Then there was the swing set and the corner of the house. I'd just have to take my medicine when he got home.

It was about two in the morning when I heard Daddy's Ford pull into the driveway. I pulled the covers up under my chin and waited. I heard him walking around the house and then I heard the garage door open and close. The next thing I heard was his footsteps on the way to my bedroom. And then there was the sound of breathing. The kind of breathing somebody does when he's madder than hell. He didn't say a word, and even though my eyes were closed so hard that the skin was pulled tight around them, I knew he was standing in the doorway with his arms folded. Then he went away. Must be something to this praying, I thought to myself.

The next morning Daddy said very little. In fact, what he said was about the last thing I expected: "I guess you're gonna be a race driver, A.J. Well, you gotta promise me one thing: Always drive good equipment. If you're not gonna drive the best race cars in the best shape, then don't even bother. And, oh, yeah, stay the hell out of the yard with the midget."

I passed the next few years impatiently. Every kid wants to grow up fast, but I was impossible. I had a career waiting for me, and I thought I'd *never* get to driving age. While I was waiting, I tried to learn as much as possible about engines and suspensions and cars in general. I worked at odd jobs around and saved enough money to buy an old motorcycle. Daddy let me ride it around the area of his garage, which was near what is now the Southwest Freeway in Houston. There was some wide-open space in those days, and I used to ride that motorcycle for all it was worth. The guys who hung around the shop would needle me into going faster and faster. "That all the faster you can ride, A.J.?" they would say. So I'd try to go faster on each lap. I would get back a block or so farther and go like hell, down the street and right through the garage, in one end and out the other. One day I had made about eight runs through the garage at just about what I considered the limit. The speed of sound. "Aw, come on, A.J., you can run faster than that," one of them said. So I got back even farther, and I opened it up. When I came in the door, going as fast as the bike would run, I saw doom. Doom: oil all over the cement floor.

It was too late to brake, so I stayed right on the throttle, hoping to beat hope that the bike would stay under me. Wasted hope. The bike slid out, skidding clear across the garage and into the wall on the other side. I went the other way and hit the other wall just as hard.

I pulled myself up as quick as I could so they wouldn't think I was hurt, and I stood up as tall as I could. But I'll tell you right now, I hurt to beat hell. It felt like every bone in my body was broken. But I wasn't going to give them the satisfaction of letting them know how bad it hurt.

"Now, I'd like to see any of you son of a bitches get off a bike any faster than that," I said.

Daddy had been under a car, and he was peering out from somewhere near the muffler. He laughed so hard he hit his head on the frame of the car. "You think that kid ain't tough?" he told them.

In the summer of 1947, Dale Burt expanded the B & F racing activities. The Midwest Racing Association had a midget-race-car circuit that operated throughout the entire Midwest. They not only paid good purses but they raced almost every night up there. In fact, Dale had raced against many of the drivers when they had come to Texas in the winter months. So they decided: Daddy would run the garage and Dale would go up there and win some money.

They got the midget ready. I watched every move without saying a word. When the car was loaded on the trailer, hooked up to the Oldsmobile and ready to go, Dale asked Daddy, "Can he go, Tony?" And he cocked his head in my direction.

Go?

"Aw, he wouldn't want to go all the way up there," Daddy said. "Would you, A.J.?"

I wasn't there to answer. I was on my way home to pack.

The trip to Decatur, Illinois, which was to be our Midwest base, took the better part of two days. We left Houston about ten o'clock in the morning and drove up U.S. Route 59 to Texarkana, on the Texas-Arkansas border. We stopped to eat on the other side of the border, which in itself was a thrill because it was the first time I had ever been out of the state of Texas. I remember the little old drive-in restaurant well. It had a small dining room as well as some outside car stalls covered over with tin roofing. We went inside. The furniture was made from hickory branches; you know, the kind where they bend them around to form the back and the legs and then they put cane bottoms in them. They hurt when you sit in them.

I ordered a hamburger, French fries, and a Coke. To that order Dale added a salad and a side dish of black-eyed peas.

"A salad and black-eyed peas?" I protested. "Listen, I don't eat that kind of stuff."

"Well, you might just as well get used to it," he said, "because you're gonna eat that kind of stuff when you're with me. You wanna get strong enough to drive a race car or not?"

I wasn't sure if it was worth it.

We slept in the car that night, somewhere north of Poplar Bluff, Missouri. It was the sleep of a contented youth. I was two states from home with a race car on the trailer behind me. From that moment on, my life was like nobody else's I knew.

We stayed at the Pine Lodge Motel in Decatur for three weeks. Most of the time we ate at a diner across the street. And by then I had milk added to my menu. Can you imagine? *Milk*. But I didn't get dessert unless I had my vegetables and milk. I liked sensible things, like Karo syrup on my sausages and wieners. On almost anything, in fact. Dale didn't understand. At night I listened to the radio for hours and hours. I drove Dale crazy, but it was the price he had to pay for the milk.

Within a radius of a hundred miles of Decatur there were fifteen racetracks. In Houston we had to drive farther than that to get to San Antonio, which was about the only track worth running outside of Houston. So, economically, towing up to Decatur and working out of there made sense. Our motel cost $25 a week, and meals weren't much more than that. Even with the vegetables and the goddamn salad. By joining the Midwest Racing Association you could make $100 a night racing, even if you ran last or didn't even make the show. They paid you for showing up.

There were good drivers, and they all went from track to track, racing almost every night: Chuck Wyant, Rex Easton, Red Hamilton, Duane Carter, Frank Burany, Eddie Duncan, and Russ Fox. They were the heroes of my youth. It was nothing for sixty cars to show up for a race, with maybe forty of them Offys. It was unbelievable. I never knew there *were* that many Offys.

Only some of them could run each night, so the ones who

didn't run fast enough to qualify for the show loaded up their cars
and headed for the next race. Maybe they made the show the
next night. But the association paid them all for showing up. If
you won a heat or—happy day—the main, you could make
pretty good money.

The drivers were good guys and we became sort of a family.
What I liked most was that they didn't treat me like a kid. I was
one of them. I played practical jokes with the best of them; I
played the jukeboxes with them in diners and cafés where we ate.
It was the basic training of a racer.

You could buy fireworks almost anywhere in those days, so
there were always firecrackers around. A man couldn't live without firecrackers. Why? Well, for one thing, they gave you something to do while you were waiting to race. The guys would wait
until a driver was in the car, all buckled up, and then they would
toss a lighted firecracker in the cockpit with him. Even though
they all knew it was too late to get out, they always tried.

I think it was in East St. Louis where I bought the biggest
firecracker anybody had ever seen. The guys called it "A.J.'s
bomb." The man I bought it from said it was as powerful as, say,
a quarter stick of dynamite.

I kept it for the right moment.

That moment came right outside Kansas City one afternoon.
We had stopped at this old service station that had the rest rooms
in the back. I went to the men's room, which was like a big old
hallway, with the john clear at the back end. When I came back
to the car, Dale said, "I'll be right back, A.J. Gotta go to the
john."

The time had come.

I gave him a minute or two and then went back there. When I
opened the door, there he sat. As I lit the huge stick he yelled,
"No, you son of a bitch. No!" But it was too late. I had made up
my mind. I tossed it inside and it landed about five feet from
where he was sitting. I can still see him getting up and trying to
get to it before it exploded, but his pants were down around his

ankles and he fell flat on his face. He just covered his head with his arms. When it went off, it sounded like an atomic bomb in that hollow room. As I came back around to the front, I heard one of the guys yell to the other drivers who had stopped, "A.J. set off the bomb." And then Dale came into view. "God damn you, you little bastard," he was yelling.

Dale couldn't hear for two days. I was a hero. One of the guys.

The drivers would do anything to you for a laugh. They also would do anything *for* you. I saw them take tires off their own cars to give to a guy who had a chance of winning when they didn't. But they would beat you anytime they could.

It was a rough life, and everybody was tired and dirty all the time. The guys drank and raised hell together; then they went out and tried everything in the book to beat one another. And if somebody crashed real bad, they took up a collection for him.

It was maybe the best summer of my life.

In the winter months, many of the drivers from the Midwest circuit came to Texas. They all stayed in San Antonio because the racing was good and they couldn't race at all up north. Besides, most of them couldn't do anything else. Or wouldn't. It was a good place to winter.

Dale and Daddy and I went to San Antonio every week. It was a half-mile dirt track and the cars went like the hammers of hell. It had once been an old horse track, and they had just hauled in some dirt to cover a creek bed that had washed through and put up a fence around the whole thing and proclaimed it an automobile track. But it was a good one, and everybody liked it. Drivers even came from the West Coast to run there.

Dale raced the midget there on Labor Day, after we got back from the Midwest. It must have been 110 degrees in the shade, and there was no shade. The track was in the prairie outside of San Antone.

There wasn't any such thing as a quick-change rear end then. At least not in the Burt-Foyt stable. The Ford midget had what they called an over-and-under rear end, so they took the gearbox out and ran the drive shaft direct. Well, the car was going real well, but it was so hot that the drivers were making pit stops just to get water. For themselves. About midway through the race, Speedy Matheney pitted for a drink of water. His pit crew gave him a wet towel to hold on his face and forehead, and he still had it when he pulled back onto the track. He saw Dale coming and he pulled alongside and threw the towel to him, so Dale wouldn't have to stop. Dale was out front and Speedy thought he was doing him a favor.

The problem was, Dale didn't know what Speedy was throwing, so he ducked. When he jerked, he lost control, and the car went through the wooden fence. It sailed over the embankment and rolled about four times. Dale had come partway out of the car, and each time it rolled, it crushed his legs under the drive shaft.

He was in the hospital nine months, in traction most of the time. I visited him at the hospital. And I painted his toenails.

His bones eventually mended, and he didn't even have much of a limp—about the same as most real race drivers, just enough that you could detect it if you looked closely. The limp, and the fact that they all were a little broke, was the way you could tell race drivers from the rest of society.

Dale never charged as hard after that crash. I didn't think so, at least.

I wanted to get in that race car so bad I could taste it. And I waited impatiently. While I was waiting, I prepared myself by collecting all the information I could get my hands on. I must have been a complete nuisance around the shop, because I quizzed everybody who came in. I knew everything there was to know about the tracks and the drivers and their strong points and their weak points. I felt like I could have driven any track in any kind of car in the country, which is not bad considering I didn't even have a driver's license yet. But I was close.

As for experience, I was getting that, too. I started by driving Daddy's car and the parts truck around the garage and the lot, and graduated to taking one or the other to pick up parts. The trips began to get faster as I improved my technique.

By the time I was fifteen, there wasn't much I didn't know about building and tuning race cars, which also was planned. When I did start racing, I was going to know every little detail, every step it took to get to the top. It was already a familiar path, almost like I had already been there. And, in my dreams, I guess I had.

②
U. S. Route
59 North

In the '50s, the best way to get to Indianapolis from Texas was U.S. Route 59 North out of Houston, up to Texarkana, and then on to St. Louis on U.S. 67. From there it was an easy drive across U.S. 40, right to Washington Street. A left on Moller Road would take you straight to the Speedway.

That was the best way on the _map._ I studied that.

Actually, for a race driver it was a lot tougher route. In those days. Automobile racing, like the drivers on our highways, has taken a lot of shortcuts, and, unfortunately for the sport, it's pretty easy to get to Indy today. As easy for a driver as picking up a map. But in the '50s, you started at some dog-ass quarter-mile dirt track in an ill-handling piece of equipment, and you ran there for as long as it took. How long it took was simple: You had to be good enough to beat everybody there on a regular basis. Only then did you move on to the next plateau.

You had to develop a skill with cars that didn't have the first bolt of sophistication. You *made* them into race cars yourself, right on the track. It took balls and a heavy foot. But everybody had more or less the same car, so if you had enough ability or determination, you got to the top. If you had both, you got there quick.

I had both. I knew it as sure as I knew my own name.

And I had done my research. I knew what it took to get to Indy. I planned to start in street racing and then go into stock cars.

After street racing, the route would be the same one that everybody else took: bigger tracks and faster cars—still dirt— and then midgets and then a shot at the national scene in sprint cars. Still not Indy, but a whole lot closer than the local scene. This route was dotted with a trail of grubby restaurants, nights spent sleeping in the back of pickup trucks, and a sea of broken race cars. But it was the time-honored pattern of getting to the top in automobile racing.

The American Automobile Association sanctioned midget and sprint-car races all over the country, and a driver needed to run as many places as possible—as much as his body and his tow vehicle would stand. Otherwise you didn't get a crack at Indy. And then, if you did, it was for a series of tests. *Tests.* If you screwed up anyplace, it was back to the minors.

It was a hell of an apprenticeship—I knew that—but it was what I wanted. So I decided early that the things that normal kids do in high school—you know, things like class plays and proms—were things I didn't have time for.

My friends were mostly the people who came to Daddy's shop or those I met at races. The people I associated with had one thing in common: hot cars. They either raced cars or they built them or they *talked* about them. The few high-school friends I had fit the mold.

I hung out at Stewart's Drive-In on South Main Street or at

Prince's across the street. We all hopped from one super street machine to another, talking speed and drinking Coke—but not the speed and coke kids know today.

It was at Stewart's Drive-In that my drag-racing career got its start. It began with talk of racing on Old Spanish Trail—or OST, as it's called in Houston—and quickly spread to actual racing. It wasn't long until the guys were racing every night. And I was champing at the bit. I didn't have a car.

By the time I got my driver's license, I could already outrun almost everybody at the drive-in. I learned that within the first week. By driving other guys' cars. So I took every cent I had saved over the years from working for Daddy and from doing all sorts of chores in the neighborhood, and I bought a used Oldsmobile.

Most kids drove Fords in those days, and the ones who didn't were considered sort of renegades. I guess I have always been a renegade. But I followed the hot-rod formula: Take the car apart. That's the first thing everybody did—take it all apart, even if you didn't change anything. You just needed to see what all those parts looked like, I guess. But most of the time it went back together differently from the way it had left Detroit.

The whole thing was a lot like childbirth. Everybody waited patiently to see what your new offspring was going to look like; or, better yet, what it was going to run like. My Olds got me a pretty good reputation with my high-school buddies. The fact that it impressed a few girls along the way didn't bother me either.

I was a mechanic the day I was born. What I didn't inherit, I learned. It was the advantage I had over other kids my age. I learned hop-up tips from the experts and engineered them into my own car, not saying too much about it to Daddy. If he knew anything about my racing, he kept it to himself. It's not likely that he knew, because he wasn't one to keep things to himself. All I knew was that I wasn't going to volunteer the information.

Usually we waited until late at night, and at times we met before daylight, for our races on OST. And they were *races*. Even when I look back now, I'm amazed at how some of those cars would run. If you had a shabby or, heaven forbid, a slow piece of equipment, you weren't even recognized. You weren't there, man. And it had to look good, too. Mine always looked better than anybody else's. Of course, I spent more time on mine. That Olds had about a hundred coats of hand-rubbed lacquer, and, I'll tell you, it was beautiful.

We ran top end, which meant it was a standing start, run wide open—which was over 100 miles an hour—to a certain point, and then shut down, hoping that all the valves and pistons were still inside the engine block. It didn't always happen. But we were doing the same things they were doing on drag strips in California. The sport of drag racing hadn't gotten to Texas that big yet. I ran some drag strips, but it was easier to run OST. Besides, a quarter of a mile wasn't enough to satisfy my appetite for speed. We got more and more competitors who felt the same way.

Enter John Law.

The fact that we got by with street racing for as long as we did was a miracle in itself. But it didn't take too long for the cops to make OST one of their regular trips. We kept people stationed around to warn us, so the real race was often between us and the cops, which would have been all right if it hadn't been for license plates. They are to street racers what fingerprints are to burglars. There was more than one visit paid to Daddy's garage by the Houston cops. So much for keeping it from Daddy. I got yelled at a lot in those days.

We moved our floating race game across town to Stella Link Road, just to outsmart the cops. It didn't, of course. It just brought a new and different batch down on us. And a new and different batch to Daddy's garage.

I wasn't sure if all the yelling was worth it, just to be a hero at school. Actually, I guess I was sure. I was a back on the football team, but it was my racing I was best known for. And it felt good.

I was a king most mornings when I drove my Olds into the school parking lot. But I left my crown at school because I didn't want Mother to know anything about my racing. And Daddy was hearing enough about it from the cops, so I didn't say much around him either. In fact, Marlene was the only one I could share it with at home. The only thing was, she used it to blackmail me. She was as much into dancing as I was into racing—ballet mostly—and she threatened to tell Mother if I didn't help her with her adagios, or whatever you call them. She made me dance with her. Hell, if my buddies had found out about that, well, you can imagine. . . .

But I was protective of Marlene; that's what it was. I even screened her dates. You see, I was four years older and I knew most of these guys. More than once I went to the door, saw who it was, and slammed the door right in his face. It pissed her off, but it was something I had to do. She told me one time, "It's gotten pretty bad, A.J. Boys have to get permission from Daddy, and then they have to come to you."

Jimmy Greer played a big part in my early racing career. He was a friend of Daddy's and one of the people who stopped in the shop almost every day. Jimmy had the first automobile air conditioner I had ever seen. It was an old ARA unit that he had installed, and he always drove around until the car was colder than hell before he came by to pick us up and take us to Dugan's for coffee. The air conditioner impressed me.

Somehow Jimmy found out that I was breaking into the Arrowhead racetrack at night and racing my car there, but he never told Daddy. He used to say to me, "A.J., goddammit, if you don't quit racin' at Arrowhead at night, I'm gonna have to tell Tony." But he never did.

One night I had borrowed Daddy's car because the engine was out of mine, and a couple of buddies and I were racing it at Arrowhead. *Backwards.* It's not that unreasonable; I was *leading.* I was leading right up to the time I flipped the car. Man, the top was level with the doors when we towed it back to the garage. Jimmy saw the car the next morning, and he mentioned it in the air-conditioned car.

"What happened to your car, Tony?" He knew damn well what happened to the car.

"A.J. Leadfoot there flipped it in the ditch out on Stella Link last night," Daddy said. "Says he went to sleep."

"I'll bet he did," Jimmy said. "Went into that ditch straight as an arrow, didn't you, A.J?"

No way I was going to answer that question. I tried to change the subject, but Jimmy kept after it.

"Tony, you might as well let the kid race. He's doin' it on his own anyway, and he's gonna get hurt," Jimmy said.

"Whattaya mean he's doin' it on his own?" Daddy asked.

"Well, if you buy that 'Stella Link in the ditch' bullshit, you're not as smart as I think you are," he said. "Let him race where he'll learn it right."

I figured the best thing to do at this point was to keep quiet.

Daddy thought about it. For a long time. "Okay, goddammit, A.J.," he said. "I knew this day would come sooner or later, and I'm gonna let you race, but you gotta promise me one thing."

"Name it," I said.

"You gotta stop racing on the street," he said. "I'll tell you right now, if I catch you racin' on the streets again, I'm gonna whip your butt. Right in front of your buddies."

He meant it. And he would have done it. So I never raced on the streets again. That is, if you don't count rental cars.

It was time to get started on the road to Indy. I did two things: First, I quit high school in the middle of my senior year. There just wasn't a thing that participles and logarithms were going to do to help my racing career. Or Wordsworth, for that matter. Second, I found a race car. Actually, it was a sort of a junker of a 1939 Ford coupe that I had seen parked alongside the road over near Austin. I bought it for $100 and started to work on it in Daddy's garage.

I had to do every bit of the work myself. Daddy didn't have much to do with the whole project. But then, he was busy making a living. At the time, he was working on Ebb Rose's and Archie Lacey's race cars. It was only when he saw that I wasn't getting anywhere that he started to take an interest.

I think for a long time he felt the whole thing might go away and I would come to my senses and do something else.

He told me some things to do to the car, like putting in Ardun overhead valves. It ran like a million bucks. And looked like two million. That may have been part of my original problem: It looked *too* nice. It was always somewhat of a problem with my cars; they looked so nice I was afraid I was going to get them scratched.

But that car stood out at the racetrack, in a sea of grubby-looking stock cars—most of which were outrunning me. The car was gleaming black with a big gold number 1 on the sides. I won the best-looking-car award for four straight weeks. No racing trophies, just best-looking-car awards.

Finally, Daddy said, "Listen, if you wanted to build a show car, you should have built a show car and showed it down at the Coliseum or somewhere. You know, where they have car shows."

He had a point.

"You got any ideas?" I said.

"Yeah," he answered. "Me and Jimmy'll go with you this weekend."

Come Friday night, the three of us went to Playland Park. I didn't know what to expect. After the first heat, where I didn't do a damn thing, Daddy said, "A.J., why don't you let M. J. Burton here drive your car in the next heat?"

M.J. was one of the top drivers around. He also was one of the hardest chargers, which meant bent fenders. Maybe even bent doors. I had been set up.

"Whattaya mean, let M.J. drive?" I said. "I mean, hell, he'd beat the car to death."

"Yeah, and he might also *win*," Daddy said. "And at this rate, you're never even gonna find out if it *can* win."

Right again.

"Besides," he said, "we can straighten out any body work before next week's race."

"We?" I asked.

"Yeah, we," he said. "Body work ain't tough."

I had a partner. Daddy.

The story wouldn't be worth repeating if M.J. hadn't won. He took the heat and then the main in that car. And he beat it all to hell. But we straightened out the body work the next week. It all taught me a good lesson: If you're gonna build show cars, show them; if you're gonna build race cars, race them. From that day on, I always had good-looking race cars, but I also ran the ass off of them. In fact, for a while I was maybe a little too rough on machinery. But I started winning regularly.

That's about the last advice Daddy ever gave me. The rest I picked up on my own. Oh, I'd always follow somebody I thought was pretty good, just until I found out where the top drivers were running; then I'd find my own groove. I always felt that I could improve on anybody's technique.

A lot of people asked me to drive their cars. I was a bush-league hero. But it wasn't coming close to fulfilling the need I had to race. The midget in Daddy's garage was going to be the only thing to do that. That was what racing was all about: open wheels and single seat, where the driver sat right up there where God and everybody could see him. It was going to be an impossible program to sell, though.

So it was back to Arrowhead to race by myself.

I was working for Daddy, and every time he left the garage, I sneaked the midget out and raced it. This went on for weeks. As I raced imaginary competitors, the sheer power of that light car with the powerful Ford engine was almost more than I could stand. Man, I wanted to drive it in front of a crowded grandstand so much I could taste it.

For one thing, it came natural to me. There was nobody there to tell me what to do, but I knew I looked good in it. You can tell things like that.

Dale came to my rescue, with an approach to Daddy that was about as blunt as Jimmy's had been with the stock car. "Tony," he said, "I think I'll quit drivin'."

"Quit?" Daddy said. "Who'll drive the midget?"

"The one who's puttin' more miles on it right now than I am," he said.

Daddy looked at Dale and then at the midget and then at me. He hitched a thumb in my direction. "Him?" he said.

"Yep," Dale replied.

"When?" Daddy asked.

It was a simple conversation.

I was very busy with a carburetor all of a sudden.

"Every time you leave the shop for more than an hour," he said. "Ever wonder why the tires are wearing out with the car sitting there?"

I spent a lot of time waiting for Daddy to hit me in those days.

"I don't know; I'll think about it," Daddy said. "In the meantime, I think you'd better drive, Dale."

I said, "Well, to hell with it; I'll get my own ride."

I couldn't stay out of the conversation forever.

"Go ahead and get your own ride," Daddy said. "Just make sure it's not a piece of junk. I mean, if junk's all you can find, you better stay with stock cars."

I went straight to Red Fondren's place. Red had midgets. I took the direct approach: "I want to drive one of your midgets, Red," I said. "I've had it with stock cars."

"Tony won't let you drive his, huh?" Red said.

"Well, to tell you the truth . . ."

"Okay, we'll give you a try this weekend," he said.

That wasn't so tough.

The car wasn't as good as Daddy's, but it was a midget, and I was determined to show him. Can't do anything with a second-rate car, huh? I thought. Well, we'll see.

I drove the hell out of that midget. And what a chapter it would have made if I had won. Anything. But I did learn that most basic lesson: If a car doesn't handle, you make it handle. It wasn't like today, when you come into the pits and hand it over to a team of engineers and say, "Work on this pig." You hunkered down in your seat and you threw that bastard into a turn, hoping it came out headed in the right direction. And most of the time it did.

It was a little squirrelly at times—most of the time, in fact—but I stayed right with it, and I didn't even run up over anybody's wheels. The tricky part about open-wheel cars is to stay away from the other cars' wheels. The wheel rotation works against your own tire and wheel like a set of gears, and it pulls your car up and over. Usually *way* over. On your head. It's very dangerous. And it certainly keeps your attention.

This particular midget pushed a lot, which means that it had a lot of understeer, which really means—in honest-to-God street talk—that the car tends to go straight no matter how much you steer it. Considering that all of this is happening at a time when you would very much like to turn, it can be interesting. But I found out that by crossing it up a little sooner and sliding more, I could run with most of the other cars. It just took more work and a lot more concentration.

If you screw up in a situation like that, the outcome is predictable: You crash. If you crank the car sideways too late, you hit the wall with the front of the car; if you crank it too soon, you hit the wall with the back of the car. And if you're not in exactly the right groove going into the turn, and you do everything else right, you hit the wall with the side of the car. The odds aren't as good as you'd like them to be.

I put on quite a show for a few weeks. Red knew how I was manhandling the car. "Kid, you're a hell of a race driver," he said. "If I didn't know better, I'd swear you'd been on this racetrack a hundred times. You look like you've got as many miles in a midget as, say, M. J. Burton over there."

I probably had *more* miles in a midget than M.J. It's just that I never raced at night with the track lights on. And driving in the dark really hones your style.

Daddy watched all this as long as he could. "Jesus Christ, A.J.," he said, "I told you to up and quit if you couldn't drive the best equipment, and here you are out there in that shitbox just working yourself to death. You gotta get something better under you or quit."

"Any suggestions?" I said.

"Yeah, quit," he said, knowing full well he might as well talk to the race car.

Jimmy Greer watched and listened in silence. When Daddy finished, Jimmy said, "Tony, you're as right as rain, but you're overlookin' one thing: The kid's drivin' that shitbox like it *was* a winner. You know, he set a track record out there tonight."

Daddy grumbled something and walked away. God damn, but the old man was stubborn.

"Thanks, Jimmy, for tryin'," I said. "I'll get a good ride. You'll see."

"You know, A.J.," he said, "your problem is that you're just like that stubborn ol' bastard. I mean, have you one time *ever* gone to him and said, 'Daddy, I know you can build good race cars. Can you help me with mine?'"

"Well," I said, "has he ever come to me and said, 'Son, I know you can drive the hell out of a race car, let me help you'?"

"See!" Jimmy said. "You know, you two are so damn much alike that I don't think the racing world can take both of you anyway. But lemme go talk to him."

It was a long time later when I found out Jimmy had told Daddy that he knew where they could buy an Offy engine and that they could put it in the Kurtis-Kraft chassis, which would make a car worthy of my driving. Daddy couldn't afford it; neither could Jimmy, for that matter. But he told Daddy he had a little in savings, maybe $400, and if Daddy could raise that much, well, they were in business together.

Eight hundred dollars might not sound like a lot of money, but it was in 1953, particularly if you were poor. And most racers were poor. Oh, we weren't mashed-potato-sandwich poor, but $800 was a big chunk of cash to us. We had the necessities, and maybe a *little* more. And we had a ton of pride. Hell, we had fifty tons.

Jimmy and his wife, Dot, were in about the same fix. They had a redwood picnic table with two benches for their kitchen—and dining room—table. And they had sheets on the windows. Oh, yeah, and an air-conditioned Oldsmobile. The $400 was in a savings account marked "Security."

Enter Offenhauser, exit security.

Cecil Green had been killed in a sprint car a few weeks earlier and Jimmy knew his widow. That's where he bought the engine.

There weren't many racing teams in those days that just went out and *bought* a car, or even built one from the ground up. Most cars were put together from the remains of other cars and from parts picked up wherever you could find them. In most cases, the other drivers and owners were scraping around, trying to put together the best car they could with the least amount of money involved. Our kind of racing was a low-bucks operation. There wasn't enough money in the winner's purse to lift it above that level.

You had to love racing. And we had a combination at that point that spelled "winning."

Now all they had to do was tell Dot and Mother. Figuring that there was strength in numbers, they went together. First, to Dot, who just came unglued. She cried awhile and then she cussed awhile. Jimmy and Daddy looked at the floor a lot. "Listen, Dot," Jimmy said, when he could break in between the crying and the cussing. "Just look at A.J. over there."

They had brought me along because they figured she wouldn't raise as much hell if I was there. "Just keep quiet and let us do the talking," they had told me.

I wasn't sure it was working, but Jimmy went on. "He could

get hurt in that old car of Red Fondren's he's driving. You wouldn't want that on your conscience, now, would you?"

No comment. She looked at him, and then at me. She stopped crying.

"Besides," Jimmy continued—he was on a roll—"he's good. It'll be a good investment, if nothing else. Hell, we'll have curtains and a real dining-room table in no time."

"Well . . . well, you be careful, A.J.," she said. "But you better be fast, too. I'm not going to eat off a damn picnic table the rest of my life."

First hurdle.

The second hurdle was a bigger one: Mother. Daddy and Jimmy hit her with the same logic. First she said, "Absolutely, no!" Then, "No." Then she cried. "This thing has gone too far already. I can't think of my boy out there in a midget."

She had seen a midget flip one night, and she never forgot the image of the driver with his head crushed.

"You know he's better off on the track than he is racing on the streets, Evelyn," Daddy said. "And you know he's gonna be racin' everywhere. Why, right now that Oldsmobile of his is gonna kill him. Our race car will be *safe*. And the drivers know a lot more than those kids on the street."

"But my baby in one of those . . . those midgets," she said. And she cried again.

Daddy looked at me and winked.

Break out the tools.

I don't think there has ever been a happier time for me than when I was building that midget. I knew what a big step it was—right in the direction of Indianapolis.

There wasn't anything in those days that drew attention to a race driver like a midget. There was something about them that said "macho." It was an important move to me. So important, in fact, that the car had to look better and run better than any other midget.

The days and nights of preparation—sometimes all night, long after Daddy and Dale had gone home—were capped when the sign painter showed up to put the numbers on the car. I handed him an empty Lucky Strike cigarette pack I had found on the shop floor.

"Number Two," I said. "Just like the Two here on the tax stamp. Lucky number."

Another couple of days of detailing and the car was ready for practice. We went to Arrowhead, where Daddy had made arrangements with the promoter to let us use the track. Man, we went right in there through the front gate, with the red and blue number 2 midget behind us. In broad daylight.

It has been a long time, and I have driven dozens of midgets since, but I get a feeling that if I went back to that car today, I would still think it was a hell of a race car. It was more than boyish enthusiasm; it *was* a hell of a race car.

There is something about a really good race car that makes it stand out from the others. It's not any different sensation or anything like that. It's just the feeling of everything working perfect—a solid, smooth, quality feeling you get only from the best. No matter what it is. You don't feel it often.

Some race drivers have it, too.

The day finally came to race the car. I can remember it sitting there in the driveway beside the house, strapped to the trailer and gleaming like a million bucks. When I came out of the house, I was in my racing clothes. And I gleamed like the car.

"Jee-zus," Daddy and Dale said at the same time.

I was wearing white pants and a red silk shirt. Get ready, race world, A.J. Foyt is coming through.

When we pulled out of the drive, Mother was standing on the porch, crying. I leaned out the window. "Don't worry, Mother," I said. "This first one's for you."

And we headed for Playland Park with the best-looking race car behind us anybody had ever seen.

There's nothing like the feel of a really good dirt car under you. I thought it then, and I think it now. It's a sensation you can't get doing anything else. Well, with your clothes on, anyway.

The feeling of a race car on asphalt is thrilling. No question. It gives you a sort of dull sensation in your chest and a tingling feeling over the rest of your body. I highly recommend it. But the feeling of a dirt car—well, now, that's something even better. When you go charging down the straightaway and you pull the wheel hard left and the rear end starts coming around, the feeling starts building. When it's in a complete sideways slide, you crank the wheel the other way and you get back on it again. By then you feel ten feet tall.

Knowing that you are sliding sideways, with the car going one way and the wheels pointing the other, gives you a feeling of strength. You're making the car do something it really shouldn't be doing. It's like you are overriding some basic law of physics. Your left-front wheel is off the ground and you're sliding through a turn on three wheels. If you have time to look in the rearview mirror, you can see a rooster tail of dirt kicking up behind you, and I'll tell you, you are in heaven. There are very few things that a man can do that are as rewarding as driving a dirt car. If you do it right.

And I did it right. I did all of those things. The race car handled just like a good race car should. The left-front wheel came right up there off the track. The rooster tail of dirt kicked up halfway to the top of the light poles. Still I didn't get the feeling that the whole picture was complete. I mean, I had my foot in it all the way and it didn't feel *fast* enough. The car wasn't as fast as it had been a week earlier in practice.

I came in just raising hell. Daddy let me rave on for a while. "When you're through makin' an ass out of yourself," he said, "I'd like to let you know you just broke Johnny Parsons' track record. You're on the pole."

I shut up. But I knew the car wasn't right.

It was the next day before I found it. They had retarded the magneto so I couldn't run flat out. Can you believe that? It was a deal they made with Mother, because they all knew I would go out there in the first race and run it as fast as it would run. They thought I might get in trouble the first night. What a bunch of crap. I wonder what that thing would have done if they hadn't screwed around with it?

But I put on a show for the fans. They filled the stands and they lined up along the fence. That's where die-hard dirt-track fans watch a race from—right at the edge of the track. As close as they can get. They stand right there where the spray of dirt is the greatest, and they only move when they have to—like when a race car comes sailing along through the air at them. Then they run, but after it's over, they come right back and line up, like birds on a rail. When the race is over, they're all speckled with chunks of mud. It's a badge of honor.

When I broke the track record, the mud-stained fans cheered like mad. It is the reason we race—the cheering crowd. Not to mention the record-breaking part.

I gave the crowd something to cheer about.

Everything in my life seemed to come together that night: the nights at Stewart's Drive-In and the blown engines on OST and the chases from the cops on Stella Link; the long nights of building engines and painting and polishing cars; the busted knuckles and the burns from the welding torch. And the torn-up back yard in the Heights. It all meshed together in that midget, roaring around the quarter-mile dirt track.

The first race was the trophy dash, which was a four-lap race between the fastest qualifiers. With only a few laps like that, you have to get out front fast. Or forget it. I took the lead on the second lap, and it was all over. I got my first checkered flag in the midget. I patted the cowl of the car like it was a good horse. It was one hell of a mount.

The next race was a regular heat race, and I took that one, too. And I took the semi-main, which is the next-to-biggest race on the card. By then the public-address announcer was having a field day: "Can you believe it, ladies and gentlemen! Here he comes around for his victory lap, waving that checkered flag. Houston's own A. J. Foyt. The kid has won everything he's been in tonight in that red and blue Offy. And he's only eighteen years old. We're seeing history made tonight. There's only one thing left for him to win: the main, the feature event. And that's coming up just as soon as we can get those race cars lined up. Can A. J. Foyt do the impossible? Can he sweep the card in his first night in this new car?"

"You're damn right he can," I said to Daddy.

I got back in the car, buckled up the seat belt, and put on my helmet.

"Stand on it," Jimmy said.

You don't wish a race driver "good luck." It's bad luck.

I nodded and pulled down my goggles. And I wheeled the car out onto the track. It was an inverted start, with the fastest cars in the back. I started dead last. There were a lot of cars I had to get past, so I busied myself looking over the field as we waited, figuring which ones I could blow off on the first lap and which ones on the second, and so on. The power of positive thinking. Also, it kept me from getting nervous.

When they gave us the signal, we fired up and pulled away. The pace lap seemed like it took an hour. It was only a quarter of a mile but it seemed like fifty. I wanted to get started. It was a long way to Indy, and this was only the next of several steps. But it was a big one.

When the starter dropped the green flag, cars went in all directions, trying to get past others—up high, down low, in the grass, everywhere. I shot up high, near the fence, and I nailed it. I had sailed past four cars by the time I got to the first turn. On a short track like that, there are really only two turns, one at one end and one at the other—unlike the traditional four turns on bigger tracks—and the straights are not very straight, because the track is so short. It gives the feeling of being on a circle. By the time I got to the second turn, I was about in the middle of the pack.

Two cars spun in front of me and I had to slide down through the grass to miss them. But I got it gathered up and was able to improve my position by about four cars, because I was alert. I breathed a big sigh of relief and nailed it again. I passed three more cars and took dead aim on Buddy Rackley, who was leading.

I followed him lap after lap, trying to get past him, but he was a veteran. I went high. He went high. I went low. He went low. I saw the white flag, meaning one lap to go. We came down the front straightaway bumper to tail—my bumper, his tail—and when we came out of the first turn, I pulled alongside him. We ran wheel to wheel down the back straightaway.

There was one turn left. Now-or-never time.

I rammed my accelerator foot up to about the front nerf bar and started past him on the outside. Buddy was also determined to win. I mean, those guys would do about anything to keep you behind them. He eased his car a little higher, trying to pinch me and make me back off. No way I was going to back off, but if I stayed there beside him, I would drive the midget right into the fence and probably flip it. If I came down, I was sure to run over his front tire with my rear, and *that* would probably flip me. But it was still the best choice, because I might make it. If I did, I would have the race won.

I turned left.

I felt my rear tire go up over his and I took in a deep breath. A *deep* breath. I also stayed on the throttle. The rear of my car went up, but it came back down right side up. I knew I had pulled it off. My heart was in my throat all the time, but I intended to *win* that race, and this was the only way.

I swept the entire card, but we came close to a fight in the pits after the race. Buddy said I chopped him off and I said he tried to drive me into the wall. You could usually count on a fight a week, but they were clean fights—no guns or knives or any of that bullshit. It's just that hopes were always high and tempers were at the point of breaking. If you weren't man enough to take care of yourself, you got the shit kicked out of you.

For once, I walked away. That night was reserved for celebrating, not fighting.

From that first night at Playland Park with the midget, it was a quick trip to the top of the field. We raced all over Texas and Louisiana and Oklahoma. I won a lot and I lost some, but win or lose, I became the driver to beat. I drove hard and rough, and that in itself tends to cause tempers to get out of hand, but the complaint office was always open in my pit. A lot of people called.

One night in San Antonio, some guy came up and hit me while I was still strapped in the car. I couldn't get to him, so Daddy beat the hell out of him.

He was as bad as I was.

We both fought a lot. And when we weren't fighting, we were arguing. With each other. We argued about everything—how the car was going to be set up, how the engine was to be set. Everything. Mother said one day that if we didn't quit arguing about the race car, there wouldn't be a race car, because she was going to "take a sledgehammer after it." That was her favorite saying. I can't say that I blamed her, because it was hell all the time. But, over the years, in spite of all the arguments we've had, I think Daddy is the only one around a race track who has fully understood me. He was always there to help me if he thought I needed it. And a lot of times when I didn't need it.

I built a new Oldsmobile stock car, and some guy ran into it, which is all right, but I thought he did it on purpose. So when I got to the pits, I came out of the car like a rocket and lit into him. About six of his buddies came to his aid. The next morning, on the front page of the Houston *Post*, there was a picture of Daddy holding me over his head to keep me from jumping into the whole gang.

It wasn't *all* fighting; there was a lot of fun, because our racing became a family affair. Mother and Dale and his wife and Marlene always came to the races. In fact, Mother became my biggest fan. We ate chicken and had a great time. There seemed to be closer family ties in those days.

There were a lot of families like that. The Tilotta brothers, for example. They came en masse and they raced everywhere. We fought with them everywhere. The Tilottas owned the System Garages in Houston, and Buddy raced their car; the rest of the brothers were his crew. Their car wasn't as good as mine and Buddy got in my way a lot on the race track, so I ran into him a lot. Then we fought. Racing was a lot different then. We all worked on our cars; we had fun, we raced, and we fought. In that order. But we were still friends.

Since everybody had about the same equipment, we were always looking for an advantage. Everybody looked—a shortcut here and there. Everybody cheated, every chance he got, but that was part of the game. And if a team found out about it, they screamed like mad to the track officials and then they went right to their cars and did the same thing. Pretty soon everybody was doing it, and it became accepted.

The day we got our second engine was the day we got *our* advantage. We had one engine punched out—the cylinders were bored out a little and oversize pistons installed—which gave it a little more displacement. And more power. When there wasn't anybody around checking engine displacement, we'd put that rascal in and just go like hell. Other days, somebody who didn't have as fast a car as ours normally would blow by me, and I knew immediately that he was running a punched-out engine. There might be honor among thieves, but there sure isn't among race drivers.

At San Antone one night, I was just raising hell because the car wasn't handling right. Daddy said it was. I said, "I'll show you," so I took it out and just threw it into the turns. I was beating hell out of it. When I came back in, he said, "Okay, smart-ass, I'll fix you," so he started to load the car up.

"Go ahead and load the son of a bitch," I said.

I went over to R. L. Furnace and said, "Who's drivin' your car?"

"You are if you want to," he said.

So I took the car out and won the feature.

Man, did that bug Daddy.

I said Daddy was as bad about fighting as I was. Well, here's an example: One night at Playland Park, I pulled the midget off to the edge of the track after the semi because the oil pressure was low and I didn't want to run it around the track again to get into the pits. Daddy said to leave it and he would add oil right there. One of the off-duty cops they hired to watch over things at the track came up while he was putting in the oil and told Daddy to move the car. "They're gettin' the cars ready for the feature," he said.

"I know," Daddy said. "We're *in* the feature. I'll just put this oil in and then we'll run it around and line it up."

That wasn't good enough. "I said, *move* this shitbox," the cop said.

Big mistake.

Daddy put down the oil can and walked over to this cop, who wasn't a little man. And he looked right in the cop's eyes. There was an eight-foot fence right behind him, and Daddy literally picked the cop up and threw him over the fence. Threw him *over*. When the cop hit, the dust flew. He didn't even come back inside the track.

I get it honestly.

Daddy was tough. And stubborn. In Oklahoma City one night, Jud Larson and I got to clowning around. They had a white board fence all around the track, and I came in after a practice lap and showed Jud where I had gotten so close to the fence that I rubbed a streak of red from my helmet along the boards on the back straightaway. "Shit, that's nothing. Watch this," Jud said as he went back out on the track. When he came back in he said, "Look over there at that." There was a blue streak from his helmet. Longer than mine.

I went right back out there and put a red streak on longer than his. Then he went out. Then Daddy got into the act. "Cut out the bullshit, A.J.," he said. "We came here to race, not play around. Besides, you're gettin' so close to the wall you're gonna crash."

During the heat race, Jud and I put more streaks on the wall. "Once more," Daddy said, "and I'm gonna load that son of a bitch up and we're goin' home."

"He's just bullshittin' you, A.J.," Jud said. He was egging me on, but it didn't take much, because I sure as hell wasn't going to let Jud get the best of me.

So I went out in the semi-main and put the longest red streak yet on the wall. And I won the semi, which meant that I had a good chance of winning the main. After the race, I went to get a Coke, leaving my helmet with all the white streaks on it in the race car. I was proud of that.

When I came back, Daddy and Jimmy had just finished loading the car on the trailer.

"What in the hell are you doin'?" I screamed.

"We're goin' home, that's what we're doin'," Daddy said.

"The hell we are," I said, and I started for the trailer to unload the car. "I'm gettin' this son of a bitch off there and I'm gonna' win that main."

With that Daddy hit me right in the chest and knocked me down, and, do you believe, he and Jimmy actually sat on me until they started the main, so it was too late for me to get into it. They *sat* on me. I was never so angry in my life. But I didn't do anything like that again.

Daddy was pretty tough on me, but I think that he had a lot to do with my desire to win, because there were many times when I wanted to win just to show him I was right about this or that.

My mother had a lot to do with it, too. She always encouraged me in everything. She didn't want me to drive race cars, but she stood behind me when I decided to do it. And she told me how good I was. She gave me some pride in what I was doing. Up to that point, the race drivers I knew were greasy, second-class citizens. "You're as good as anybody else, A.J.," she told me. And I knew she was right.

I felt as if I was better than most, in fact. So I decided to try to change that image of race drivers. It's why my cars were always sharper than anybody else's. And it's the reason I wore silk shirts and white pants to race in, while everybody around me wore dirty T-shirts and torn jeans. A lot of people laughed at me for a while, and they called me "Fancy Pants," but they learned when and how to say it. I mean, you can only carry this good-guy shit so far. I had to straighten a few of them out.

I get bored very fast after I've mastered something. I need to move on. Another mountain to climb, another hurdle to clear. You've heard all those clichés before. Well, with me, they're true. And in 1955 my next hurdle was sprint cars.

In case you're not familar with them, sprint cars are about the most ferocious race cars you can find. They resemble midgets— open wheel, front engine—but they are bigger and more powerful. And they usually run on larger tracks, so that means they can go a lot faster. And they go a lot farther in the air if you flip one. More people have been killed in sprint cars than in any other type of race car. That very reason is why a lot of us look at them with so much respect. It's also why we drive them—the challenge of all challenges.

In the days when I was on my way up, there was no better way to draw attention to yourself—national attention, particularly around Indiana—than with sprint cars. You can see the picture. Well, my problem was that Daddy and Jimmy Greer couldn't afford to build me a sprint car at that point, so I had to keep running the midget trail until somebody "discovered" me and offered me a sprint-car ride, or until I made enough money from the midgets to build my own. The latter wasn't likely, because I was winning only about $300 a night. And that's if I swept the whole card.

I think what made me drive harder was the hope that somebody would come along and say, "Would you look at that son of a bitch run! Sign him up for the sprinter."

While I was waiting for all this national acclaim, I was eating beans and sleeping in old garages. Many times we towed the car all night to get to a race and then slept in the back seat of the tow car until it was time to unload and race. Then we wheeled the car off, got qualified, and, more often than not, I blew their doors off and loaded it back up. When I wasn't racing the midget, I was running my Olds stock car.

I was impatient, sure; but there was a good reason for this impatience: Fame seemed to be taking too damn long getting there. But I was determined, and I believed that a man could do anything he wanted to do, if he made his mind up to it. I still do. My mind definitely was made up, but the impatience made me hard on equipment, because I ran as hard as I possibly could. It took me a long time to realize that you have to take care of the car if you want to be around at the finish of most races. That knowledge—maybe "maturity" would be the word—hadn't reached me yet. I ran the hell out of the car until I got the checkered flag or broke the car.

I won a lot of races. Still, nobody was beating down my door to drive his sprint car. What the hell did it take?

Dale said it first. "You're doin' a hell of a job around the Southwest, but if you ever expect to be a champion, you're gonna have to get out of here. You're gonna have to get up to the Midwest or the East or somewhere where they really *race*. Somewhere they're gonna notice you."

Hell, I could have told him that.

"Got any ideas? It takes a ride, you know," I said.

"Matter of fact, I do. Go see Harry Ross," he said. "I hear he needs a driver for his second sprint car."

I was out the door.

Harry Ross worked for Daddy at one time, so he was no stranger. "Harry, ol' buddy," I said. He must have known what was coming after the "ol' buddy" because he had already started to nod. But I continued: "Now, I know you're looking for a driver for your sprinter—a good driver—and I'd like—"

"Okay, A.J.," he interruped, "I'll give you a *try*. We're racing in Minot, North Dakota, next week. You can drive the Jimmy."

Hot damn!

Harry's number-one red-hot sprint car was powered by an Offy engine; his number-two, not quite so red-hot sprinter had a GMC engine—Jimmy, for short. I got the number-two car, but it didn't bother me a bit. It was a *sprint* car. And that was step three. The stock car, the midget, and the sprint. Three down, one to go.

I was like a kid out of school as I waited for the trip to North Dakota. For one thing, I had never raced outside the Southwest; for another, I had never been in an airplane, and they were *flying* us up in a single-engine Cessna 182. That in itself was a big step up.

The morning we left, Tex West said, "You'd better take a razor with you. They might just keep you up there in Yankeeland."

"I don't *shave*, Tex," I said.

"Well, you'd better not let 'em know it, because you're gonna be racin' against *men* up there."

I wondered if they were that good. I forgot about racing when they closed the door to the Cessna. Man, I was all eyes. "You sure this thing is *safe?*" I asked Harry.

"Jesus Christ," he said. "My hero race driver's afraid of a goddamn airplane."

"Listen, Harry," I said, "if God had meant me to fly, he wouldn't have invented the Offenhauser." I was cocky, but it was a cover-up. I would have been a lot happier going up with the guys who were towing the race car. I consoled myself with the fact that I was in the big time now and there wouldn't be anymore sleeping in the back of cars and eating beans. That's what I told myself.

The track at Minot was the first half-mile track I had ever been on, and it looked as big as, say, Oklahoma City. And I found that the IMCA (International Motor Competition Association) circuit *was* a whole lot tougher than any place I had ever raced. The quality of the cars and the drivers was way ahead of anything we had in Texas. My work was cut out for me.

But the first time I sat in that sprint car, any doubts that I had vanished. I could do it.

"Now, listen, A.J.," Harry said. "Don't expect to run as fast as the other car. I mean, don't get upset if you can't keep up, because, well, because it's a Jimmy, you know, and Jimmys just can't run with Offys."

"Sure," I said, "I'll remember that." That was the wrong thing to tell me. I would have busted my ass before I let the Offy outqualify me. I pulled up the bandanna from around my neck to cover my mouth and as much of my face as the goggles didn't cover. I wore a bandanna over my mouth and nose because the tracks were so dusty and the cloth helped filter the air. A lot of drivers wore scarves, but the red bandanna had become a sort of trademark with me.

I not only outqualified the Offy, I also won the race. Why not?

"Tell me the part again about Jimmys not being able to run with Offys, Harry," I said.

Listen, it's beginning to sound like I never thought about girls. I want to set that straight right now. I *did* think about girls. Hell, they were almost as important to me as carburetors and manifolds. There was even a special one: Lucy Zarr. Well, she wasn't special at first. In fact, after a friend introduced us, we didn't take to each other for a while. We made dates and broke them, and neither of us was sure if we even wanted to go out or not. But there must have been something there—something psychologists would put a long name on. Whatever it was, we kept talking about going out until we finally did.

The difference in our backgrounds was right out of a soap opera. I came from the Heights. She came from River Oaks, which is one of the most exclusive sections of Houston. My father was a mechanic. Hers had been a doctor—he had died—and her stepfather, Elliott Flowers, was a prominent lawyer. I was four years older and out of school. She was in high school. And one other thing: I was a race driver.

"It'll never work," we kept telling ourselves. But we went out several times. And we fought like cats and dogs. It was only when I announced to Mother and Daddy that I wanted to take her to the next race that people began to take our relationship seriously. It was only then that *I* began to take our relationship seriously.

She wasn't wild about racing, and it was life itself to me. Everybody who knew us said there wasn't a chance in the world that we would stay together. We didn't have a thing in common. So we did the only sensible thing: We got married.

With romance clearly defined in my life, I could get back to racing. If Lucy was my first love, Harry Ross's sprint car was my second. There were times, Lucy said, it was the other way around.

My next race was in Omaha, where I won a heat race and was running well in the main when somebody spun me out near the finish. But that showing was good enough to prompt Les Vaughan, who had a van-and-storage business there, to offer me a ride in his sprint car. It was an Offy and a good one. And he wanted me to run at St. Paul, Minnesota, which is the Indianapolis of sprint-car racing. I jumped at the chance.

There were sixty cars at that race. Sixty. Less than half would make the show. I figured if I was going to do it, I would really have to hang it all out. So I did. I put the Offy on the pole, which shocked the hell out of everybody. Everybody but me, that is. I could have told them I was going to do that all along.

It was amazing to me how good race cars had started to sound. When you're driving your own car, you hear all sorts of sounds, like it's falling apart. But when you're driving somebody else's, you seldom hear a thing. I didn't hear anything that day.

It was a good day. I won the race and planned to go back to the motel and continue my honeymoon with Lucy. There was a detour.

During the race, I had a brush with Jack Jordan, a more experienced driver but one I considered a friend. Wrong. After the race, Jack said, "If you chop me off again, punk, I'll put you right over the fence."

Some friendships only go as far as the checkered flag.

"Listen," I said, "you drove under me and you automatically

spun yourself, so I don't know how you can figure I chopped
you."

It hurt me that he would say that, so I just walked on toward
the ticket office where we got our purse money. I went from hurt
to upset. Then to flat mad. I told Lucy to go on back to the motel
with Les Vaughan. "I think there's going to be some trouble," I
said.

Buzz Barton, a friend of Daddy's, saw me steaming. "What's
wrong?" he asked.

"Jordan called me a punk," I said.

"Oh, shit," Buzz said. "You know there's five of them over
there, don't you?" he said, pointing to Jack, who was on the other
side of the pits. It was too late. I was on my way. Somebody told
Buzz, "They're gonna kill that kid."

"Don't worry about *that* punk," Buzz said. "That punk can
take care of himself."

I walked up and put my nose about two inches from Jack's and
I said, "What did you call me in the pits?"

"Listen, punk, I meant just what I said, and if you got any
swingin' to do, you better get started," he said.

I hit him right in the mouth.

The fight was on. One of his crew grabbed me and I decked
him. Another got me from behind and held my arms and Jack hit
me so hard that blood ran down into my eye, but I got loose and I
beat the hell out of Jack and two of his crew members. The others
quit.

I went back to collect my purse and Buzz said, "Not bad for a
punk from Texas, huh, kid?"

"Well, hell, Buzz," I said, "I can't have people thinkin' I'm a
punk, can I?"

After all, a man's got his reputation to think of.

The next year, Lucy gave birth to Anthony Joseph Foyt III. I
was so proud I didn't know what to do. But it added another
dimension to my responsibilities. I had to make more money, so
I got a job as a mechanic at Jim Hall Jaguar. And I made the

decision to move on up a notch from IMCA.

The United States Auto Club had been formed to take over when the AAA had pulled out of racing. USAC was running midgets, sprint cars, and a National Championship (Indy car) Series, so I joined up and proceeded to drive sprint cars all over the country, particularly the East.

I couldn't believe how tough some of those guys in the East were. It didn't make a damn to them if they had helmets or belts or roll bars or not; they ran balls out every lap. Guys like Tommy Hinnershitz and Johnny Thomson and Van Johnson and Buddy Linder were hard to beat on dirt. It was a dangerous sport then. In fact, Linder and Johnson got killed in sprint cars within a few months of each other. There were a lot of fatalities in those days. Cars sailed over my head and right out of the track. And I went out a few times myself. Drivers went over fences and they went through them. Keep in mind, they were doing all this with almost no protection. Those guys were race drivers.

Back then there were no roll cages or shoulder harnesses. We wore old cotton seat belts that we got from Army surplus stores and crash helmets that were so flimsy you could squeeze the sides together. They make me cringe when I see one now. There's one hanging in one of my ranch buildings, and I can't believe we actually wore those things.

Of all the drivers on dirt, Tommy Hinnershitz stands out in my mind as the best. Man, he had that sprint car up on two wheels, one wheel, up on its side, whatever it took. And he almost never turned it over. One year, they actually sold advertising space on the *bottom* of his car because it was up on two wheels so much.

The fans at tracks like the ones we ran in Pennsylvania—Williams Grove and Langhorne and Reading—thought Tommy hung the moon. I broke the track record one night at Langhorne, and when they announced on the PA system, "Ladies and gentlemen, A. J. Foyt, the sensational young driver from Texas, has just broken the track record," the crowd cheered like mad. Then the guy said, "That's right, ladies and gentlemen, he has just broken the record held for so long by Tommy Hinnershitz," and just as many people booed. They did a 180, man, because Tommy was an idol of theirs. I'm sorry I didn't get to race against him a few years earlier, because he was really on his way out by the time I got to the Eastern circuit. It would have been fun to race him in his prime. I always felt I could beat most of them without too much trouble.

I needed a bigger arena to prove it.

③
Mecca

In 1956 I made it to Indianapolis. Not exactly the Indianapolis 500, but I made it *across the street* from the Speedway, to the old quarter-mile asphalt track on West 16th.

Well, it was close. And, after all, there was a tremendous spillover crowd there from the 500. Actually, they were waiting for the 500 the next day, but they were Indy fans, nevertheless, and they heard the name A. J. Foyt. I hoped. Maybe some would carry it across the street.

If the midget had only cooperated. But it ran like it was made out of brick. I didn't even make the main. Can you believe that? I had dreamed about Indianapolis nearly every day of my life from the time I could walk until I was twenty-one years old, and right there I was, in the shadows of the hallowed ground, and I couldn't even make the feature race at an asphalt track.

I did qualify sixth fastest for the late-night show. The only problem with that was that the fans who were still there for the late race were so drunk they wouldn't have known the difference between "A. J. Foyt" and "Harley-Davidson." I placed fourth in the first heat race and thirteenth in the late-night show. And I won $68. Shorty Templeman swept the card.

I stayed for the Indianapolis 500 the next day. I did have sixty-eight bucks to spend. On race morning, I went to the garage-area gate and told the guard that I was a race driver and that I had driven across the street the night before. "I'd like to get in the garage area," I said.

"Listen, kid," he said, "there are probably a hundred thousand people out there who would *like* to get in the garage area. Come back when you've got a ride here instead of across the street."

"That might be a lot sooner than you think," I told him. And I walked away. Actually, I stomped away. Things weren't turning out like I expected.

I stood outside the fence at the back of the garage area for a long time, and I watched as they pulled the Indy cars out of the tiny wooden garages and got them ready to take out to the pits. The cars looked even meaner than sprint cars, and I wanted to get in there and touch one. Just sit in it. There was no way in hell that any apprenticeship should take so long. When I had tortured myself for as long as I could stand, I fought my way past hundreds of people who were trying to get a glimpse of the cars the way I had. And I bought a ticket to see the race.

I sat in the grandstands at Turn One along with half the population of Indiana and part of Ohio. And I watched my first Indianapolis 500.

When they lined up the thirty-three cars on the front straightaway, I think it was the most beautiful sight I had ever seen. And when they started the thirty-three engines, the hair stood up on the back of my neck. I knew I could run that race. It was impressive as hell when the green flag dropped and the field charged into the turn, but I couldn't believe how early the drivers were shutting down when they came into the first turn. I thought they were all a bunch of balloon-foots. Hell, they shut off in the middle of the front straightaway, and they *coasted* into the corner.

Of course, I had never driven a track anywhere near that big, and I guess I had never driven that fast, but I thought to myself, Shit, these guys don't even drive down into the corner. Was this what I had waited for all my life?

Paul Russo was leading the race in the Novi when right in front of me he came into Turn One on lap twenty-two and blew a right-rear tire. It sounded like a cannon, and the next thing I knew, Russo slammed into the wall. I thought the car was coming right into my lap. They immediately brought out the yellow flag, but Sam Hanks and Keith Andrews tangled in front of the pits and Troy Ruttman spun to miss them. Then Johnny Thomson spun into the pits and hit a mechanic.

It was only then that I realized the magnitude of the 500. I sat there, sort of stunned by how quick it all happened. I had been involved in sprint-car crashes and had seen many from the cockpit of a race car that were worse, I'm sure. I had seen drivers killed; one, in fact, was killed in a car that sailed right over mine. But to be a spectator and see all the cars spinning was almost too much. It seemed like it was happening in slow motion.

I wasn't sure if I wanted to do this or not.

Pat Flaherty finally outbattled Pat O'Connor to take the lead, but during the course of the race Ray Crawford hit the wall in Turn Four, Al Herman hit the pit wall, Andrews spun again, and Bob Sweikert and Jimmy Bryan spun; Jimmy Daywalt hit the wall in Two, and Tony Bettenhausen hit the wall in front of me. Hell, it was like they were taking their turns crashing. A demolition derby. And I'll be damned if Dick Rathmann didn't hit the wall in front of me *after* the checkered flag.

Pat Flaherty barely beat Sam Hanks to the checkered flag.

I left the Indianapolis 500 grandstands wondering if I wanted to come back or not. Somehow it didn't seem like the kind of thing a man spends a lifetime getting to.

Nearly anybody who was anybody—or had been, for that matter—had had a Wally Meskowski ride. Here are some of the men
who had driven for him: Jimmy Bryan, Don Branson, Tony Bettenhausen, Ed Elisian, Rex Easton, Jud Larson, and Andy
Linden. And a lot of others I'm sure I didn't even know about.
Add one more name: A. J. Foyt, Jr. I had never even met the car-
builder, but he came in search of me to drive his sprint car in
1957. What made this important to me was that he wanted me to
drive it on the USAC National Championship Series trail. It was
the trail to Indianapolis—the *other* side of 16th Street, the one I
had been aiming for since the fifth grade, back when race cars
were homework.

Any doubts I had after watching all the crashes at the 1956
Indy 500 completely vanished when Wally called me. A man's
got a right to change his mind, hasn't he? Wally wanted me to
drive his car at Salem, Indiana.

The car was slightly obsolete, but I pushed it to a fourth-place
finish at Salem. And that was against the big boys. The next race
was at the Illinois State Fair in Springfield. I finished ninth in a
hundred-miler. This wasn't going to be as easy as I thought. I'm
sure a lot of baseball players have felt the same when they've gone
from a Triple-A club to the major leagues.

I drove the hell out of every car in every race, and that was a
bunch, because in 1957 alone I drove thirty-five midget races,
five Championship Series, and four sprints. And half a dozen
stock-car races. The fact that I survived said something for my
ability. Or my luck. It was so much more dangerous in those
days. Oh, there have always been crashes in automobile racing
and there always will be, but with the primitive safety equipment,
it meant that there were far more disabling injuries. And deaths.

If you flipped a sprint car or a midget, it was just you and the
race car and the ground. There weren't roll cages. I don't think
people realized the chances they were taking. But some of those
early guys were stronger than mules. You almost had to be be-

cause the cars were so physical and you needed a lot of strength to handle them. I weighed only about 160 pounds when I started, and I'm sure that those cars are what developed me physically, particularly my arms and shoulders.

Drivers didn't talk as much about death and suicide complexes and all that bullshit then. In fact, it was about the farthest thing from anybody's mind. If you did think it, you didn't talk about it. I think all that came about with *Sports Illustrated*—athletes making like college professors. I mean, did you ever hear of Babe Ruth talking about psychology or Sugar Ray Robinson getting into death wishes? Hell, no. They just did their thing and went home. Racing used to be like that, too.

I remember some female reporter interviewing Jimmy Reece at a Championship car race at Trenton, and she asked him how he handled the constant threat of death.

Jimmy said, "Lady, when I'm out there racin', I'm too damn busy to think about dyin'."

It turned out to be a lot more timely conversation than either of them realized. Jimmy went out in the race and flipped his car clear out of the racetrack. And he was killed. I wish I had had a chance to ask him if what he said was really true, because the thought of death had crossed *my* mind.

But it was just passing through. Once the green flag dropped— I don't care what kind of race it was—I had one thing on my mind: winning. And the lengths I went to would have scared Dick Tracy. It scares *me* to look at the films of some of those early races. I remember one night in particular—it was a midget race at San Bernardino, California. I took the lead, and no sooner did I get up front than somebody tapped my rear and I spun. Well, I drove like an absolute maniac and got in front again. And I spun again. It made me so damn mad that I just threw the car into the corners. I didn't give a shit. I was mad. But I got in front again, and I'll be damned if I didn't spin another time. It took me four more laps, but I got back to the front by the time they waved the white flag—one lap to go.

I came out of the final turn and had the race won and some-body hit me right in the side. The car was totally sideways and I was still on it, just madder than hell, when somebody hit me from the other side. And—would you believe it?—the force from that straightened me up and I won the race.

It was typical of my "don't give a shit" attitude. I drove every race like it was the last one. It's one reason I got the reputation I did when I was coming up. But, I'll tell you one thing, I wouldn't have gotten where I did if I didn't feel that way. You couldn't be careful and catch up in those races. You had to be a little wild if you were going to be a winner.

I always figured that if I had spun, I had already as much as lost the race, so what else did I have to lose? I might just as well get back in and drive like hell.

So much for winning and losing. The time for the 500 was coming around again, and there was no call for A.J. Wasn't any-body paying attention? I decided to run some USAC races in the Midwest and wind up at Indy again in late May; maybe some-body would notice that I was hanging around a lot up there. It turned out to be a good decision, for two reasons. One, I won my first USAC race, a hundred-lap midget race on a quarter-mile dirt track in Kansas City. It was a perfect kick-off for the month of May. We'll get to reason two later. From there I went to In-dianapolis, to hang around some more and wait to be noticed.

More people knew me up there by then. Some fans and some of the drivers I had run against asked if I had a ride at Indy. I didn't, of course, but it was a good feeling to know that people were starting to connect Foyt and Indy. Everybody, that is, but the people who pass out credentials to get into the pits and garage area.

This time, I had a USAC victory under my belt when I went to the office. Didn't make a damn bit more difference than the year before, when I had run sixth in the late-night feature across the street.

"Jesus Christ," I said, "what do you guys want up here?"

"Your name on the side of one of the race cars," the guy said.

Back to the grandstands in Turn One. Those people up there were starting to look like family, which is more than I could say for some of the other people at the Speedway.

USAC had come up with some half-assed plan to try to avoid another of those first-lap crash-'em-up derby scenes that had become so familiar at Indianapolis. They devised this single-file pace lap—instead of the traditional three-abreast start—and it worked just fine. There wasn't a first-lap crash. It happened even *before* the cars got the green flag. The crash took out Elmer George and Eddie Russo. I think they had one man whose only job was to screw up the start of the race. And another to keep me out of the garage area.

After they finally got the race started, it was a hell of a show. Pat O'Connor, Troy Ruttman, and Paul Russo fought lap after lap, with first one and then another taking the lead. For a while there it even looked as if Andy Linden might have a chance. I liked Andy because of a story somebody told me about him. Andy had started in the second row in 1953, and he was running like hell when, for no apparent reason, he lost it in the back straightaway. It was one of those long, agonizing slides that seem to take all day. But it was obvious that Andy was going to hit the wall. It was just a question of where.

He finally slammed into the wall just as he approached Turn Three. Somebody asked him later what he was thinking of while he was sliding along there.

"Well, I thought about gettin' out," Andy said, "but I figured a man's apt to get hurt at that speed."

But this time Andy just couldn't keep up the pace and he ended up finishing fifth. The man none of them could beat, it turned out, was Sam Hanks. It was his day, and that made me feel good.

Sam Hanks had been trying since 1940 to win the 500, and when he took the lead along about the fortieth lap, the fans went wild. Sam was driving what was considered a revolutionary car. It

was a "lay-down" roadster. They had actually laid the Offy engine over on its side, allowing a lower hood line and making the
car a little more streamlined. It was the beginning of a trend to
make cars sleeker, and it worked. Never before had they paid that
much attention to things like aerodynamics. Oh, they tried to
round off the corners as much as they could, and they put
shrouds over everything that stuck out a whole lot—everything
but the wheels, that is. But as for actually trying to design a car
that had less frontal area and wind resistance, well, the lay-down
was a starter.

All of the drivers in the race had Offy roadsters, except Paul
Russo and Tony Bettenhausen, who were driving the Novis. But
the George Salih car that Sam was driving had been built by
Quinn Epperly, and you could just tell to look at it that it was
going to be fast. The nose was low and it had a slim, tapered look
about it. Sam had started back in thirteenth position because he
didn't get qualified the first day, and if you don't qualify on the
first of the four days allotted for time trials, you don't get a crack
at the pole position—no matter how fast you run. It's part of the
ritual.

Once Sam got in front, he was there to stay. There were several crashes during the race, but, aside from the comic start, it
was a pretty safe 500.

I said earlier that there were *two* good things that happened to
me in May. Well, the second one came in victory lane after the
500. Sam Hanks, with tears in his eyes, announced that he was
retiring from racing. He had finally done the one thing he had
wanted so much to do. He had climbed his mountain, stormed
his beach. He had won the Mother Earth of all racing. And now
he was going to sit back and watch some other people bust their
asses for a few decades.

The reason it was important to me was that it started a chain
reaction. Since the Sam Hanks car was so fast, Jimmy Bryan,
who was the current USAC champion, asked George Salih if he
could take over the Belond Exhaust Special. Salih couldn't have

done much better than Bryan, so since he was left high and dry by Sam's retirement, he jumped at the chance.

"What the hell am I going to do for a driver?" asked Al Dean, who owned the Dean Van Lines Special Jimmy had been driving since 1954. (And driving well, I might add. He finished second in '54 and third behind Sam in '57.)

Bryan told chief mechanic Clint Brawner, "Why don't you get that kid A. J. Foyt? I've seen him hanging around the Speedway."

Now, that's more like it.

It turned out that Clint Brawner had seen me race, too, and had already suggested that Al take a look at me, "in case we ever need another driver."

Clint phoned me. They had a driver. It all seemed so simple when it finally happened. The Kansas City *Star* had referred to me earlier in the month, when I won the midget race there, as an "overnight sensation from Texas." I thought of that when Clint called. It had only taken five years of hard work and sleeping in old garages and going hungry and a couple dozen crashes and every goddamn ounce of energy in me to become that "overnight sensation." A quick rise like that deserved a shot at the Indianapolis 500.

The car wasn't as fast as the Belond Special—otherwise Bryan wouldn't have switched—but it was a competitive car. Eddie Kuzma had built it, and with Clint Brawner as mechanic, it *could* win the race. Longer shots had won.

Wives didn't go to Indianapolis in the '50s. Well, some of them didn't go. The only ones who did were the ones who wanted to check up on their husbands. Just to make sure they didn't get laid or killed. In that order. And if some of the ones who stayed home had shown up unexpectedly—at any race, for that matter—there would have been hell to pay. You see, race drivers work hard, and they play hard. Besides, there are all these honeys around all the time. They're called "pit poppies," because they hang around the pit area, just on the other side of the fence, hoping to get to talk to one of the drivers.

It is easy to get one in the sack. If you're so inclined, of course. One of the guys said that you can tell which ones are pit poppies when you get their clothes off because they still have the imprint of the hurricane pit fence on their stomachs.

Auto racing may have invented groupies.

I was on my way to the big show. It seemed like I had waited for that moment all my life. Hell, I don't know what I'm saying. I *had* waited all my life.

This time when I got to the Indianapolis Motor Speedway, it was with a lot more confidence that I approached the office where you got pit and garage-area credentials. No more second-class citizen, hat-in-hand bullshit for A. J. Foyt. I had a *ride* and there was no longer anything they could do to keep me out.

I did everything but pound on the desk when I went in. "I'm A. J. Foyt, a *driver*, you know, an Indy *driver*," I said. Damn, it sounded good. "I'm drivin' the Dean Van Lines Special."

The guy behind the counter—I think Frankie Bain was his name; I don't remember anymore, although I should—anyway, the guy said, "And?"

And?

And? Where's all the respect that goes with being an Indianapolis driver? "And, I want my goddamn pass," I said. I couldn't believe this guy even questioned me.

"Is the car here yet?" he asked.

"No, the car isn't here yet. But I am. I came up early. And I want my pass. I wanna sign in on Al Dean's team."

"Al Dean's not here yet," he said.

"I *know* that. I'm his driver," I said, getting more upset by the minute.

"Sure, kid, you're like all the other rookies. Everybody's a *driver*," he said. "What's your proof?"

"Proof?" I said. "My word's my proof."

"Come back when you've got a car and a car owner," he said. "That's what I call proof."

I couldn't believe it. The same old bullshit as the two years before. What really made me mad is that this year I really *did* belong in there. What the hell did it matter if the car was there or not? I went to every office I could find at the Indianapolis Motor Speedway and I never did get the badge I needed to get into the garage area or the pits.

I could see these guys in there that weren't doing a damn thing. Just telling stories. And I saw some people I knew who didn't have the first goddamn reason in the world to be in there. But I couldn't get in. That's how chickenshit they were then at the Speedway. You know, I'm glad a lot of those bastards are gone now.

Today everybody and his brother can get in.

Here I thought May 2, 1958, was a day that should be marked in red on calendars from then on, with a little note down under, like they do on Arbor Day and Mother's Day. This one would say "The day A. J. Foyt first appeared at the Indianapolis Motor Speedway." Scratch that. I couldn't get in.

The car arrived two days later and I got my badge.

The first thing I did was walk up and down through the garage area, very slowly, trying to take in everything but, at the same time, trying not to look too impressed. But I was so impressed I almost couldn't stand it. For one thing, it was so big. Not only the track—I had seen all that before—but the garage area and the pits. And everything was concrete and wood and, well, *permanent*. More than anything else, I felt that it was something solid and traditional, like, say, Plymouth Rock—wherever that was— or the Liberty Bell.

Everything was old, but it was freshly painted, and even though you could tell it had been there for a long time—fifty years, in fact—it was well cared for. Like a shrine. The garages were four long rows of frame buildings, partitioned off into individual stalls or small rooms with heavy wooden doors and sturdy padlocks. Some of the garages were newer than others because a

fire the night before the 1941 race destroyed several of them—
and some race cars, too—but for the most part they had been
there for a long time.

There *was* something permanent about the Indianapolis 500.

I recall when I was a kid seeing pictures of movie stars at Indy.
I particularly remember Clark Gable being there, and I could
finally understand why. Indianapolis was a *man's* place. And Gable was a man's man. It's only natural that he would come to
Indy. I mean, the place had this masculine feel to it. It even
smelled tough. It was like a big old three-masted sailing ship.
Sailing was a masculine thing to do. So was Indy. I thought
maybe I should name my car *Mayflower*.

When I had soaked up about all the atmosphere my brain
could stand, I decided to look for my garage. "Where's A. J.
Foyt's garage?" I asked a guard.

"Who?" he said.

"The Dean Van Lines Special," I said. Shit.

"Row of garages on your right. Back side," he said. "Garage
Forty-eight," he called after me.

When I got there, Clint Brawner already had the car mostly
apart. It's a thing they have always done at Indianapolis. They
show up with a car that's completely assembled and ready to race
and the first thing they do is take it all apart. But they had been
doing it for half a century, so there was no reason anybody could
see to stop. Like I said, there was all this tradition about Indianapolis.

"Hi, Clint," I said. "Gettin' 'er ready, huh?"

"Oh, hello, A.J.," he said. "Yep, gotta take this all apart here
and make sure everything's okay. I'll have 'er ready for you . . .
maybe tomorrow."

Tomorrow? I had already spent two days waiting. I thought I
was never going to get out on that track.

Just then the sign painter showed up. More tradition. But this
one I liked. They always paint the name of the race car over the
garage door assigned to that car. And the name of the driver.

"Got any name other than A.J.?" he asked.

"Yep. But A.J.'ll do just fine," I said.

Somehow I knew that it was going to be one of the last times anybody would ever have to ask my name again at Indianapolis. I planned to see to that the next day when I got that race car out on the track.

The next day, it rained. It rained for the next four days, and there probably has never been a period in my life when I was so dejected. Each day began and ended the same way: I woke up early—say, six o'clock—went to the window of my Holiday Inn room, pulled back the blind, cussed, and went back to bed. Later in the morning I went to the track and sat in the garages all day and swapped racing stories with all the guys who were in the same boat I was. We played cards a lot.

I got to know them. They were friendly, for the most part, but only two of them took the time to give me any driving tips—Tony Bettenhausen and Pat O'Connor, both top Indy drivers.

O'Connor told me some things to look for and to listen for in the race car. "That track out there does strange things to a car," he said. "The brick pavement sets up a sort of vibration pattern that can drive you crazy if you listen to it. But you have to be aware of it, and if it changes, you know something is happening to the car."

I would have liked to have found out. Jesus, I wouldn't have been surprised to find some guy building an ark in the garage area.

But I had to console myself by listening to race stories. And more race stories. Paul Russo drove the 500 before World War II, so he had driven with Wilbur Shaw and Rex Mays and Ted Horn and Mauri Rose and Ralph Hepburn and some guys who went back to the '20s. Russo was my link with the past at Indy. He actually *knew* these old-timers.

He repeated what had been told to him—of the old days of riding mechanics, for example—and that impressed the hell out of me. I mean, it's one thing to drive a car at Indy speeds, but to ride along while some other idiot is driving it is just flat crazy. Can you imagine somebody crawling around on the hood of an Indy car—while it's running? Well, a guy named Harry Martin—I looked it up in the record book, and it's true—this Martin was the mechanic for Charles Merz, who finished third in 1913, and he was actually out on the hood of the car when it crossed the finish line. What was he doing out there? He was beating out flames with an oily rag.

I had some act to follow.

And then there was the Novi Special. It was there—two of them, in fact. It *was* history. I heard of the earliest days when drivers just went to their local car dealer and bought a car. They took it right off the showroom floor, stripped it down, and raced it. Joe Thomas did that with a National in the second Indy race. He crashed his car the day before the race and went to the factory, which, fortunately, was in Indianapolis, and bought another National passenger car. Just *bought* it. Everybody knows the rest. He won the Indianapolis 500 the next day. They raced Stutz and Duesenberg and a lot of other street machines in the early days. Ray Harroun won the first Indy 500 in a Marmon Wasp, which he drove because he was a friend of the man who owned the factory. Harroun went over there and supervised the building of the car, making a few suggestions when they got to the engine, and he went out and won. He *invented* the rearview mirror while he was at it because he had the only car without a riding mechanic and he didn't have anybody to tell him who was about to run over him.

I was becoming a historian, if not a famous Indy driver. Did you know that Ralph DePalma and his riding mechanic pushed a Mercedes that must have weighed two tons across the finish line? Pushed it. They didn't win, but they sure must have wanted to.

On the fifth day, it stopped raining. Finally. It was time to have a crack at the brickyard. The main straightaway was still paved with brick in 1958. I felt all of the history when I went out there, every record and every hero of the past.

Clint Brawner and the crew towed the race car out to the pit area with a nylon strap attached to an electric golf cart, which was painted white and had flying red horses on it, like the race car. I always thought the Mobil horse was a perfect symbol of Indy, like Champion spark plugs and Firestone tires.

The white Offy roadster had a big blue number 29 painted on its nose and tail. My ride.

Pat O'Connor came over and said, "Go get 'em, A.J. And don't forget what I told you about those bricks." He suggested I follow him for a few laps, just to get the feel. Pat O'Connor was all right.

Indy cars don't have on-board starters. It means your pit crew has to start it with an auxiliary starter—just like a jet airliner. I was buckled in the car, with my crash helmet snug and the red bandanna pulled up over my mouth and nose, and I was ready to go when they stuck the long snout of the starter into the nose of the race car, like they were giving it a big shot of adrenaline or something. Clint looked straight at me. I could see the word form: "Ready?" I nodded. I *was* ready.

The starter whined and I felt the engine catch and roar to power. I could feel the vibration in my fingertips on the steering wheel. It was like taking the car's pulse. I could feel a strong heartbeat. The Offy was ready, too.

I saw the big blue Kurtis-Kraft race car go by. Number 4. It was O'Connor. Indy cars had only two gears forward. No reverse. They were meant to go in two directions: forward and to the left. The first gear is a lot higher than the first gear in a passenger car, so that if you have to use it, you won't overrev your engine. But it's almost too high to get the car off the line from a dead stop, so the crew had to help push the car to get it started.

I motioned toward the first turn with my left hand, and I felt the car start to move slowly forward. I let the clutch out easily and I was rolling. At the end of the pit road, I stepped down harder and the car fishtailed slightly as it approached the track. Three cars were coming down off the bank in Turn One, so I stayed down low on the apron and accelerated through the short straightaway they call the "short chute." And I shifted into high.

I thought, for just a fraction of a second, how far I was from the Heights.

I could see O'Connor's car in the long back straightaway, tooling along, waiting until the oil in the engine got warm enough and the parts got all heated up so he could nail it. I eased down a little more on the accelerator and took aim on the blue car. As I pulled in behind him, he gave me a thumbs up. He wouldn't have seen me if it hadn't been for Ray Harroun's handy-dandy invention, I thought.

After a couple of laps, I saw a slight puff of blue smoke from O'Connor's exhaust, and I knew we were on our way. I pushed the pedal hard to the floor and I felt the power of the four-cylinder, 255-cubic-inch Offy engine. It pushed me back hard in the seat. We went up high in Turn One, down across the turn and into the short chute, down low through Two and out toward the concrete wall coming into the back straightaway. I was limited to 120 miles per hour because I was a rookie. I was being observed all the way around the track.

We turned two or three laps at this speed and then O'Connor waved. I knew he was moving out. He had shown me his way around the Speedway and now he had a job of his own to do.

A race driver can't train another race driver. You have to be born with it. If you don't have it, there's only so much anybody else can do. After that you're on your own. O'Connor and I both knew that. I watched the rounded tail of his Offy fade away and I went about my business, too. I needed to get the driver's test over with. Hell, I hadn't been shackled like this since Daddy and Jimmy Greer had retarded the magneto on my first midget.

The car felt big, but, at the same time, it felt surprisingly agile. I could tell how much power it had even though I was a long way from its top end. More than anything else, it felt natural. Everything felt as if I had been there as long as the bricks themselves. The only thing that was different to me was the sheer size of the

Indy track. It was so big—compared to what I had been used to—
that the turns looked like mirages down at the end of the straightaways. It was like looking out across a Texas prairie.

And I felt just as much at home on that Hoosier track as I did
on the prairie. You've found a home, A.J., I thought to myself.

By the time I had moved up through the proper order of the
rookie driver's test, plateau by plateau—ten laps each at 120,
125, 130, and 135 miles an hour—I felt like an old-timer. I'm
not into the—what do you call it?—occult? Whatever it is, I'm
not into it. But I had this weird feeling that I had done this before. I don't mean driving a race car. I mean driving a race car at
Indy. It all felt so natural, the going down into Turn One and
turning left down across the bank and through the short chute—
all of it.

Maybe it was just that I had been thinking about it for so long.
There were the days in fifth grade when I daydreamed about it;
and all the times at Stewart's Drive-In when Indy was all I talked
about; and the times in the midget when I imagined it to be an
Indy racer. Maybe that was it. I had been living this life in my
mind for so long that it all seemed real. Still, I felt I had been
through those turns before. A long time before.

I knew how a race car should feel. It didn't make a damn if it
was an Indy car or a jalopy; I knew just what it was supposed to
do. Daddy had taught me some of that. But only some of it. I
knew it from the beginning. It's just something that some people
are born with. So I was able to tell Clint Brawner what it was I
thought the car needed. Most of the time I was right. And the car
got faster. I got faster.

In some ways, the big track was easier—after you got used to
going that fast. You had more time to think.

Indy has always been the same. Run as fast as you can and
come in and change it all, trying to run faster. And if someone is
out there running faster than anybody else, you try to figure out
what he's doing to run that fast. You can tell the guys that are
running fastest, too, because they're the popular ones. They're

the ones whose pits are crowded with other drivers and mechanics. Buddy-buddy. Hell, they're not buddy-buddy. They're just trying to find out what he's doing. They're just trying to see if they can pick up something, some little hint, so they can go back and put it to work on their car. And if they find out, it's the last time you see them in the other guy's pit.

Dick Rathmann and Ed Elisian had so many people in their pits there was hardly room for the race cars. They were the ones who were going faster than anybody. So much faster, in fact, that the rest of us just watched in amazement as they went out each day and outran each other. Rathmann would go out there and run like a son of a bitch, and then Elisian would go out and run faster. Then Rathmann would go out and go faster yet. I couldn't figure out where those guys were finding the speed.

Jimmy Reece was another one who was going fast. But he did it in a sort of quiet way. He just went out there and went fast and came in. Rathmann and Elisian made this big show about it. They raced *each other*, lap after lap, day after day. The press picked up on it and the fans mobbed the place, just to watch these two idiots. You can figure, once the press gets involved, it's going to get blown all out of proportion.

While all this was going on, I was out there working my ass off to find the groove that felt best to me. And it was starting to work. I was running as fast as most of the top drivers. I was only a mile or so under Pat O'Connor's speed. But I found out that once you get to a certain speed, you've sort of reached your limit for a while. It's difficult to get that extra mile an hour or so, and that's what makes the difference between drivers. Some never find it, and they're destined to run in the middle of the pack all their lives. Every race. Other drivers—a select few—find the mile an hour or maybe two, and they're winners.

The track is difficult. Every turn is different. The wind blows from all directions. And the grandstands are so big that they block it at times and change it at other times. The track can change on you very quickly, just because of the wind. And the traffic.

But you always keep trying. You try one thing and you go

faster; you try something else and you slow down. It's why you see drivers—even veterans—out there going fast one lap, then slower, then faster. They're trying everything they can think of. And the track is changing on them.

Both Clint Brawner and Al Dean seemed happy with my driving. For a rookie. Al told the press, "I think this guy can do it for me. One of these years, he's going to bring home the bacon right here."

Clint said, "It may take a little time, but A.J. can do it. I mean, you don't become a Jimmy Bryan overnight." They all said Clint was hard-boiled, so words like this meant something.

One thing that pissed me off: Everybody kept telling me what big shoes I had to fill—Bryan had won so many races, including the one in Monza, Italy—but I felt I was filling them pretty well.

I didn't think it was going to take all that long. I sure as hell didn't plan to make any career out of getting to the top. I already had my eye on it.

The first qualifying day was just like it had been all month. Elisian went out there like the hammers of hell and qualified at a new track-record speed: 145.926 miles an hour, and that's a four-lap average. You have four laps under the clock, and they actually take the time you are out there running and they simply divide it by the distance—ten miles. So Ed's speed meant he was going probably 180 or more in the straightaways.

Dick Rathmann went out and turned a 145.974, to break Elisian's record.

Jimmy Reece, just like he had been doing all month, quietly turned a 145.513, which was only a shade off Pat Flaherty's 1956 track-record speed, the one that Elisian and Rathmann broke. The front row was filled.

I qualified at 143.130. Twelfth fastest. That put me on the outside of the fourth row. In fact, it was the best rookie qualifying speed. I was the youngest driver in the field. There were fifty-six drivers at Indy that year, so that meant that I had gone faster than forty-four of them.

Not bad for a punk kid from Texas.

The sun was shining and it was warm on race day. When I left the hotel, it was the usual scene of bedlam outside. It was only six o'clock in the morning and already traffic was backed up as far as I could see in all directions. The traffic jam was worse than either of the other times I had been there. At least it looked that way to me.

I had been awake since four.

The motel was just across the street from the Speedway, and our crew had decided the night before to walk to the track. We had all been there before. It's just that I had never gone to the working part of the Speedway on race day.

I ducked between cars in the bumper-to-bumper traffic on 16th Street and went to a pedestrian gate. I showed them my badge and went inside, working my way through a sea of people in the infield.

The infield at Indianapolis is much like the infield at any racetrack, only bigger. There are more people. And more drunks. They open the gates sometime before dawn, and people who have been lined up for hours start streaming into the place. Many of them have been drinking all night, so they find a good spot in the grass and they zonk out. There are a hell of a lot of people who miss the race entirely. They wake up after it's all over and say, "Well, there's another 500 under my belt," and they go back to Little Rock and tell everybody how great Indianapolis was that year. "Best yet," they say. Well, it might have been the best hangover, but they didn't *see* a thing.

There were many acres of people like that, and as I waded through them, somehow I felt like I was parting the waters.

The sober ones had all the fried chicken and beer in the free world. I mean, there wasn't a single drumstick left in America. And not a can of beer. All of it was at Indianapolis on that day.

By the time I got to the garage area, people were starting to mill around. There was a coffeepot going in every garage, and the drivers who were there already were starting to mill around. That's what you do early on race day. You mill around. First you go to the garages to needle the other drivers. And then you come back to your own garage so people can come in and needle you. It's a very nervous time.

You pee a lot.

There finally comes a time when there's no more needling to be done. No more milling around. The race car had been taken out to the pit area and was lined up neatly with the thirty-two other cars. Three abreast. Eleven rows of gleaming, flat-assed nasty machinery. It was easy to see why the Indianapolis 500 was the greatest spectacle in all of sports. I mean, as I stood there in the pits and looked up at the grandstands all around me, it was like being in the Grand Canyon. The walls of seats and grandstands stretched as far as you could see, and they towered over the people down on the track. And every seat had a body in it. *Three hundred thousand people.* There was a dull roar just from the talking, and every once in a while a cheer went up.

Jimmy Bryan came out on the track. And they cheered. Pat O'Connor came out. They cheered again. I came out, and there was polite applause from some of them. Just because I had on a driver's uniform.

The Pontiac pace car was parked along the pit wall. And there were celebrities from all walks of life. They were milling around, too. Shirley MacLaine was brought in in another Pontiac convertible. And the Purdue University marching band came by, with the world's largest drum, right there in the bed of a pickup truck. There were bands from all over, and marching groups. And they played "On the Banks of the Wabash," and everybody got quiet.

By the time they got to "Back Home Again in Indiana," all of the drivers were out on the track, near their cars. It had gotten very solemn. There were some people cracking jokes after the band quit, and there was some shallow laughter, but nobody was paying a bit of attention to anything anybody else was saying. I could have gone up to any of the other drivers and said, "Listen, buddy, I hate to tell you this, but your engine just fell out," and he would have smiled and said something like, "Sure, pal, me, too."

They played the "Star-Spangled Banner" but nobody heard the words.

Somebody said we should get into our race cars, and I walked over, threw my right leg over the cowl, and got in. I worked my way around in the tiny, cramped cockpit and reached around and took the shoulder harness Clint was handing to me. Nobody said anything. A few people came up and I saw their mouths moving and they smiled and tapped me on the helmet. It's the nice part about having earplugs in and a helmet on: You don't have to answer a lot of bullshit questions. I nodded to all of them.

And then most of the people were gone. It was just my crew and me. And the car. The starter was ready in front of the car. The crowd had gotten quiet. Or maybe I just didn't hear them. I looked out over the long hood of the car. That son of a bitch looked two feet longer than it ever had before. I refocused my eyes on the inside of my goggles, and tried to see where the plastic lenses touched the sponge-rubber frames. Then I worked my gloves down tight, pushing between the fingers with the side of my other hand. Still, nobody said a word.

I tightened the shoulder harness a little and leaned back, letting my helmet touch the tiny roll bar that arched slightly over the back of my head. And I stared up into the restless crowd.

Then I heard the words. It was Tony Hulman. "Gentlemen, start your engines."

Jesus.

I felt the starter clank into place and I flipped the toggle switch for the ignition with my right hand. I pumped the accelerator very slightly as I felt the engine begin to turn over. It caught and I felt the power run through the entire car. I zapped the accelerator. Hoodin! Hoodin! Hoodin!

The starter was moved away from the car, and in a second I

saw Tony Bettenhausen's dark-red lay-down roadster move out. I turned and winked at my crew, and I eased the clutch out. I felt my car moving. And I looked way ahead into Turn One, where we would all be going full bore very soon. The nervousness was going away.

As we followed the Pontiac around the track for the pace lap, I could see Dick Rathmann and Elisian. They were pulling away from the field. Jimmy Reece moved up with them, and there was a big gap between the first row and the rest of the field. As we came out of Turn Four, we got the sign for one more lap. They were trying to close the gap between the first row and the rest of us.

I thought, "Those two bastards are going to ruin everything." But by the time we got out of Turn One, the field was together again. Everything looked good until we came out to Turn Four. The starter hadn't even waved the flag yet, but Rathmann and Elisian were gone. There were other cars going fast. Some thought the race had started; others weren't sure. But they waved the green anyway, and the race really *had* started.

I hit the accelerator hard and steered up high, near the wall, as I came down the front straightaway. Bettenhausen was there, too, so I followed him into Turn One. I could smell burned rubber and exhaust. It is the thing racers get high on. And I could see the crowd on its feet, cheering. We accelerated smoothly out of the turn and down across the banked track into the short chute. I looked ahead to see what was happening in the front of the pack. Dick Rathmann had beaten Elisian to the turn but Ed had pulled right in behind him. By the time they got to the back straightaway, Elisian had pulled alongside, just under him. They were running wheel to wheel.

There is more than one place to go through any corner on a racetrack. But there is only one place—or groove—where you can go through it wide open. Any other place and you will either spin or somebody will knock you into the wall or the infield. It has something to do with some law of physics. And the size of your balls.

Elisian and Rathmann were approaching this spot in Turn Three, still running wheel to wheel. It looked like the biggest game of chicken in the world. It *was* the biggest game of chicken in the world. While they were at it tooth and nail, I had moved up a few places in the field. I had a good seat for the game of chicken.

They got to the turn. Rathmann backed off slightly, and Elisian, who was in the groove—that's the only reason Rathmann backed off; there was no place for him to go—well, Elisian was in too deep and too fast. I saw Elisian's car bobble slightly. That's the sign of trouble at Indy. There just wasn't time to turn the car. He slammed into Rathmann and the force took both cars into the concrete retainer wall. Rathmann's car was chopped in two; parts from Elisian's car were sailing everywhere.

I saw Reece slow down, and then Bob Veith hit him, sending Reece's car directly into the path of Pat O'Connor. Son of a bitch. O'Connor's car went up and over and sailed fifty feet in the air, and when it hit the track on the other side, upside down, it burst into flames.

Everything was happening so fast. But I could see everything, and I remembered everything I had heard in the driver's meeting. "If you see a car spinning on the start, look for a place to go," they had said. "Be careful of the first lap," they had said. "Watch the lead cars," they had said. I did all of those things, and it was *happening*. Just like they had said.

I thought, Oh, shit, I've come this far and it's all over. I didn't even make a lap.

I looked for a place to go. There were cars sideways in front of me, so I spun my car to keep from hitting them. There was a hole and I sort of pulled myself up straight in the seat, trying to make myself as thin as I could. Somehow I thought it might make the car thinner. While I was sideways, I saw a car go up over another car and flip right out of the Speedway. I found out later it was Jerry Unser going over Paul Goldsmith.

My car was still sliding through the hole between Johnny Parsons and Tony Bettenhausen. I got through without touching a thing. The slide had scrubbed off a lot of my speed, like I hoped it would. The car was still spinning to the right, so I turned the wheel right and it started to straighten out. And then I saw it. A clear track ahead.

I had made it.

The yellow lights were all on, of course, so I kept it at about 100 miles an hour. When I got back around to the crash scene, I counted fifteen cars that were involved. They were sending traffic above, below, through, anyplace you could go without hitting a car or a broken part or a tow truck or an ambulance.

O'Connor's car was still burning.

I tried hard not to look at it. Goddamm it, I didn't want to look at it.

The next time I came around, the fire was out, but it was still smoking. I looked. Shit. Why did I look? Pat's arm was frozen in midair. Everything was black. His car, his helmet, his uniform, everything.

Son of a bitch, I thought. I wasn't sure I was tough enough for Indianapolis. It was going to take some thinking.

It took them twenty laps under caution to clear the debris from the track. Long after his car and his body were taken away, I could see Pat's arm sticking up in the air. I felt sick. When I came by the pits, I could see Ed Elisian sitting on the pit wall. His helmet was off and his head was in his hands.

I wondered how it could have happened. But I knew the answer just as well as any of the drivers. You race all month with a guy and you build up this rivalry. It almost becomes a hate. But it isn't. Only race drivers feel it. Maybe some people feel it on the highway. There are just some people who don't like to be passed. But in racing it builds up so much stronger. It becomes an obsession. I guess that's what happened to Elisian and Dick Rathmann. They just got overcome with the obsession to beat each other.

The rest of the race was hollow for me. I was running as hard as I could, but I wasn't comfortable. I was petrified, to tell you the truth. And I've never said that before. I ran hard; I just didn't feel like I had in other races. The spirit wasn't there. I was within sight of the leaders most of the time, but the race was all between Bryan and George Amick and Johnny Boyd.

On lap 148, a water hose broke in my car, spraying water not only all over the car and me but on the track as well. A race car running in water—even its own water—does not do well. I felt it start to go. It's a feeling I know well. And I knew just as well that there was no saving it. There's a difference between being squirrelly, knowing that you can save it by turning the wheel this way or that, and being out of control. You reach a point where all the superior knowledge and skill in the world can't save it. I had reached that point.

The car skidded out of the first turn, across the short chute and toward the wall. I kept seeing that first-lap crash. And the fire. The car missed the wall and spun the other way, down into the infield. It was then that I realized I had been holding my breath. I guess I always held my breath when I was sliding. But I didn't realize it until then.

I wound up in sixteenth place, and I won $2,919 for my efforts. Half of that went to Al Dean, the car owner. Jimmy Bryan went on to win the race in the Belond Special—the laydown car. It was the second year in a row that the car had won. Jimmy won $100,000.

If I had stayed in the race to the end, I might have won Rookie of the Year honors. The way it was, George Amick, who finished second, was the top rookie. You might have heard a lot more about George, but he was killed the next year at Daytona.

I vowed one thing when I left Indianapolis: I would never get close to any race driver again. And I've stuck to it. I've never run around at night with any of the other drivers. I've always been by myself. A lot of people think I'm stuck-up at times, but it's not true. It's a bad thing to see some driver get killed—real bad—but you just have to walk away from it and not let it play on your mind. You can't have something like that on your mind when you're out there going 180 miles an hour. I found that out.

④
Indianapolis Revisited

It was amazing what driving in the Indianapolis 500 did for my image. I was asked to speak at women's-club luncheons, both Houston newspapers interviewed me, the television stations sent cameramen over, and I even got fan mail. I heard from relatives I never even knew I had. I wonder what it would have been like if I had won?

Everything was starting to work for me. I went to Monza, Italy, with a team of American drivers with Indy cars to take on the best Europe had to offer. The year before, Jimmy Bryan had blown everybody's doors off. I thought it was a damn nice thing for them to take me.

I wish I could have had the chance to show my stuff. The car broke, and I ended up driving the car Juan Manuel Fangio was supposed to drive. I got a sixth overall in the three-heat event.

Jim Rathmann won all three, which was a hell of a feat. Bryan was second. Again it was a complete sweep for the Americans.

We drove a lot faster than we did at Indy because of the high-banked turns on the Monza track. You could drive right down into those turns, just like I thought the drivers should have been doing at Indy when I watched that first race from the grandstands. That was before I drove Indy, of course. After I started driving it, it was a different story. At those speeds, things are happening fast, and with a relatively flat track, you have to back off much earlier, or you'll wind up in the grandstands with all the would-be drivers who think you're a balloon-foot.

When you're in the car, you don't feel you're slowing down that much when you go into turns. It might *seem* that way from the other side of the track, but it doesn't in the race car, I'll tell you. You get off the throttle, but the car actually doesn't slow down too much. It just sounds like it because it gets so much quieter. You can't feel much change in the sensation at all. In fact, you really don't *have* that much sensation of speed. It's not like a dirt track, where you're sliding sideways most of the time; those are G forces you feel, I guess, because of the sudden change in direction. You don't have that at tracks like Indy and Monza. Besides, all of the cars are going roughly the same speed. It's not like being out on the Interstate at, say, 90 miles an hour and blowing by everybody. Look at the qualifying speeds and you'll see that there's only about a three- or four-mile-an-hour difference from top to bottom. It proves what I said about the last mile or two being the hardest to get.

On the highway, you've got a guide. On the track, you lose those reference points. Sure, if you look at the grandstands—I mean, really take a long look—you see everything going by very fast. But you don't have time to take a long look at the grandstands. If you do, you'll be *in* them.

At Monza, there was more sensation of speed. For one thing, we were going past the Europeans about like you pass slower cars on an Interstate. For another, we were driving deeper into the turns, and it was a more sudden change of direction. It gave the feel of a dirt track. The banks there were probably three times higher than the 12-degree banks of Indy. But, then, Indy was built in 1909, and 12 degrees was fine for the speed of the cars then. The average speed of the first race at Indy was 74 miles an hour.

It was a tribute to the drivers in the '50s that they were going twice that fast. I had to go all the way to Italy to realize that.

The 1959 Indianapolis 500 had all the earmarks of a banner year for me. I was going to drive a new lay-down Dean Van Lines Special. You see, I had completely gotten over any doubts I had after the big crash the year before. If anything, I was more excited about the '59 race than I had been about the first one. There was no doubt: I was hooked. I imagine it's like being hooked on drugs or booze. I don't know, because I've never faced that problem, but I wonder if you get hooked as quick as I did on Indy.

And a lay-down car—man, that was it. The last two 500s had been won with that kind of car, so I knew that was all I needed. I always felt that it was a lot more the driver than it was the car— maybe 75 percent to 25 percent—so with a top car, I really thought I could win. I knew I had the ability.

Another nice thing about the second year at Indy is that they *knew* me. I got my badge without any trouble. Not being the new kid on the block any longer was a damn nice feeling.

There were some changes. For the first time, USAC required roll bars and fireproof driving suits. Many drivers—like me— had used both before, but there were an awful lot who drove in T-shirts, right up to the time they were forced to change. Not me. I got that out of my system before my first race. You remember the silk shirts and the white pants.

But the mechanics screwing around with the race cars hadn't changed. It still took a couple days before I could get the car out on the track to see what it would do. When I finally did, I was like a kid with a new toy.

I made two laps and came in. Clint rushed over to the car, about as excited as I had been. "How's it feel?" he asked.

I didn't know how to tell him. I figured the plain truth was best.

"It doesn't handle worth a shit," I said.

Clint and Al and everybody on the crew said it in unison: "It doesn't handle worth a shit?"

"Whattaya mean it doesn't handle worth a shit?" Al said.

"Yeah, whattaya mean?" Clint said.

"I mean, it doesn't handle worth a shit," I said. "You know, like crap." I never was much on mincing words.

"Wait a minute," Clint said. "You mean to tell me that car doesn't *handle*. How do you explain the fact that lay-down roadsters won the last two races here?"

"Well, they didn't win them in *this* car," I said. "And I'll tell you one more thing: I don't see how they won at all. I mean, I don't think they're as good as the old-type roadsters."

"Listen to the *expert*," Clint said. "One race and he's an expert."

"Screw you," I said. "I'm out there drivin' it and I know how it feels." Eddie Sachs came over and joined in our friendly little conversation. "That sled handle any better than my lay-down?" he asked. "I mean, mine doesn't handle worth a shit."

Eddie Sachs knew what he was talking about. Here's a guy who had been at the Speedway six times. You can't tell a goddamn mechanic a thing. You really can't.

Elmer George took over the ride in the old roadster I had driven the year before, and I'll be a son of a bitch if he wasn't going faster than I was. I didn't let up a bit on Clint. We worked every day in trying to improve it. Even with the lower profile, there still wasn't that much aerodynamics involved in Indy race cars. They were all about the same—the same suspensions, the same engines, the same gearboxes. So it pretty much depended on how the car was set up.

"Set up" is a term you hear around racing all the time. What it means is how the suspension parts are adjusted and how the weight is distributed on each corner of the car. Most of the time the term should be "screwed up" instead of "set up." I've already said that the cars are sometimes better when they arrive at Indy than they are on race day. It's really true. Even the best of mechanics and the best drivers have to change everything, all the time. It's as much a tradition at Indy as, say, the drunks in the infield.

When you change the weight distribution, they call it "jacking weight." You can balance the car differently, so that there is more weight on the right front, or less on the left rear—whatever it takes to make the car stick better in the turns. It varies on every car. And with every driver. It depends on a lot of things, like how far a driver is driving into the turn before he lifts, how soon he gets back on the throttle coming out of the turn, the line he takes going through the turn. A lot of things.

We jacked weight here and we jacked it there and at times we had it so screwed up that we had to go back to square one and start all over again. There was a lot of tension in our garage. I mean, I was right there, grease up to my armpits, working with Clint to try and get the thing straightened out. We worked in the garage with the doors closed so nobody would come in and steal our secrets. Everybody does that, too. A guy can have the worst-handling pig that ever hit the track at Indianapolis, and he thinks somebody wants his secret formula. Why Clint thought anybody would want to use the combination we had was beyond me. You would have had to be crazy to set up a car the way we had ours.

But we would get it all set up—all jacked around—and then we'd tow it out to the pits, and I would climb in and go like hell out on the track. Then I would come back into the pits to report. Everybody in the crew always stood around on one foot and then the other, sort of leaning forward. They all leaned forward a lot, waiting to hear what I had to say.

"Not worth a shit," I said each time.

The argument was on.

There isn't a mechanic in the world that gives a driver credit for knowing a goddamn thing about race cars. They think that a driver is just a necessary evil, and they would be a whole lot happier if you just ran all the race cars by remote control. I can see the whole picture: You've got thirty-three mechanics, sitting along the pit wall, each one with a little black box with two controls, and they're running this Indianapolis 500. Two-thumbing it. "Look at that son of a bitch go," they'd yell. "Man, he's got the best *thumbs* in the business." And then they would have this banquet and they would give the Golden Thumb award. That's how mechanics feel.

Race drivers, of course, are just the opposite. They've never changed from the time Joe Thomas went into his local National automobile dealership and bought a car and went out and won the 1912 race with it. He didn't even need a mechanic to jerk off the fenders and the running board.

Drivers and mechanics almost never agree on a damn thing.

I said it then, and I say it now: That lay-down roadster I had was a dog. You won races in those days by driver ability and pit strategy. But you also had to have a car that would go through the turns. We continued jacking weight and adjusting everything. And we continued fighting.

A lot of teams were having problems. Jerry Unser, another of the many in a long line of racing Unsers, started at Indy the same year I did, but he didn't qualify the first year. He went out about the middle of the month and it looked like he had it all put together at last, but he came out of the fourth turn and lost it. The car spun and hit the wall, sending it end over end down the front straightaway. There were parts flying everywhere. The car caught on fire.

When a car crashes like that and then catches on fire, you know the outcome. It's a miracle if you survive an end-over-end crash, but to combine that with fire—particularly in those days, when you could carry so much fuel—well, you didn't have much of a chance. Jerry didn't make it.

The same day, Bob Cortner removed the yellow tape strips from the rear of his car, indicating that he had passed his rookie driver's test. Two days later, he hit the wall in Turn Three and was killed.

We all started to get a little paranoid. The minute the car got a little squirrelly, the driver came in and started yelling at his mechanic. It was a full-scale war. And by the time we got to the first of the two qualifying weekends, half the cars were screwed up.

Everything about Indianapolis is either bigger, longer, or more complicated than at any racetrack in the world, so it is only natural that it would take twice as long to get the cars qualified. If you don't get qualified on the first weekend, then you've got a whole week to screw up your car even worse before you try again.

By the time the first qualifying weekend got there, my car wasn't a bit better. I went out there on the track to take my turn at the four-lap run, and the car was handling so bad that I waved off the try on the third lap. You can do that. If you're not satisfied with the way the car is performing or you think you can better your speed, you can wave it off, simply by coming into the pits instead of staying out there and going through the timing lights in the front straightaway. You can come in, jack some weight, or whatever, and get on the tail end of the qualifying line again.

My time was poor, so I came in. We worked on the car some more and I took it out to practice. Scratch one engine. I blew up the Offy like a bomb. Also scratch any chance of sitting on the pole, because there was no way we could get the car ready again for that day, and, like I said before, if you don't get qualified the first day, you can plan on being back about the middle of the pack on race day. Tradition.

We got a fresh engine. I didn't have much enthusiasm because I had missed my shot at the pole, so I decided not to try the second day either. Might just as well wait for the next weekend, I figured. Maybe some miracle would come along and get it straightened out.

Like I said, a lot of other drivers were having problems. Tony

Bettenhausen flipped his car through a wooden barrier upside down, and there was blood everywhere when the emergency crews got to him. It turned out that all he had was a bloody nose. Sometimes you get lucky.

Jimmy Bryan's car was as bad as mine, and he missed the first day of qualifying, too. So I figured I was in good company, if nothing else.

I qualified the second Saturday, settling for seventeenth spot. That meant the sixth row, along with Paul Goldsmith and Pat Flaherty. Johnny Thomson was on the pole. Eddie Sachs and Jim Rathmann filled out the first row.

I was glad to get the whole qualifying mess over with. I wish I could say that after you finally get qualified at Indy, all you have to do is sit and wait until the race, but it's not that simple. Nothing is at Indy.

They give you another whole week to screw around with your car. And then, at the end of that week, you get to go out for what they call "carburetor tests." You can make your final runs and do your final adjusting. One last shot at completely screwing up your car.

You also run for the first time with a full fuel load. Up to this point, you make your runs with only a partial tank, for two good reasons: First, the car is lighter, since fuel weighs seven pounds per gallon, so if you multiply this by, say, sixty or seventy gallons, well, hell, it's like hauling around your lard-assed brother-in-law in the race car. Second, if you crash, it's safer if you have only a small amount of fuel. And when you're still screwing around with suspension changes, the chances of crashing are good.

On carburetor-test day, you go out with a full fuel load to see exactly how the car handles and what changes you might have to make. The stands are always crowded because there are usually crashes.

But if you get through that, then you can sit back and relax until race day. Two days away. This means that you have spent the entire month in Indianapolis. You have been at the track every day, made every change in a race car that can possibly be made. If you're trying at all to live up to the race-driver image, you've been drunk twenty times, laid thirty-five, had twenty hangovers, and blown two engines. And they give you one day to rest. Damn, racing is fun.

They managed to get through the pace lap and the official start of the race without a crash. It was the first time in three years. Starting way back in seventeenth place is not that bad, really. After all, you've got 500 miles to get up front, so why not just take your time and work on a car at a time, and by, say, mile 300, you can knock off the leader and win. Almost nobody does that.

I like to get up front as soon as I can because it's a lot easier to *stay* there than it is to *get* there, so why not get the hard part over with first? I always eat the crust of the pie first, too. That saves the best part for last.

But coming from seventeenth position is not as easy as it might sound, because there are sixteen other guys in front of you who have exactly the same idea that you do. You have to outdrive every one of them. And then you've got all those guys in back of you who are trying to do the same thing. It's why some guys qualify so well and then seldom do a damn thing in a race. Either all the race traffic intimidates them or they just can't figure it out fast enough. You've got to think fast. The second you see a hole or the instant some guy in front of you has a slight case of brain fade—say, he just hesitates a second—well, you have to make your move immediately, and it has to be the right one, because you don't get a second chance. Either the hole fills up or, if you've made the wrong decision, you screw up.

I was able to play on some mistakes in some cases and some slight hesitations by drivers in other cases.

On about the fifth lap, I got past Paul Goldsmith going into Two and then blew off Don Branson in the back straightaway, all because I had such a good line on the turn and I came out of it so fast. Goldsmith wasn't expecting it, and Branson flat didn't see me coming. On the next lap I tried to go past Jimmy Daywalt on the inside, but he used up all the groove and wouldn't let me past. In racing, you just don't get many guys who will say, "Why, yes, sir, Mr. Foyt, you just come right on past here. Pardon me, sir." You get more who say, "Screw you, Foyt. This here's my groove. Go find yourself another one."

I found another one. I tried time after time to get past Jimmy low, so when we went into Turn One, he was expecting me to come charging down there again. For one thing, it's a lot easier—and safer—to pass low. Well, I moved the car down where I had been for the past several laps, and then, just as we got into the turn, I moved that rascal up high and went right by him. There wasn't much room between him and the fence, but I got past.

I had moved up six places in the first ten laps. By the twentieth lap, I had gotten past Jack Turner and Bob Veith, to move into eighth spot. The rest of the way was tough going. It's just like getting to a certain speed. I mentioned that the faster you go, the harder it becomes. It's the same thing in passing cars. The more you pass, the tougher it gets. You've got to figure that the guys in front of you are there because they're running well. Otherwise, they'd be behind you. So you're going to have to work harder with each one you pass.

It took me to the halfway point in the race to get past Tony Bettenhausen and Bobby Grim. Then, ten laps later, I passed Bill Cheesbourg. I was in fifth place. But there was still a long way to go, and even though I was driving as hard as I had ever driven a race car, I started to get pretty cautious, too. It wasn't that I was afraid of making a mistake; it's just that I knew other drivers can make mistakes, too, and I didn't want somebody else to take me out with him. You never do.

Duane Carter had been following me for many laps, trying to get by me, and Duane had been running at Indy since 1947, so he knew every trick in the book. I knew a few, too. And I used them all to keep him back there. It was lap 130. Of 200. I saw him coming hard, and I punched it, too. I felt him hit me in the rear. It wasn't that hard, but it doesn't take too much when you're in a turn. You're always right on the edge anyway. I thought, Oh, shit. You always think, Oh, shit.

The car started to slide, but I was ready for it. The tires were squealing like hell and I was steering for all it was worth. I was definitely out of shape, but I could feel the tires starting to get a bite again. You can tell when you've got it gathered up, just like you can tell when you've lost it. And I knew I was going to be able to save it.

There's never a time when you have to work so hard, but, at the same time, you have to do it gently. It's like making love to a porcupine.

But I saved it. Unfortunately, I had lost about four places while doing it. And even though you avoid a crash, it always takes something out of you. You have all that work ahead of you again. You have to go right after the guys you worked so hard at passing, and, well, it's just hard on your spirit.

It was time to pit. They gave me the board, which had on it in big, block, chalk letters "A.J. P 2." What it meant was "Pit in two laps."

I pitted, but I came in so fast that I almost overshot my pits. You don't have any reverse, and your crew can't go get you and push you back, because there's other traffic in the pits and they would get run over, so you have to go out and come back again, and you can just kiss the race good-bye if that happens. But I was within reach of the gasoline hose. The crew could tell that I was starting to struggle with the car, and the race. The near spin and the 400-plus miles and sheer exhaustion had started to take their toll.

I saw Rodger Ward and Johnny Thomson and Jim Rathmann go by on the track while I sat there waiting for the crew to change three tires—both rears and a right front—and fill the car with fuel. If everything goes right, it only takes about 20 seconds for all that service, but it always seems like it takes twenty *minutes*. Everything went right, and I charged out of the pits to try once more to catch the leaders, but I knew, just like everybody else, that it was too late. There just wasn't enough time to work my way past all those cars. But I never give up, so I drove like hell.

There was a glimmer of hope when Pat Flaherty crashed and Eddie Sachs's car failed and Dick Rathmann's car caught fire in the pits. Johnny Thomson's car started to go sour, but my car started to slow down, too. That happens late in a race; many cars just get tired. Johnny Boyd went past me. And then Eddie Johnson. And then Paul Russo. Shit, I wondered if I had *stopped*.

Way up front, Rodger Ward had gone into the lead to stay.

I finished tenth.

That's not bad. I was in the top ten in my second Indianapolis 500. But, I *had* been as far up as fifth. And, from there, I could *see* first place.

One more thing before we leave Indianapolis for 1959.

There was a big crash on the forty-fifth lap. Mike Magill was trying to pass Chuck Weyant on the outside and he got squeezed into the wall. It goes to show what I said earlier about why it's better to pass low. Well, Magill's car flipped end over end down the short chute between Three and Four. That took care of those two cars. Jud Larson and Red Amick ran together trying to miss the other two cars, taking them out. Nobody was injured, despite how hard the cars hit. Then Bobby Grim, who was named rookie of the year, came along and, in the excitement of the spinning cars, threw his arm up so hard to signal the other drivers to slow down that he dislocated his shoulder. Explain that one.

The rift that started between the Dean Van Lines team and me didn't get any better, despite the fact that I came close to winning a couple of races. I thought it was the car; they thought it was me.

When George Bignotti called me near the end of the season and wanted to come to Houston to talk about teaming up, I told him to come on down. I felt Bignotti was one of the best mechanics in the business. He was a lot like me in that he was very independent. He didn't have any ties with anybody, and I felt that was an advantage. He could do exactly what he thought should be done without having to cater to this person or that sponsor.

I had already signed a contract for the 1960 season with Al Dean, but a problem had come up between us. It involved some parts they had promised to sell me for my sprint car. They hadn't lived up to their end of the bargain, so I didn't look at my contract as all that binding, either. I was ready to talk to George.

Bignotti brought a message from Bob Bowes, who owned the Bowes Seal Fast Special. There was a ride there if George and I could work out a deal. The deal appealed to me because Bowes Seal Fast was one of the most respected names at Indianapolis. They went clear back to the *beginning* of sponsorships at the 500, and the list of drivers who had driven Bowes Seal Fast cars included Wild Bill Cummings, Shorty Cantlon, Rex Mays, Louie Meyer, and Troy Ruttman. Lou Schneider won the 1931 race in a Bowes Seal Fast Special. Johnny Boyd had finished third, sixth, and fifth in the past three races in the Bowes car.

I called Al Dean and said, "I know I signed a contract for 1960, but you all backed out on your deal with me on the parts for the sprint car, so I quit." End of conversation. End of me and the Dean Van Lines Special.

If there was ever a period in my life that stands out above the others, it was the Bignotti years. And I'll bet it stands out in George's, too. And in the minds of just about everybody around racing. It started off on the quiet side, but it didn't stay that way long.

When I got to Indianapolis in 1960, the car was there, and, much to my surprise, it was *ready*. I'd never heard of such a thing. George was chief mechanic on two cars that year. Johnny Boyd drove one and I drove the other. They were both lay-down roadsters, but George and I had talked the whole thing over and I was convinced that his version would work.

I wish I could say that I jumped in the car and from that moment on my problems were over in racing. It's never that simple. The Bignotti car was a lot better than the car I had been driving, but it still wasn't as good as it should have been. Troy Ruttman and Dick and Jim Rathmann and Rodger Ward and Johnny Thompson and about half the field were going three or four miles an hour faster than I was. It was getting frustrating as hell.

I fumed at George. And he fumed right back. Our battles quickly became the talk of the Speedway. By qualifying time I had made up my mind that I wasn't going to set the Speedway on fire that year. I was right. I qualified sixteenth. Sixth row again, this time with Johnny Thomson and Tony Bettenhausen. Both of them were considerably faster, but they didn't get qualified the first weekend. I figured they could just walk off and leave me on the start. In fact, the three cars right behind me were faster, too.

I felt like I might run with them when the race started, because I really thought I could do better in traffic than almost any of them. But there wasn't much of a race to it. For me. Up front Rodger Ward and Johnny Thomson and Jim Rathmann were at it tooth and nail, just like they had been in 1959. And Eddie Sachs was running good.

I could see all this from the pits. That's where I was from lap 90 on—out of the race with a bad clutch.

It was a helpless feeling, being out of the race at the finish.

Rodger Ward and Jim Rathmann ran wheel to wheel until two laps from the finish, when Ward had to pit, so Rathmann won. I imagined how Ward felt, but at least he had been in the battle. I felt like I had been drafted for the war but never got to go on the battlefield.

By the time I got back to the motel, I was madder than hell. Lucy had come with me to Indy, so she had to listen to it. "I'm no better off than I was with Clint Brawner," I said. "I'm sick of this. I mean, I've worked so damn hard, and I don't have a thing to show for it. I feel like quittin'."

Lucy didn't say a word. She didn't have to, because she knew I would never quit. She just let me blow off my steam. The next day I was ready to go again. But that's the way I've always been. I don't keep anything bottled up inside me. If I feel something, I say it. If I feel like raising hell, I raise hell. And then, five minutes later, I'm over it. I don't hold grudges.

And it was a good thing, as it turned out. George and I really got our act together by mid-season. I won my first Championship-car race at DuQuoin, Illinois. Then I won the Hoosier Hundred at the Indianapolis Fairgrounds. Then I won the Championship-car race at Sacramento. I had won three of the final five Champ-car races since Indianapolis. It came down to Rodger Ward and me at Phoenix.

I really had the championship all but won. There was a possibility on paper that Rodger could take it away from me, but he had to win the race and I had to finish farther back than fifth place. So everybody I talked to said the same thing. "Now, A.J., we know how hard you want to charge and we know how you want to win that race, but just get out there and stroke it, for chrissakes. Take it easy. You've got the championship all won, so take it easy."

Bignotti said, "Take it easy." Bowes said, "Take it easy." I wouldn't have been surprised to get a telegram from President Eisenhower saying, "Take it easy."

The telegram would have helped. I wouldn't have taken it easy, but I would have thought about it for a second.

When they dropped the green flag, I shot into the lead. I was going to win. There was no way I was going to back into my first championship by "taking it easy."

In a 100-mile race, if you have to pit, you've as much as lost. So when I saw Ward go into the pits about halfway through, I knew I was the USAC champion for 1960. It would have been a perfect time to listen to all the advice everybody had given me.

So I kept right on hammering it.

It felt so good. I kept it sideways longer than anybody else on the mile dirt track. I drove deeper into the turns than anybody else. I accelerated sooner coming out of the turns. And I won that race.

I was the champion.

I stayed right on it, even after the checkered flag. I took my victory lap—you know, the one where you tool around once more, waving to the crowd—well, I took *that one* wide open. And I *slid* right into victory circle. Bignotti said, "You son of a bitch, you're crazy."

The next year at Indianapolis, my car would have a great big number 1 on it.

After the race Bignotti said, "God damn, A.J., you sure had that son of a bitch under control all day. It looked like you were right on the verge of losing it on every turn, but you had it under control, buddy."

George was right. On both counts. I had it under control. But—and I've never admitted this to anyone before—I *was* right on the verge of losing it. All day.

I remember going by Sachs one time completely sideways.

After the race, he said, "Man, A.J., that time you went by me sideways, you were going so fast the wind damn near pulled my jockey shorts off."

⑤
My Badge, Please

The most important thing that comes with winning the USAC championship is respect. It meant I didn't have to take any more crap. And there were a lot of people at Indianapolis that I told to kiss my ass. The guys who wouldn't let me into the garage area and the guys in the offices who wouldn't listen to me. I tried to tell them.

I know: They probably hear it all the time. But a lot of guys who get only a few days in the sun—only a short time to show their authority—turn out like some of the guys at Indy. Parking-lot attendants are like that. I mean, they have this really lousy job, but they get to tell you what to do with your car. Traffic cops are the same. But some of the guys at Indy could have been a little nicer about it; I don't care if they heard it every minute of every day. And I wasn't going to let them forget about it. Four years after I went there the first time, trying to get in, I was back as USAC champion.

Sweet revenge.

USAC did a worse thing to Leon Clum than not give him a badge. You probably don't remember him. The reason you don't remember him is because some guy at USAC got a hard-on for him, just because he had run a lot of outlaw tracks—you know, tracks that weren't sanctioned by USAC. Leon was a very capable race driver; he had run sprint cars and Championship cars and he came to Indianapolis to take a crack at the big one, which he deserved. But he did some little thing they didn't like on his driver's test. It was so small I can't even remember what it was. Nit-picking. And they flunked him. Sent him back down to the minors.

That wouldn't have been so bad, because Leon was a tough guy. He planned to come back and show those bastards. The only thing was, by the time he came back the next year, he had been in a terrible crash and lost an eye. He kept trying—three years, I think—but he never made it, because the loss screwed up his depth perception, along with whatever else you lose when you lose an eye.

Here was a guy who ran better than a lot of guys who passed their driver's test—hell, he beat a lot of them on other tracks—and just because somebody didn't like him, he got screwed.

There was so much jealousy then, and people like Harlan Fengler—who was a friend of mine, and chief steward of USAC then—took out their frustrations a lot of times on people like Leon. The little guy. Like I *had* been.

Racing is a strange business. A lot of guys who should make it don't, some who shouldn't do, and a whole lot of others stick around too long. They may have had it at one time or another, but for some reason—age, a loss of nerve, or, worse yet, loss of determination—they slow down. And rather than quit, they just keep going, dragging it all the way down the other side.

Jimmy Bryan wasn't like that. He decided to quit while he was still a winner. After the 1960 season, Jimmy announced that he was going to hang up his helmet and watch the rest of us bust our asses.

If he had just stuck to it.

But race drivers, most race drivers (well, almost all, if you have to know), never stick to it. I don't know what it is. Maybe it's just that they can't do anything else. Maybe they can't stand being away from a crowd that's cheering for them. They can't face driving a truck the rest of their lives, or doing any other uncolorful thing. Maybe they can't hack truck-stop coffee. And you don't get too many cheers at a truck stop. Whatever it is, they come back.

Jimmy came back to "run one more" at the dirt track at Langhorne, Pennsylvania. He loved that track more than any other he had ever raced on. He told me one time, "If I could drive a sprint car every weekend at Langhorne—I mean, no place else—I'd do it in a minute."

He drove it once more. Once. The car hooked a rut and he went flying through the air. The car came down on its nose and his shoulder harness broke, and the car literally beat him to death.

I heard Richard Petty say one time, "I'd rather stick around a little too long—I mean, just till I'm sure I want to quit—than quit too soon and then come back."

We were losing too many drivers. Death is something that you have to think is going to happen to somebody else. If you're a race driver. I never felt it was going to happen to me. None of us do. But you have to face it from time to time.

I knew one thing: The 1961 Indy race wouldn't seem quite the same without Jimmy Bryan.

Or Johnny Thomson.

Johnny was killed in a sprint car at Allentown, Pennsylvania, after the 1960 Indy race. Damn, it really makes you think.

I put it all out of my mind.

It was bad luck for some, but very good for me. I told Lucy, "This is the most money I'll ever make. The only thing that could be better than this would be if I won Indy."

I made $60,000 in 1960. I never, in my wildest dreams, expected to make that much money in auto racing. I was drawn to it because I loved it, right from the start. That was a lot of money in 1960.

Not many make any money racing. You *have* to do it for the love of the sport. Because for every driver who makes as much as I was making, there are a hundred—maybe a thousand—more who are losing their asses. They will sleep in the backs of cars and eat beans all their lives. And their families will never have a dime.

There was something different at Indy in 1961. There was a bright-*green* car there. I wouldn't even get close to it. I'm not a real superstitious person, but I have always believed—just like a whole lot of people—that green is a very unlucky color. You don't even wear green socks around a racetrack. Or drive a green passenger car. And here was this green race car. Right there at Indianapolis. I didn't realize how significant it was.

It was a British Cooper Climax. Jack Brabham, who was a top driver in Europe, brought the damn thing. And aside from being green, as if that wasn't enough, the son of a bitch was rear-engined. It was supposed to be similar to what they drove over there. The car was sponsored by Jim Kimberley, the guy who inherited the Kleenex company. Actually, the whole idea had been Dan Gurney's. Gurney had driven a lot over there, and he was always trying to get those guys to come over here and race. I guess he thought we didn't have enough good race drivers here. Gurney was auto racing's self-appointed ambassador to the world.

But the car ran well. And Brabham was a pretty good driver. He ran right up there, and speeds were getting closer and closer to the magic 150-mile-an-hour average for a lap. Here was this old track that was built for 75 miles an hour, and now they were about to go twice that fast. Eddie Sachs and Don Branson and Tony Bettenhausen and Jim Hurtubise, who was in his second year, were all running fast. I was running fast.

Jim Hurtubise was one of those guys who come along and

don't give a damn about anything. Pretty much like me. He enjoys racing. Mauri Rose, one of the old-timers, who had won the race three times, said, "Hurtubise doesn't feel like he's strapped in an electric chair when he gets in the car, like lots of guys do."

Well, Hurtubise went out and qualified in the front row. When he came back in, Tom Carnegie, the guy who sticks the microphone in your face and says, "What's it like out there?" was right on the spot. "What's it like out there?" Tom said.

"It's not so tough," Hurtubise said.

I liked him immediately.

But it wasn't going well for everybody. Paul Russo, who had driven about seventeen or eighteen races, couldn't figure out what was wrong with his car. It was handling bad. His crew had tried everything. We were all sitting on the pit wall, listening to Tony Bettenhausen, who *had* it all put together. Russo said, "Listen, Tony, maybe you can help me find out what's wrong with my car. Would you drive that son of a bitch for me and tell me?"

"Sure," Tony said. Tony Bettenhausen was one of the few drivers who would help other drivers. Most of them wouldn't give you the time of day. But I think that's what comes of really being good. If you've got real talent, you don't have to hide it.

It's bad to drive somebody else's race car. We all knew that. Every car has its own personality. It does little things that are different from any other race car. The goddamn things have minds of their own, it seems. But you get used to it, and you compensate for it. But with a driver like Tony, well, we all felt he could overcome anything like that.

He went out in Russo's car, and it didn't look bad. He was going a couple miles an hour faster than Russo had gone in it. We saw him come out of Four, down low on the track, getting ready to come in. That's what you do at Indy. You get down out of the groove in the short chute, and by the time you get to Four, you're down on the apron. That way you're out of the way of the fast cars. And it's the only way you can get the proper angle on the entrance to the pits. There are concrete walls on either side, and it makes a pretty damn tough gate if you don't approach it right. At 100 miles an hour—which is how fast you're going as you get to the entrance—you'd better have it right.

Tony had it lined up just right. He approached the pit entrance at the right speed and at the right angle. All of a sudden, he swung back to the right, like he had decided to make one more lap. The car got squirrelly and started to spin. He hit the wall in the front straightaway and the car flipped end over end. We all stood there and watched in horror. Nobody said anything. The car ripped out five of the fifteen-foot-high steel posts and about three hundred feet of steel wire. When it finally stopped, it was all wrapped up in the wire.

We didn't even have to go over there. You get to know when the big one has happened. You can just tell. Eddie Sachs just sat down on the pit wall, and he put his head in his hands and cried.

I walked back to my garage. I remembered something Tony had said once about crashes: "I never worry about crashes, as long as I can count them. And I've crashed twenty-eight times." He couldn't count the twenty-ninth one. I stood alone in my garage. And I threw my helmet as hard as I could against the back wall.

The part where somebody has to tell a guy's wife is the toughest.

Somebody called Tony's wife. It was a simple conversation: "There's been an accident," he said.

"Tony?" she asked.

"Tony," he replied.

"All the way?" she asked.

"All the way."

After the first year, all my family went to Indy with me—Lucy, Mother, Daddy, and Marlene. It was like the early days. They loved it because Indy is special, not just because of the race but because of the color and the excitement. It's like nothing else in

the world, and people who go to only one race a year make it
Indy. There are people there who have been going for years.
They get the same reserved seats each year. They *know* everybody
in their section. They develop patterns.

We did, too. I got up early race morning, had my usual big
breakfast of eggs, toast, and steak—it's a big, tough day, and you
have to start it right—and I went to see Mother. This day I kissed
her and said, "You're gonna drive that gold Thunderbird home."

The Thunderbird was the pace car that year, and, along with
the purse, they always give the car to the winner.

"I'm gonna win that car," I said.

"I know you are," Mother said.

She was always good for my ego.

The pattern I developed for the race was the same one I had
used from day one: Get up front early and stay there. It's simple,
but positive. I would probably make three pit stops. It takes three
for tires and gasoline. Any more pit stops than that and you're in
trouble.

Eddie Sachs was on the pole in my old Dean Van Lines Special. Don Branson and Jim Hurtubise were beside him. In the
second row were Roger Ward, Parnelli Jones, and Dick Rathmann. Those were the six cars I had to pass to get out front. It
couldn't have been much tougher, but that's what makes Indy
the race it is. If it was easy, nobody would give a damn about it.
It's like trying to catch that big bass that's been in your favorite
fishing hole for years. If it was easy, the fish wouldn't still be
there.

When we got out on the track, you could still see the skid
marks Tony Bettenhausen's car had made. The crews had gotten
the fence back up to protect the crowd, but the image of Bettenhausen's spinning and flipping car was vividly brought back to
mind.

It all bothers a race driver. But nobody talks about it. You just
talk that much more about how you're going to win and how fast
you're going to go. Eddie Sachs was telling everybody that he had
found a secret way around the Speedway. I think he believed it.

But nobody else did. If there was one driver at the Speedway who wanted to win as much as I did, it was Eddie. And he was one of the best drivers.

But on the start Jim Hurtubise jumped out in front of Sachs and Branson and led the pack into Turn One. Branson lasted only one lap. He bent two valves, I found out later. He must have really nailed it when they dropped the green flag, just trying to catch Hurtubise. I tried to move up, but it was tough to do. The cars in front of me were as fast as mine and the drivers were good, but I stayed right with the pack of leaders, waiting for my chance—the time when somebody moved too slow to close a hole or when something caused somebody to get out of shape. I knew it would come. I would get up there.

About the fiftieth lap, Don Davis blew his engine in the front straightaway and spun in his own oil. The car headed for the wall, and I'm sure the fans sitting in those expensive box seats were glad the fence was put back up. The car hit the wall and a wheel came off. Several cars missed him. It all happened behind me, but I caught a glimpse of it in my rearview mirror. When the yellow came on, I looked around for what had happened. You learn to do that. It's flat scary to come sailing around a corner and find the track covered with spinning race cars. It's bad enough when you *know* about it, but if it surprises you, there's more of a chance that you're going to be part of it.

A. J. Shepherd hit his brakes and slid into Bill Cheesbourg. Before it was over, Jack Turner, Roger McCluskey, and Lloyd Ruby were involved. After the green flag went back out and the action resumed, Hurtubise's car went bad and Parnelli Jones took the lead, followed closely by Sachs. Parnelli had led for a couple of laps when somebody's tire threw up a piece of metal from the track that had come off another car and it hit him right above his goggles. We found out later that he was bleeding so bad that his goggles filled up with blood and he had to empty them two or three times. But he stayed out in front, until his engine went to hell.

While all this was going on, I was steadily moving up. I passed

Sachs and went into the lead. I couldn't believe the feeling. I was leading the Indianapolis 500. I thought about the radio broadcast of the race. I knew exactly what Sid Collins was saying on the radio, because I had heard his broadcast of the race almost all my life. I knew he was talking about me.

Troy Ruttman moved past Sachs and challenged me, and for the next several laps we switched back and forth. He would pass me, and then, down at the end of the next straightaway, I would go past him. His clutch let go and that was it.

With less than 200 miles to go, Sachs got past me. I knew how much he wanted to win, and I knew he was going to be as tough to get past as I would be if he was on my tail. I drove down underneath him, with my wheels on the apron, almost in the grass, where it would have been a sure spin, and I got by him. He stayed right on my tail pipe, for three laps. If I went high, he went with me. I couldn't shake him. Then he shot down low and went past in the straightaway.

There was no question that his car was faster than mine, so I knew I would have to outdrive him in the corners. I went way up high in the short chute between Three and Four and was right up against the wall when I went by him in Four.

For the next 100 miles, we traded the lead ten times. He passed me in the straights and I passed him in the turns. Rodger Ward pulled up for a while to run with us, but he fell back after a few laps. I guess he could sense that here were two guys who were going to win that race or bust their asses trying. He didn't want to be around if we did take each other out.

When you're out front in a race and there's somebody chasing you real hard, you hear all kinds of noises from your car. You hear rattles that were never there before, and you feel vibrations you never felt in your life. You're sure everything is falling off your car. And mine sounded like it was about to explode any minute. But it was really running like a charm. That's the thing about a George Bignotti–prepared car: It's built to run 500 miles. I had that confidence as I pushed the car to its absolute limit.

I was out front for two or three laps, which was the longest I had been there, and I got a feeling that I was there to stay. I got paranoid. I was afraid every car I passed was going to crash into me. And I thought every car I pulled up behind was going to spin in front of me. But you do that: You start looking everywhere for something that's going to take you out of the race. Hell, you get to thinking that something's going to come out of the bushes and get you. For one thing, you're getting tired, and your nerves cause you to sort of hallucinate at times. For another, you know that other drivers and other cars are getting tired. It's late in the race and you figure every other car in the race is going to explode. Right in front of you. You watch for every bobble. It's like squirrel-hunting. I mean, if you sit there in the woods, quiet and not moving, looking for a squirrel in a tree, pretty soon every leaf is a squirrel. And every branch that moves from the wind is one running. That's the way it is when you're leading: Every car is out of shape.

But as much as I wanted to keep the lead, I knew both of us were going to have to pit. The tires and fuel on neither car would make it to the end of the race. There weren't any mandatory pit stops; you just stopped when your crew chief told you to stop. You lived by those pit signs. And Sachs and I had been going at it so hard that neither of us wanted to give up the lead for a second.

The pit stop would make the difference. If either one of us was in there for over twenty seconds, it was all over. Sachs went in first. Exactly twenty seconds later, he was roaring down the pit again, heading for Turn One. I was way ahead now, but that was only temporary, because I had already gotten the sign a lap earlier: "Pit 2." I had to come in the next lap. I was giving up the lead in the Indianapolis 500. What made it worse was that Eddie had had such a good pit stop. It all might be decided in two laps.

I slid sideways as I got to my pits because I had come in so hot. I pounded on the steering wheel with the butts of both my hands. And I yelled at the crew. And I pounded. The car went up on the right side. I could see the fuel hose in the tank opening. The car went down and I felt George Bignotti slap me on top of the helmet. It was time to go. Eighteen seconds! Man. I could see Sachs go past, down the front straightaway and into the first turn. Within two laps I was right on his tail again. For some reason I was suddenly faster than Sachs, even in the straightaway. I didn't know why, but to hell with reasons, I thought, and I sailed right past him. I glanced over and I could see his teeth clenched. I've never seen a look of determination like the one that was on his face. I'm sure I had it, but I couldn't see that.

I had that race won.

Sachs was right on my tail. He just couldn't muster up quite enough horses to get by. But he didn't drop back. Then I saw the pit sign. Oh, shit. I couldn't believe it. It read "A.J. Fuel low."

What had happened? I stayed out there, hoping they would take the sign away, but they didn't. Something must have happened in the pits on my last stop. It must be desperate. They put up a sign, "Stay there," and I knew they must be working on whatever it was that went wrong. I knew I was running out of fuel. That was why my car was faster than Eddie's all of a sudden. I was lighter because he had a full tank—enough to go the distance.

The sign I feared went up: "Pit A.J. 1." Next lap.

There were tears in my eyes when I came roaring down the pit road. They put in just enough fuel to finish the race. Eight seconds later I was moving again.

There were fifteen laps to go.

I got within sight of Eddie and I drove deeper and deeper with each lap. I was right on the edge. Eddie was, too, so it didn't look like I was going to catch him.

Four laps to go. Run, you son of a bitch. Run.

I felt the vibration. It wasn't the car. It was the crowd. You can *feel* it. You don't hear it; you feel it on your skin. You can feel it when a crowd is standing and screaming. There were 300,000 people screaming. I knew something had happened to Sachs. I knew I had won. I knew it.

When I came around, I saw Sachs's car in the pits. The right side was up in the air and they were changing a right-front tire. Race tires have a layer of white rubber beneath the tread rubber, as a warning to let drivers know if they have run the tire into the danger area. At the speeds Eddie was running trying to stay ahead, and later trying to catch me, he had worn through the tread rubber. Also his extra fuel load had made his tires wear faster than mine.

It must have been the toughest decision of his life. If he had stayed out there the last four laps, he would have won. But if the tire had let go he certainly would have crashed, and maybe he would have been killed, at those speeds.

I won the race by eight seconds.

There's no use even saying how I felt. You couldn't help but know.

In victory lane, when they were telling the world I had won $111,000, I remembered the first feature I won in a midget. I got $8.

The question for the next year was "What would you have done in Sachs's place?" Al Dean said he would have stayed out there. Clint Brawner said he would have stayed out there. Sachs said he would rather finish second than finish dead.

A man's life is the most important thing in the world to him. Is any race worth going that far out for—I mean, far enough to look over the edge? Even the Indianapolis 500?

Everybody asked me, but I *never* gave anybody an answer. Until now.

I would have stayed out there.

⑥
The Good
Years...

I won nineteen USAC races in 1961—that's counting the Speedway, of course. I didn't change my life-style a bit. The only big
chunk of cash I took out was to pay off what Mother and Daddy
owed on their home. It was the least I could do for them. They
had given me about everything I ever wanted: nice clothes, cars,
a good life. I wanted the first big thing I ever did financially to be
for them. Lucy didn't question it.

There were a lot of times I would have liked to have bought
George Bignotti a house, too. Say, in Singapore, or anywhere a
long way from a racetrack. There were other times, of course,
when we were the best of pals. That's the problem: It was one
extreme or the other. We were yelling at each other or we agreed
on something completely. The latter didn't happen too often.

I think our biggest problem was that George was an absolute

genius on engines and I knew enough to bother him. I questioned many of his decisions. On the other hand, I was an expert on suspensions, and that caused a lot of arguments. I was supposed to be the driver; George was supposed to get the car ready. It never worked that way.

I came in from one of the first practice runs at the Speedway in 1962, and that car didn't handle at all. The conversation went something like this:

BIGNOTTI: Jee-zus, A.J., can't you drive that goddamn car? I mean, you're all *over* the track.

FOYT: Whattaya mean, can't I *drive* that car? Hell, there's not a race driver in the world who could drive that son of a bitch. Why, that pig is the worst-set-up race car in the history of the Speedway.

And from there we got nasty.

I threw things and George cussed.

But, when you got right down to it, we were a hell of a team. Otherwise, there wouldn't have been a number 1 on the side of the roadster for the second year in a row. To everybody in racing, it meant that I was the USAC champion. To George and me, on the rare occasions when we agreed, it meant that *we* were the champions.

I qualified fifth for the 500, less than a mile an hour off the fast pace set by Parnelli Jones, who turned in the first 150-mile-an-hour qualifying speed. Obviously, by qualifying time, our car felt good. Together we had worked out the handling problems, and I was ready to bring Bob Bowes another Speedway victory.

There was one odd car there again that year. Dan Gurney—naturally—had a European-type car. It was a Buick-powered rear-engine car built by Mickey Thompson. At least it wasn't green.

About as many Indianapolis races have been won or lost in the pits as on the track. A pit stop means so much when you have so many cars that are capable of just about the same speeds, especially when there are several drivers who could win the 500. So if nobody runs into you, and if you don't run out of gas or brains, and if something doesn't break on the car, the pit stop could mean the difference between winning and losing.

It's why drivers try to wait until the yellow flag is out before they pit. If you get into the pits and back out on the track before the pace car comes around again with the field, you haven't lost a lap. You'll notice that every time there's a yellow light out, the pit action is frantic. Just about every car pits, and usually there's more excitement right then than during the race. Why else would the seats directly across from the pits cost more than those elsewhere on the track?

You can't always time your pit stops for a yellow light, but you try. And, sure as hell, at times when you pit under green—when you've stayed out there just as long as you possibly could and you finally come in—the yellow comes out the next lap. But that's a big part of the strategy—the pit stops. No matter if it's under green or yellow, you hope to get out in under twenty seconds. You usually change right-side tires only, because with most of the force going to the right in the constant left-hand turns, they wear out three or four times quicker. But you try to change tires at every pit stop, even if you've been in. It's not that they're worn out; it's just that you always want fresh tires, because the more rubber you have on the tires, the more protection you have if you run over something on the track, like a part from another race car.

There's always the fear of something going wrong to screw up a pit stop. Fuel hoses get stuck; cars catch on fire when the fuel sloshes down on the hot exhaust pipes; air-impact wrenches jam; cars fall off jacks. Anything can go wrong. And often does.

There are all kinds of stories about pit stops at Indy. In 1923 Tommy Milton's crew screwed up the fuel cap, so they made a replacement cap by running a copper tube through an orange and stuffing it into the fuel-tank opening. Where the hell they got the orange I don't know. It seemed like a good idea, but when they sent him back out on the track the pressure from the fuel system sucked the orange inside the tank. Well, the crew wasn't about to give up, so they ran over to a wrecked car, stole the cap, and brought Milton in again. They replaced the cap, and he won the race.

A few years later, one of the crews took some sticky tar from a crack in the pit wall and repaired a leak in a Novi radiator.

But if it all goes well—and our crew practiced a long time to make sure it did go well—you're out in under twenty seconds.

Here's what should happen in a perfect pit stop:

I usually come into the pits so fast that it's hard to find them, so I have one man there with his hands out like he's going to *catch* the car. I haven't run over him yet. The second the car stops rolling, five men fly over the pit wall that separates the crew and the fuel tank from the actual pit road.

There is a sixth crew member out by the concrete wall at the edge of the track. His job is to keep me informed of what's happening in the race and what I should do. He has the pit board, which is just a big old blackboard that he writes on with chalk. Big letters, and fat, so I can read them in a hurry. A seventh man stays on the grandstand side of the pit wall by the big fuel tank. It gets a little complicated, because all the services have to be performed in under twenty seconds. Otherwise it's not a good pit stop. And I get pretty upset.

I'm the eighth member of the crew. My job may be a little more important than the rest, but I couldn't win the race without the rest of them.

One man takes care of the right-front tire. That's all, just the right front. It's his job to get a tire-and-wheel assembly, along with the pneumatic wrench and air hose, over the wall when the car comes in. He spins off the single big nut that holds the wheel on and bolts on a fresh tire and wheel. Another man has exactly the same job at the right rear. Since there aren't as many left-side changes, we don't worry too much about them, but, if necessary, the left front is handled by the right-front man, and the left rear by the right-rear man. It's the only simple part.

One man handles the pipe-frame jack that fits under the right or left side of the car, raising the whole side of the car, so both tires can be changed at the same time. Then there are two men to handle the fueling: a vent man and a fueler. The fueler inserts the big hose in the tank, and the vent man puts a pipe in the tank to get the trapped air out. The man over the wall at the tank shuts off the valve when the tank is full or if it overflows for any reason. He has one other job: to get the starter over the wall if the engine stalls or the car comes in dead—like out-of-gas dead. In either case, he hands the starter to the man in charge of jacking, and the rear-tire man takes over jacking. I said it was complicated.

George Bignotti would watch over the whole operation like a coach on the sidelines, making sure everything went perfectly. He also kept an eye on the sight gauge on the side of the tank, so he knew how much fuel was in it. Running out of fuel before the race is over tends to get everybody pretty upset. Particularly me.

The whole pit-stop operation is practiced for days—weeks, in fact—until the crew can do it with their eyes closed. They probably do it in their sleep. One of the guys said he got so wrapped up in pit-stop practice that he laid this broad the other night in less than twenty seconds.

Some teams are better than others, just like some drivers are better than others. But the good ones are determined; they work harder at it. It's like the Wood brothers, in NASCAR, who are so good that they have been brought to Indy just to handle the pit work for certain cars. That's how important a good crew can be. My crews have always been good because they *have* to be. If they screw up—any one of them—it's "hit the road" time.

But most pit crews stay together for years because they love it. They get to know how everybody else works, not only on their own team but on all the other teams as well. It's a dangerous job and it's hard work, but there is a lot of pride in what they are doing. Maybe they are frustrated race drivers and this is the only way they can get right in the middle of the action, but, whatever the reason, they can make or break a driver. Take my crew in the 1961 race, for example: The foul-up with the fuel wasn't their fault; it was a nozzle that went bad. But they fixed it in record time and brought me in. What's more important, they had me out in eight seconds with enough fuel to win the race.

I don't have time to figure out when to stop and when to back off a little to conserve fuel, so I put my faith in my crew. I'm busy enough trying to keep my car out of the grandstands or keeping somebody else's car out of my lap. The whole thing of the pit stop is like a ballet. If it's done right.

I've told you how it *should* go. But let me tell you how it *did* go for me in 1962—the year my crew proved Murphy's Law.

The big race had been between Parnelli Jones and me. He drives a lot like I do because he came up through the same basic training. All the newspaper articles about him said he started his career by flipping dune buggies. For fun. Sounds like fun to *me*. From there he went to dirt tracks. The same school of hard knocks that I attended. People started to compare him to me, so it was only natural that I wanted to beat him more than I wanted to beat anybody else at that time.

I never did like it when anybody compared somebody to me. When they start saying things like "He's another A. J. Foyt," that's when I start trying to show them he isn't. I guess the press has had about as much to do with my success as anybody. They piss me off so much that I go out there to "show them." I'm almost glad they're around. Almost.

I started in the middle of the second row. I had to get past Len Sutton, Bobby Marshman, and Rodger Ward to get to Parnelli. Ordinarily that would have been tough, but not that day. I had another *mission*. I got right behind him in a few laps, and I chased him for fifty laps. His magic 150-mile-an-hour qualifying record didn't mean a damn thing to me.

He tried every way to shake me, but there was no way. We ran nose to tail and wheel to wheel, abusing the hell out of our equipment. We slowed down some when Jack Turner flipped his car down the main straightaway for the second straight year. But after the green came out again, I was right back on Parnelli's tail.

I took the lead for the first time when he pitted. When he came back out, he tried just as hard to get past me, but it took a pit stop by me to get him there. It looked like it was going to be that way all day. It looked that way until I hit my brakes as I came into the pits. I felt something snap. That was followed by the helpless feeling of having no brakes, which always makes me mad more than it scares me. Most drivers quit at that point, in spite of the fact that they all say they never use their brakes at Indy except in the pits or if somebody gets out of shape in front of them. Not me. I use my brakes on every lap. I touch them as easy as I can when I'm going into One and Three, just enough to set the front end of the car and not enough to slow it down a whole lot. Slow it down too much and you're gone, another statistic at Indianapolis.

At the speeds the cars go at Indy, there is a lot of air going under the car. No matter how low they make the cars or what they do to keep the air out of there, some of it still goes under, and it lifts the car slightly. If I touch my brakes, it brings the nose down, and the steering works a hundred percent better. Maybe two hundred.

I've never given away many tips like this, but maybe this is a good time for it.

After I heard the snap, I knew it was going to be tough getting the car stopped. It was, but I scrubbed the left-side tires on the wall and got it whoa'd just in time. That's when the ballet started to go to hell. I yelled at the crew that something had broken in the brakes. They stood there with their mouths open, doing nothing. "Get the goddamn wheel off!" I screamed. "See what the hell's wrong!"

They pulled the right-front wheel and stood around some more. I had already been in almost a minute. I ripped off my shoulder harness and jumped out of the car. They were looking at a broken bolt in the caliper. Looking. I ran to the big red toolbox on the other side of the pit wall and ripped open drawers, throwing tools all over the pits. No goddamn bolt.

"Get a bolt from the garage," I yelled.

Two guys started jogging toward gasoline alley. *"Run,* god-dammit, *run,"* I screamed. They ran. While they were gone, the others refueled the car and changed three wheels. The bolt was back on in minutes, but it might as well have been hours as far as the race was concerned. There was no way I could ever catch Parnelli now, but I clung to the dream.

I gunned toward the first turn, looking for Parnelli. If I could just get past him one more time, it would show everybody that I could have won if the car had stayed together. Just as I got up to speed, I felt the car drop hard to the left. For chrissakes, I yelled to myself. The left-rear wheel had come off. I lost my wheel at 180 miles an hour. The car started to spin, but I was ready for it. I braked slightly at what I thought were the right times in the spin, and I steered the rest of the time. It swung toward the wall in Two and I cranked at the wheel with every ounce of strength I had. The car spun the other way and down into the infield grass. And it stopped.

I got out of the car and looked at the left rear, where there was supposed to be a wheel. No knock-off spinner. Somebody hadn't tightened it in my pit stop. I started back to the pits to find out who was responsible, getting madder with each step. I was about halfway there when I saw a bunch of people yelling at me and giving me big, swooping "hurry up" arm signals. There was only one reason anybody would need me quick at this point: Some-body needed a relief driver. I broke into a dead run. It was half a mile, but I made it in a time that would have won at a track meet.

Elmer George ran to meet me. "You gotta drive my car, A.J.," he yelled. "Nobody else can get it to handle."

The car was a middle-of-the-pack roadster, but it was the kind of challenge that appealed to me. It was the only challenge left that day. Naturally, the farther up you finish, the more money you win, and even though we all do it because we love it, the money part doesn't *offend* us.

Paul Russo had taken over when Elmer couldn't fight the car

anymore, and he had given up, too, so they felt I was the one to manhandle the car into a better position. A lot of people by then had figured out what I had known for a long time: A. J. Foyt's determination makes up for a lot of ill-handling in a race car.

It was tough working my way into the cockpit, because each car is tailored to the driver. It helps hold him snug inside. The forces on you are tough, trying to pull you to the right in the constant left-hand turns, so a glove-tight cockpit holds you in place. I was bigger than Elmer, so I almost needed a shoehorn.

It is dangerous to drive a car that you don't feel a hundred percent comfortable in, but I figured this isn't tennis or some pansy sport; this is auto racing, and it's a dangerous sport. Everybody knows that.

I quickly got the car up to speed. And I just as quickly realized that they were right about the car. It didn't handle worth a damn. It reminded me a lot of some of the cars I drove in my early days, but I made *them* handle, so I figured I could make this one handle.

I passed a lot of cars, and I was doing pretty damn well. Until the engine seized. I felt the rear end start to get loose and I thought, Oh, shit, here we go again. Twice in one race. What would people think?

But I got it gathered up, and for the second time that day, I spun without hitting anything. It's unusual to spin *once* without hitting something. Twice is unheard of. It wasn't exactly the record I was after.

I climbed out of the car. Hell, I had been out of race cars more than I had been in them that day. As I walked back to the pits, the anger came right back to the same boiling point it had been at before I took over the relief driving.

I looked at the scoreboard. Rodger Ward was out front, and it looked like he was there to stay. I found out that Parnelli had had trouble at exactly the same time I did, and for the same reason: brakes. I was chasing him when my wheel came off and it rolled right in front of his car. When he hit his brakes, he found out

A.J. roars to victory in a John Mecom race car at Nassau in 1963.
(*photo courtesy Goodyear*)

A.J. on his way to a closed-circuit speed record of 200.4 mph at Goodyear's test track at San Angelo, Texas, in 1964. The car is his 1964 Indy Championship racer. (*photo by Bill Neely*)

Former Goodyear tire engineer Ed Long, left, and A.J. discuss a new racing tire during a 1965 Indy practice session. (*photo courtesy Goodyear*)

A.J. at Indianapolis in 1965. (*photo by Bob Stamm*)

A.J. tests a new car at Indianapolis, prior to the opening of the speedway n 1967. Joe Leonard, Foyt's teammate, lends a hand during the Goodyear ire tests. (*photo courtesy Goodyear*)

A.J. in his first rear-engine car, a Lotus Ford. (*photo by Robert C. Rowe*)

A.J. after increasing his world closed-circuit speed record from just over
200 miles per hour to an astonishing 217 plus in his Ford-powered Coyo

A.J. in Victory Lane at Indianapolis in 1977 as he becomes the first man in history to win the Indianapolis 500 four times. (*photo courtesy Valvoline*)

The familiar Number 14 in the pits during the 1978 Indy 500. (*photo courtesy Valvoline*)

A.J. in a routine pit stop during the 1981 Indianapolis 500. Gordon Johncock, background, heads back to the battle. (*photo courtesy Valvoline*)

Foyt heads for the pits early in the 1981 Indy 500. (*photo courtesy Goodyear*)

A.J. waits to qualify for the 1982 Daytona 500. (*photo by Martina Neely*)

A. J. Foyt the businessman flashes the famous smile. (*photo courtesy Goodyear*)

they were gone. And although it didn't take him out of the race, it slowed him down. He had to scrape the pit wall to get it stopped when he came in. I wouldn't have quit either just because I didn't have brakes, but with my wheel coming off, I didn't have any choice. It did too much damage to the car.

I guess, in a way, our hard charging took us both out.

That didn't make it any easier for me. I chewed the hell out of everybody in my garage when I got there, including Bignotti. Nobody said a word. They knew not to cross me at a time like that. Besides, what could they say? Daddy was the only one I didn't chew out. It was one of his first races at Indy as a member of my crew, and I knew he didn't have a thing to do with the foul-up. If he had, I would have raised hell with him. But he would have yelled back. He always did before. This time, he wasn't involved. And he knew I was right. Otherwise he would have been right there with his nose against mine.

There had been times in the past when I was so mad at him I could have punched him—my own daddy. And he's been that mad at me. We used to get to arguing so bad that he would just square off. He'd put up his fists and say, "Okay, big boy, come on." But that always broke the tension with me. I'd look at him, standing there so damn mad, ready to fight me, and I'd say, "Aw, Daddy, shit, put your hands down." And the argument was over. For that time.

That day he understood, because he would have done the same thing. He just went around the garage picking up the tools as I threw them.

As the defending national champion, I felt it was my responsibility to run as many USAC races as possible. It didn't matter if it was a big race like the Hoosier Hundred or some dog-assed dirt race somewhere. I ran it. If fans in Milwaukee or Sacramento or wherever couldn't get to Indianapolis to see the champion, the champion was going to come to them.

And some of those races were tough. I got tired from hustling those open-wheel cars around. The roadsters were always hotter than other cars because all the heat from the engine blew right back in your face. And sometimes hot oil as well. My feet and hands got burned because there were pipes and hoses running all over the driver's compartment—a dozen things to burn you. It got so hot that my rubber soles melted to the floor and I had to keep lifting them to keep them from sticking. I found out that if I put a Styrofoam cup under my heel, it wouldn't stick. And if I wasn't too hot, I was too tired from pushing those big old crates around. My arms and shoulders ached so bad at times I thought they were broken.

I finished races with the car on fire. But that was part of my reputation. A little old fire wasn't going to stop me. Of course, if it got bigger than a little old fire, I came in. No race driver wants any part of a fire that's going to burn him bad. The one thing that runs through my mind all the time I am in a race car is being *trapped* in it and burning to death. Physical discomfort and even broken bones don't bother me at all, but damn fire scares me. It would be an awful way to go.

Anything short of that wasn't much of a threat. It is one of the commitments I made to myself when I first started racing: If I started a race, I was going to finish it, one way or another. Why, I've finished races with scalding oil spraying over me. And, you know, I hear all the time about somebody dropping out of a race because of heat exhaustion or because of this or that physical discomfort, and I've never been able to understand it. I can't imagine it. Either you want to race or you don't. It's not always a bed of roses.

I went to a midget race in Terre Haute, and the track was so bad nobody even wanted to qualify. It had rained all the night before, and there were ruts about ankle deep on the track. They couldn't get anybody to go out. Finally they came to me in desperation. "A.J., we really *need* you to go out there and qualify. I mean, none of these other guys will, and if we don't get somebody to at least make an attempt at it, we're gonna lose our crowd. I mean, they're goin' *home*."

There were blue skies in the west and it looked like the sun might dry the track up so we could race later.

"You just qualify and you're automatically on the pole if nobody else goes out," they said.

"Well, hell," I said. "Go ahead and tell 'em ol' A.J.'ll have a crack at it."

I took the midget out, and, I'll tell you, I've never had a rougher ride in my life. The ruts bounced the car all over the track. I made about three or four laps, and every time I got the car set up for the corner—every time it was sliding just right—one of the front tires caught in a rut and just about threw me out of the car. It was tough just trying to keep the car on its wheels—shiny side up and greasy side down, as the truckers say.

But I qualified. And most of the fans who had started to leave came back and sat down. And a lot more who were sitting in their cars in the parking lot came inside. You're not going to believe the next part: The sun did dry out the track, and they let the rest of the guys qualify. Naturally they all outqualified me, leaving me completely out of the race. They wouldn't let me have another crack at it. "See, it wouldn't be fair to the other drivers," they said. "First thing you know we'd have every driver up here wanting a second crack at it. We'd never get the race run."

And most of the drivers did complain when it looked like they were weakening and about to give me a second shot at the now fast track.

"We didn't tell him to go out there," the drivers said. "Just because he's the big champion doesn't give him any special rights."

"Well, screw all of you," I said, and stomped off.

They paid $100 to everybody who started the race. This was as much as many of them expected to get, so I went up and down the pits until I found a driver who would sell me his spot. Since I was the first alternate, if any one of them didn't start, I was in. I paid a guy $200 and he was happy as a lark. He thought it was a hell of a deal, and I did, too. The only thing was, I would have to start dead last and pass them *all*. That was just fine with me. I had done it before.

I never enjoyed anything as much in my life. I ran that car like the Indy 500 was at stake. I picked them off one by one, in pairs at times, and I would have given each one of them the finger if I hadn't been so completely sideways all the time. In the end I proved my point. I not only won; I lapped the entire field. That means I passed them all *twice*.

That sort of thing happened all the time in those days. It was a tough period of auto racing, so I felt it needed a tough champion. I wore my title with pride, and nobody was going to take it away from me without a fight.

And, speaking of fighting, Bignotti and I were doing our share. Maybe more. We finally agreed on one thing: It was best that we part company. I went over to drive for Lindsey Hopkins. Jack Beckley was his mechanic. When Bignotti and I split, Bob Bowes sold his cars to Bill Ansted and Shirley Murphy, two Indianapolis businessmen who owned a company called Sheraton-Thompson. Bignotti stayed with the cars and hired Bobby Marshman as his driver.

My association with Lindsey was a pleasant one, but it wasn't getting me to the winner's circle. In six attempts, I had two second-place finishes, and that was the best I did. The last second-place finish came in Milwaukee. I was chasing Rodger Ward all day and I couldn't catch him. It was like a bad dream. I really wanted to beat Ward, so on the last lap I drove down off the corner as hard as I could, cutting right down in front of him. We were running wheel to wheel, but my car didn't have enough to get completely past him. Ward had gone into the corner in much better shape. He was in the groove and I was trying to move him over, but you don't intimidate a driver like Ward, so he had the edge on me. We accelerated as hard as we could coming down to the checkered flag, but he beat me by about a car length.

After the race, Ward went straight to victory circle. And the championship. I drove to the pits, where some reporters were waiting for me. They had started a "Who's the best? Ward, the good guy, or Foyt, the young hothead" controversy, and they wanted to interview me after a finish like that. You know, "What's the kid think of the veteran now?" sort of thing. Well, anybody who knows me also knows that right after I've lost a race is a bad time to talk to me. Period. I'm not a good loser. I make no bones about it. I've never read in any contract anywhere that I have to be a good loser—"gracious," I think, is how Lucy once put it. Well, gracious my ass. I've seen a lot of "good losers," and I'll tell you, I don't know about the "good" part, but they're "losers." To me the two words don't go together any better than "jumbo shrimp."

If you're good enough, you don't have to be a loser.

I've always just wanted people to leave me alone after I've lost a race. In time, I can smile about it and *appear* to be a good loser. But it takes time, and then it's just an act. I hate like hell to lose. So I got out of my car, threw my helmet down on the seat, and stomped off. It didn't do much for my image when I got into an argument with the track promoter and invited him outside. USAC fined me $1,000 and threatened to suspend me, but I didn't back down. In time, I figured, people would learn to just let me do what I had set out to do: Drive race cars better than anybody who ever lived. I didn't think it was asking too much to let me do it in my own way. That way just didn't happen to include the press and a lot of bullshit.

Since I wasn't around to interview after the Milwaukee race, they all went to Ward to ask about me. He said, "I was champion when Foyt was breaking in, so he set his sights on me. He won the title from me, and now that he's lost it back to me, it's really hurt him. Pride is very important to a race driver and Foyt is very proud. He's also young and impetuous. He's also hot-tempered. He's a tremendous race driver, but he often takes his anger out on equipment, and doesn't use the best judgment all the time. You have to know when to run hard and when not. But he's gaining experience. If he seems to want to beat me more than anybody else, I can understand that, because that's the way I feel about him."

I took it from the paper, so I know that's what he said.

I wanted to take exception to some of the things he said—you know, about me not using good judgment and being hard on equipment and being impetuous—but it's kind of hard to argue with a man who says I'm a tremendous race driver. He was also right about me wanting to beat him more than anybody else. I guess it was because he was good. I know I always hated to have him on my tail, because I knew it was going to take everything I had to keep him back there.

The press said we hated each other, and that wasn't true. We just didn't have a whole lot in common. I respected him, but why did we have to be friends? We were out there trying to knock each other off the track, but we did it clean and honest; to me, that was friendly enough. I didn't think we had to be drinking buddies, just to keep the press happy.

As for me being harder on equipment, we were just different kinds of drivers. But I sure as hell hated to start the 1963 season with a number 2 on the side of my car. Particularly since he had a number 1 on his. I was very eager to show him just how much experience I had gained.

It got so it wasn't just Ward who wanted to beat me. Everybody did. I don't know why, but the battle cry of racing seemed to be "Let's go beat Foyt." You think that bothered me? No, it made me feel good. It also made me that much more determined to beat *them*. I started driving even harder—deeper into the turns and as fast as I could go. All the time. I didn't let up, and if I could beat somebody by a mile, I beat him by a mile. And tried for two.

It didn't do a whole lot for my popularity with most of the other drivers, but I always figured to hell with them; they're out there for the same reason I am, and that's to win. If they're not, then they've got no business there. It's time someone separated the men from the boys.

The biggest problem I had at that stage was with the car. It wasn't as good as Bignotti's car. It's not that Jack Beckley wasn't a good mechanic; he was. It's that he and I didn't get as much accomplished as George and I did. Even with the fighting, I was better off with George. Now, I don't admit to a whole lot of mistakes, but leaving Bignotti was one of them. I'm not for one minute saying that I was wrong in arguing with him or that he was right all the time; I'm just saying that we were a good team. A team that needed to be together again.

Bobby Marshman hadn't done much with George's car, so I figured I might as well swallow my pride and patch things up. It was something we both needed. I didn't plan to swallow all my pride, though. I would give *him* a chance to make the first move.

When things were right between us, I always called him Big George Notti, so that's what I said when I walked into his garage: "How you doin' there, Big George?"

"Real good, partner," he said. "I mean, we got this car really ready. How's your ride?"

It wasn't going to be easy.

Maybe I would make the first move, just a little one. "Well, it's not bad, George," I said. "We got a few problems here and there, but it's not all that bad." Move one.

"Well, I guess things *could* be a little better over here, too," he said.

"Not working for you either, huh?" I asked.

"Nope."

"Think we oughta try it again? Together?" I asked.

"I was comin' over to talk to you in a little while," he said.

That's how Bignotti and I got together with the Sheraton-Thompson Special for the end of the 1962 season. We celebrated when I blew everybody's doors off in the final race of the season at Sacramento. That was more like it.

There were eleven rear-engine cars out of the sixty-six that came to Indianapolis in 1963 to try to qualify for the 500. Eleven. I couldn't understand why anybody would want to risk his life in one of those cars. They were supposed to be lighter and faster and were maybe better-handling. Some of that might be true, mainly because they had independent rear suspension where the old roadsters had solid rear axles. They followed the contour of the track better. All the engineers said that. But I always figured that a whole lot of those guys with college degrees didn't know their asses from Page Eight. They weren't the ones out there driving the cars, and, besides, if you had to engineer the *brains* into a car, you might *as well* let the mechanics run it by remote control. To begin with, they weighed 300 pounds less than the 1,600-pound roadsters, and they saved the weight by cutting down on the size of a lot of things—things like the front-suspension parts. If you just looked at one of those front ends, it seemed like you could bend it with your hands. They were little old spiderweb things that didn't look like they would hold a go-cart, let alone an Indy racer. They didn't look safe to me.

And those "funny cars," as I called them, ran on gasoline. Gasoline! Anybody knows that a race car runs on fuel. Stock cars and passenger cars and lawn mowers run on gasoline. Indianapolis race cars run on methanol-alcohol fuel blends. It's part of the tradition.

To make matters worse, you lay down in the goddamn things. You didn't sit up there where God and everybody else could see you. You couldn't even tell who was driving one of them, because he was lying down in there somewhere, with just the top of his helmet sticking out. Sitting down in there surrounded by gasoline, which is maybe twice as volatile as fuel.

And the Europeans who had come over to Indy in the past had had the nerve to say that the track was unsafe. They were used to open fields, not concrete retaining walls. They also weren't used to running steady speeds of 150 miles an hour. And not used to running 500 miles at all. There was one European, I'll have to admit, who did look pretty good: Jimmy Clark. He seemed to be a little more like the rest of us, and not as much like the other foreigners.

I couldn't understand why there was all this fuss over the little shitboxes. Why, Firestone even built a special tire for them. I mean, you've got this company like Firestone, whose name is synonymous with Indianapolis. They had always built the tires, and they ran these ads in *The Saturday Evening Post* and all the other magazines—double-page ads—that showed all the winning cars that had ridden on Firestones over the years. They were *part* of the tradition, and here they were building tires for the European cars and the ones like Mickey Thompson entered that were copied after them.

The thing that really did it was when they gave Smokey Yunick a special tire, because the roadster he built was lighter, they said. Mine was just as light, and they wouldn't give me the special tires. I didn't believe them. I felt it was because Smokey's cars were big in NASCAR and Firestone was battling like hell with Goodyear down there in the Southern stock-car circuit, so they were just playing favorites. Goodyear had just gotten started in racing and they had a pretty good stock-car tire, so they were starting to *bother* Firestone, who had reigned since year one.

Well, I figured if they wanted to screw around with tradition, then I could, too. There wasn't anything in the rules that said you had to run on Firestone tires; it was just expected.

I called Goodyear.

I went straight to my garage and called Tony Webner, who was director of racing for Goodyear in Akron, and I said, "Listen, we've been runnin' on these skinny, cast-iron tires for so long, and puttin' up with no bite on the track, and now Firestone's kowtowing to a bunch of foreigners, so why don't you all come on down and have a try at it. I'll run your tires. And, by the way, bring some of those wide stock-car tires with you."

I'm the last one to break tradition in racing, but I didn't start the whole thing. Firestone did. And Gurney.

Goodyear brought a supply of their Stock Car Special tires. They were wider than Firestone's, and lower. And slower. It would have made me feel real good if they had come down there and just blown everybody away with the wide tires, but they had been developed for a 3,800-pound stock car and for the high banks of the NASCAR tracks. Indy was a whole other ball game. Aside from a casual test here and there, Firestone hadn't done much development on new racing tires for Indianapolis, until the rear-engine cars came along. Goodyear hadn't done any, so I guess I shouldn't have expected them to do any better. But I hoped.

When it comes down to it, I'm as loyal as the next guy. No, I'm a hell of a lot *more* loyal than the next guy. When it's deserved. But Firestone hadn't really done anything for me personally; I mean, nothing that they hadn't done for Indy racers in general. So when they turned around and gave those other guys special tires, that was too much. It was time for me to switch to Brand X. I felt personally responsible for bringing Goodyear to the Speedway, and then they came down there and didn't do well, so I made up my mind right there and then that I was going to help them do something about it. I told them that if they would make arrangements to rent the Indy track after that year's 500, I would come and test the tires. I not only had the experience; I now had a cause. And having a cause is something that has always made things happen for me.

You might say that I wasn't number one on Firestone's hit parade for the rest of May, but that didn't worry me a bit. I thrive on controversy, so I drove on Firestone tires because they were faster. But I wore a Goodyear cap every day, and that really got to the Firestone people. But they were so damn cocky. There wasn't a thing in the world anybody could do to shake their hold on the Indianapolis 500. Many had tried over the years, and all of them had failed.

They just hadn't been up against A. J. Foyt before.

As it turned out, Parnelli was on the pole again, but his was one of the few cars that could outrun the Lotus Fords of Clark and Gurney. There were a lot of "I told you so"s going around the Speedway, particularly when they came around my garage, because I had sort of become the champion of the roadster—Jim

Hurtubise and Parnelli and me. "We'll see come race time," I told them all. "It's one thing to go out there and go fast when you're on the track by yourself, but when there's a lot of traffic, it could be a different story. And five hundred miles."

Jim Hurtubise had everybody cheering when he immediately took the lead in the Novi, but he didn't last long. The car was spraying oil and he was black-flagged to the pits to get it fixed. He was back out in record time, but had lost the lead.

I started in the middle of the third row, and I moved up to sixth pretty quick, but I could see the battle between Parnelli and the Lotus Fords taking shape, so I decided to wait awhile and see what might happen. I really thought that one of those little bitty suspension parts might let go, and I didn't particularly want to be beside one when it did. I felt that I could get up there when the time came.

At the 200-mile mark I moved past Hurtubise, and at the half-way point I passed Sachs, to move into fourth. By the 350-mile mark I had decided that it was time to move up one more spot. The time had come to challenge the first of the Lotus Fords. I pulled up behind Gurney for a couple of laps and then pulled alongside him in the second turn. When we came out of the turn, I gunned it and went right past him into third place.

Jimmy Clark was in my sights when Parnelli's car started spraying oil. Clark and I stayed right on it, but the track started getting slippery. I waited for the black flag to come out, like it did for Hurtubise. But there wasn't a black flag. Sachs spun on the slippery track, right behind me. Then Roger McCluskey spun behind him. Clark and I kept going.

I couldn't understand why the flag didn't come out, but I guess Harlan Fengler, whose job it was as chief steward to decide this, figured it wasn't as bad as everybody thought. I found out later that J. C. Agajanian, who owned the car, talked him out of it. Politics. It wasn't too bad for me, and, much to my surprise, Clark handled it well. In the Lotus Ford. But I have always felt that it was more Clark than it was the car. There are a few drivers—damn few—who can really handle a car right. There are a lot who can drive a good car and drive it fast, but I can count on one hand—and have a couple fingers left over—the ones who can take a poor-handling race car and do well with it. Clark appeared to be one of those select few. Eddie Sachs was another. I had always marveled at how he could handle a car. He could take the worst-handling pig that ever sat on a racetrack and go out and just manhandle that thing into looking like a winner. It's why he was so hard to get past. Most drivers have a bad day now and then, but more often their cars have a bad day. With Sachs, you had to fight like hell every day because he didn't have many bad days and it didn't make a damn if his car was having a bad day or not: He *made* it go.

He had even handled the oil problem fairly well. He spun in it, but he saved it enough to only brush the wall. Still, it must have damaged his car, because on the next lap his wheel came off and he crashed.

But now it was just Clark and me out there battling with Parnelli. There was no catching him. We were going fast, but we couldn't go fast enough to get around him with the track the way it was.

Parnelli won the race. Clark and I finished right where we had been for the last several laps—second and third. Parnelli's car had stopped throwing oil because the oil level had gotten down below the crack that they discovered in his oil tank. That's why they didn't black flag him at the end. But there was a lot of hell raised. Clark said, "I thought there were rules here, but now I know better. Next year I'll do differently."

American racing was a lot rougher and the drivers were a lot tougher than the Europeans were used to—nobody paid much attention to rules of good conduct—but I was glad to see Clark stand up there and say, Okay, boys, I'll play it your way from here on in. That's what he said, in effect. And that was ballsy.

The rest of us didn't get too upset about it. I felt that you won a race any way you could. And Parnelli had a fast car, so he deserved to win. I don't know if Clark or I could have caught him or not if it hadn't been for the oil, but it would have been interesting to try.

Sachs wasn't so quiet about it. At the awards luncheon the next day at the track, Sachs said that Parnelli didn't deserve to win, so Parnelli punched him. It took several people to break up the fight. Race drivers will take a lot of bullshit—I won't, but most of them will—but don't ever tell one that he shouldn't have won when he did. Winning races is a very important thing to all of us.

During the 1963 season, I started twelve races and I finished twelve races. That's not too bad for a guy everybody keeps saying is hard on cars.

It was also the year I won some races in a sports car. That's right—one of those little bitty things I've always made so much fun of. But I felt that I needed to drive one. You see, it was very important to me that I make a name for myself in all types of racing. And for a very good reason: Nobody else in the history of racing had ever done it. There were great stock-car drivers, like Richard Petty and Curtis Turner; and there were great Indy drivers, like Rodger Ward and Ralph DePalma; and there had been great dirt-track drivers, like Tommy Hinnershitz; and road racers, like Juan Manuel Fangio and Tazio Nuvolari. But there had never been a driver who had been great in all of them. I intended to be the first. And maybe the only.

It takes a lot of different kinds of driving to master each one. Over the years there had been several attempts by NASCAR drivers to run Indy, but none had ever really mastered it. And no Indy driver had ever done that well in NASCAR. As far as I know, not many Indy or NASCAR drivers had done much road racing at all.

I devoted more and more time to racing. Lucy had given birth to our third child, Jerry, so she didn't go to many races, because she wasn't going to let somebody else raise our kids. I was on my own most of the time. But I had a star to catch. Some newspaper said I was becoming a legend, and I wanted to get there while I was young enough to enjoy it. I raced championship cars and dirt tracks with midgets and sprint cars and stock cars and sports cars. In fact, I won one of the biggest USAC stock-car races of the year, the week before we went to the Speedway—the Yankee 300 at Indianapolis Raceway Park. And I took a day off from Speedway practice to go over to Langhorne and win another one.

I never did like racing road courses, but I had to do it. For one thing, I always like to keep a car at speed, and with road racing, you're fast one minute and slow the next. You're going around so many corners that you don't get to go flat out on just a little bit of the course. You can screw up one corner and make it up on the next one. Or the one after that. If you screw up two corners, you've usually got twelve or thirteen more to make it up. On an oval, you've only got four corners—two on some—so you have to be right all the time. You have to be a lot more precise.

I didn't have too much trouble finding out the formula for road racing: You have to be smooth; that's as important as being fast. You have to get a smooth line through all the turns. But you can make a lot more mistakes on a road course and get away with them. They are a lot more forgiving. I'll tell you one thing: When you get back on an oval, those concrete walls sure do look hard, because when you spin on a road course, you usually have about a thousand acres of land to slide across. The concrete doesn't give much.

Gurney was a good road racer. He won a lot of NASCAR stock-car races on the Riverside road course, but then he had driven it more than any man alive. He knew it like the back of his hand. Still, he could motor around a road course.

I won races from New Jersey to California and all the way to Nassau, where I won the Nassau Trophy Road Race. I even won a few rental-car races. Man can't live by legal racing alone. Race drivers like to get out on the highway and do a little racing from time to time. It's not like some of the television commercials you've seen.

Mario Andretti did one for the National Safety Council where he said something like "Aw, shucks, fellows, it just doesn't make sense to get out on the highway and break the speed limit. Us race drivers never do."

Bullshit.

It's one of the things race drivers like best.

A bunch of the guys were out back of the Speedway Motel one Sunday after the track had closed, and the Goodyear guys had some beer, so they were sitting there on the tailgate of the tire truck, having a beer, when Bill Newkirk of Goodyear came up with a bunch of Chrysler executives he had brought to the Speedway. I don't know what made him say it, because he knows better, but he was just telling them about the Andretti commercial. "That's the way it is," he said. "They're really very safe drivers on the highway."

Hell, I didn't know he was in the middle of saying such a dumb-ass thing or I probably wouldn't have done it. (Well, maybe I would have.) I guess he hadn't any more than gotten it out his mouth when I came sliding around the corner of the Speedway Motel, completely sideways. Just as I got to the truck, I did a 180 with the blue Ford station wagon. And I slid in backwards, right beside the truck. I threw the door open and jumped out.

"I just blew off a cop on Sixteenth and then I chopped him off. Gimme a beer," I said.

End of Newkirk's story.

We used to take rental cars and run up along the sides of the drainage canals on the way to the track outside of Phoenix. We all tried to see how close we could come to the edge, and, I swear, we would have those cars so close that if you got out the passenger side, you would have fallen right in the canal, which was about twenty feet deep. But, then, who would want to get out of a passenger door at 100 miles an hour?

I remember one night in Indianapolis, I was at Shannon's Roaring Twenties having a few beers with some Goodyear engineers and one of their PR guys, and we left the place about two in the morning. We had found out where this party was, so we decided to go. Well, I never *ride* with anybody. I just don't like to ride in a car. If I can't drive, I'd rather walk. So I insisted that I drive the rental car that belonged to one of the guys. It was a current-model Ford with automatic transmission. As we were tooling up 16th Street at about 70, I said to Ed Alexander, who was in the front with me, "Wanna see me put it in reverse?"

"You can't put it in reverse at seventy," Ed said. "They've got a lock-out to keep people like you from doing that."

Lock-out my ass.

I put it in reverse. It was a little trick I learned. Well, the car stopped real fast. And it filled up with smoke—from the tires and the transmission. Took reverse gear right out of it, but that wasn't any problem, because we were headed in the right direction. Somebody suggested that we might want to go back to the motel and get another rental car because we might have to back up at the party, so I went on back to the Speedway Motel, and when I went sliding in sideways, there was a cop parked across the street with his lights off. I guess he figured we were going to bed, so it was okay. I figured I had done my good deed for the day, so I wandered off to go to bed. "Hell with the party," I said.

When Ed Alexander went out the other side of the motel sideways in the other rental car, it was more than the cop could take. He went after him. When he caught him, Ed got out of the car and *fell down*. Good start. He got all the way to the back fender and he was just sort of laid out across it when the cop walked up.

"Where you goin'?" he asked.

"We're goin' to a party," Ed said, his speech slurred.

"Oh, no, you're not," the cop said, and he followed the guys back to the motel. "If I see one of you as much as *walk* out of this motel tonight, you're goin' to jail," he said.

Rental cars and pit poppies are just part of racing.

By the end of the season, the Lotus Fords were really starting to make a name for themselves. A lot of the old-time Indy drivers were starting to talk of switching over. I never thought I would say it, but they were starting to get on my nerves. I wasn't ready to give up on the roadster. Tradition is like loyalty: There aren't too many people addicted to it.

Right after the Speedway in 1963, Goodyear rented the track for a couple of weeks and we got started on a very tough task. It's tough to push around a company the size of Firestone—particularly one that has more experience than anybody in racing—and say, "Excuse me, fellows, but I want to play, too." Unless you've got a very good product.

The one thing we had in our favor was that Goodyear was a lot bigger than Firestone, so they had the money to spend. And it seemed to me, too, that there was more to it than just wanting to win Indianapolis. They kept telling everybody—the press and TV and anybody who would listen—that they were in racing to give their company a "vital" image for the youth market. "They're buying a lot of tires," they said. But I felt it was as much to get to their crosstown rivals, Firestone, as anything. I knew that their top brass belonged to the same country clubs as the top brass at Firestone, so what better way to get under their skins than to share in Firestone's biggest apple?

Whatever the reason, I was there to help.

Their first batch of tires wasn't much better than the stock-car tires they had brought down before the race, but we had to start somewhere. I took the roadster out and tested tire after tire, telling them each time what I thought this tire needed and what particular synthetic compound felt best, what stuck better in the turns or broke loose or whatever.

When you start an engine at Indianapolis, there are automatically a couple hundred people in the stands in Turn One. They just sort of materialize. That's how popular the Speedway is. It's open year round for tours, and a lot of people come there just to sit in the stands and pretend that there are race cars on the track.

If there happens to be one, people come from all over town the minute they hear an engine running. The word spreads fast.

Among these fans in the stands, we started to notice more and more familiar-looking faces. They wore sunglasses, and hats almost pulled down over their eyes, like in an old Alan Ladd movie, but we knew who they were: Firestone engineers. We went right about our work, and every once in a while somebody would hold up a pit board for me that said "A.J. 158.8." That sent them running like hell right out of the stands. We weren't going that fast, of course, but it was fun to keep them moving around. I'm sure they went to the nearest phone and called Akron: "These bastards are going seven miles an hour faster than the track record."

That only worked a couple of times, and then they started bringing their own stopwatches. But it was fun while it lasted.

To get a better picture, Goodyear hired a whole bunch of other drivers, including Johnny Rutherford and Don Branson in roadsters and Bobby Marshman in a Lotus Ford. They even tried an English four-wheel-drive Ferguson with Jack Fairman driving, but that didn't work too well, because he couldn't get through the first turn without hitting the wall.

But Goodyear was doing it the right way. If they were going to build improved tires for Indy, they were going to build them for all the cars, not just for a few they picked out. I became sort of the chief tire tester, for a couple of reasons: One, I had gotten there first; two, I could tell a lot better what was happening out on the track. Some of the drivers—a lot, in fact—aren't real sure which end of the car the engine is *in*. All this business about front-engine cars and rear-engine cars didn't mean a damn thing to them. So if they didn't know anything about it mechanically, they weren't able to tell if handling problems were from the tire not being right or from the way the car was set up.

They got out there and ran one fast lap and a slow one and then a fast one again. They were all over the ball park in speeds. And the Goodyear engineers said, "Man, he's runnin' good."

"Sure," I said, "but just listen to the tires in the corners." You could hear them screaming. They were getting good speeds on paper. It looked real good, but the guy was working twice as hard to run that speed, which really didn't tell them what they wanted to know.

"Just don't show them the pit board and see what happens," I told them.

They tried it, and the speeds went down. They were trying to beat their own time, not trying just to go fast and feel the tires.

"What you need is a guy who's running consistently faster speeds, and not working harder and harder to do it," I said.

I'll have to say this: They listened to almost everything I had to tell them. And it's a good thing, because the minute we got off the track, Firestone moved in. And, you know, I'll bet it was the first really serious tire test Firestone had had at Indianapolis in twenty years. They were there two weeks. And a few people with sunglasses and Alan Ladd hats appeared in the stands when they were testing.

When Firestone moved out, Goodyear moved right back in. It was a war. They had spies. We had spies. You hear about industrial espionage; well, this was just out-and-out battle. If a Goodyear tire blew, all the engineers tried to pick up every little piece. They didn't want a shred of evidence left behind that Firestone could take back to Akron and analyze. We had a crew just to watch tires and pick up pieces. Clarence Cagle, who was in charge of maintenance for the whole track, thought we were the neatest people who had been there in years.

We kept all the pieces from Firestone. Then we realized that we were losing whole tires. Somebody in our organization was selling them to Firestone. We never did find out who it was, but we countered by finding someone in the Firestone group who would sell us tires. It would have been easier if we just said, "Okay, fellows, let's just trade. That way we can let about ten guards and six sweepers go."

But we didn't. That would have taken away all the intrigue.

Besides, what we found out from their tires led us to believe that we were gaining on them. We worked late at night, getting the cars all set up for the next day, and there was always a run to the airport to get a new batch of tires that had been made that day in Akron. There were many times when the tires were still hot when we unloaded them from the airplane. They actually had twenty-four-hour shifts running in Goodyear's Akron racing-tire plant. I'll say this for them: They were dedicated to the huge job they had ahead of them.

After the late-night work sessions, the engineers had meetings to analyze all the findings from that day's tire tests. There were many days when they went straight from the meetings to the track to start testing again.

One night, when we were working at my garage, we hit the jackpot. Firestone had brought their tires in for their next tests, and our spies had told us that they had a tread design that really worked. But we hadn't been able to get our hands on one. They were all stored in the Firestone building at the entrance to gasoline alley. There was only one way. We picked the lock to the garage and took one of the tires.

The whole thing made Watergate look like a Sunday-school picnic.

Then we got to thinking that we could never get the tire out of the garage area, so I called Ed Long at the motel and said, "Get a Polaroid camera and bring it over here."

"A Polaroid camera?" he said. "You got any idea what time it is? Whattaya need a Polaroid camera for?"

"Never mind. Just find one," I said, "and meet us at the fence over by the northwest turn."

I don't know where he found one, but he did. He met us there and tossed it over the fence. "Got any film?" he said.

"What the hell would we be doing with Polaroid film?" Leo Mehl, a tire engineer, said.

"Just kiddin'," he said, and he tossed us a pack of film.

"What broad you photographin' tonight?" he asked. "Make me a print."

"It ain't no broad," I said. "Just wait right here."

We went back to the garage, photographed the tire, and returned it to the Firestone building. We took the photos to Ed and said, "Okay, buddy, here's your new Firestone tread pattern. Ask your monkeys in Akron what they think of it."

The next day, Jim Loulan, who was director of race-tire development, said, "I don't know how you guys got those photographs. As a matter of fact, I don't want to know how you guys got those photographs. But they're on a plane to Akron right now."

Tread design was important in those days, because with all the experimenting with compounds and sidewall construction, there were many times when the heat buildup was so great that the tires would blister, and the next step was chunking. The next step, after that, was "Hello, wall," if you were in a turn when it happened. It wasn't until years later that they got everything developed to the point where they could run slicks, which, after all, is the answer. No tread at all is the best tread; it gets more rubber on the track, and more rubber means more traction. But then we were fighting heat buildup.

Heat is the greatest enemy of any tire, on the track or on the highway, so racing tires are much thinner than passenger-car tires; that way, they dissipate more heat. Not many people know that.

There wasn't much time for play in those days. The battle raged, and the battlefields became other tracks like Phoenix and Trenton and Milwaukee, wherever they ran Championship cars. We tested at the track before each race, and it was all starting to fall into place. In fact, in all the tests, I never picked a tire for Goodyear that wasn't a winning tire.

The thousands of miles I put in at Indy in tire tests didn't hurt me, either. I had developed a style that was going to be hard to beat. No longer did I have to worry about some of the older guys and all their experience. I had crammed a lifetime of experience into a very short period. And the nice thing was, I had it my own way. I learned it exactly the way I had learned to win in every phase of racing on the way to Indy. Nobody told me how. I did it, and then I improved on it until it was perfect. A lot of drivers try to change their style and drive where they are told the groove is. "Move around where that groove is," they say. But I move the groove if it's necessary, because I drive a race car where it feels good to me, regardless. If I have to move lower than the accepted groove, I move lower. Or I go high.

And a lot of drivers go out and run lap after lap, each one a little faster. It takes them maybe two dozen laps to get up to a respectable speed. But I've always been impatient. I want to know what the car is going to do, so I go out there and smoke it off pretty hard to see how it's going to react. If I'm at all skeptical of a car, I'll run it as hard as I feel I can, right to the point where I know I've about halfway lost it, and then see how it recovers. I want to get that out of the way up front. Most drivers just keep creeping up on that point; they keep creeping up until they get in a rut. What they're doing is losing it a little more each time. They are saving it, but they can't tell when they're at that point where it's too critical to save. They're in over their heads, and they're into the wall.

I want to smoke in there fast enough that it will jump a little bit. That's why I try to warm up as fast as I can. If it doesn't feel good after a lap or two, I'll come in and make some changes. I'm not going to stay out there all day trying to figure it out. I mean, I know immediately what's wrong, so I'm not going to keep running *slow*. The guys who don't know that will never get much better. No matter how much experience they get. They will run in the middle of the pack all their lives.

The roadsters were pretty stable, but you didn't slide at all in them. You had to be right on top of it all the time. You look at some of the movies and notice that anytime there was a little puff of smoke from the right-rear tire, the car spun. All that changed when Goodyear got into the act. With the old, hard compound there was no recovery. If you saw a car just barely wiggle, you could bet the guy had lost it.

At Indy, I run high and I let the car drift up close to the wall, just about as far as it wants to go. I don't pinch a car, like a lot of people do. In other words, I don't turn it hard in the corner, and I think that's what gets a lot of people in trouble: They turn it too much in the corner.

The turns at Indy are all different. Turn One, for example, gives you the feeling that you are going down *into* it. It's like you're sinking into a hole, but you can go through it pretty fast. When I get into it, I get back on the accelerator a little sooner than a lot of drivers. I nail it all across the short chute as I line it up for Turn Two, which is sort of flat. The wind usually blows down the back straightaway right at you, so the front end of the car tends to push up toward the wall, giving you some understeer. I'm pretty close to the wall at that point anyway, so it really keeps my attention.

For some reason I always seem to be able to run a little faster down the back straightaway, so I'm really moving when I get to Three. This turn is flatter than One, so I steer all the way through it. In the other turns I can let the car drift up toward the wall. Turn Four always seems to me like it is banked more than the other turns, so I drive through it probably faster than any of the turns. But if you come off it too wide, there's a little hump that sort of lifts the car over toward the wall. A lot of drivers have gotten into trouble coming off Four just because they got too wide. If they hit the wall there, it usually sends them spinning across the track and right into the inside retaining wall.

In addition to its being smoother if you let the car drift up and go straighter through the turns, it takes less power to get out of them. So I go very wide as I enter the turn and then I drive down across it. In the center of the turn I barely touch the inside line and then drive straight toward the wall at the end of the corner. It brings me off the corner maybe six inches from the wall.

If I am overtaking a car as I approach the turn, I look ahead to see where I am going to be able to pass him. I try to figure out where he is going—which line—and if he's a fast car and it has taken me more than one turn to get past him, I try to judge exactly at what part of the corner I'm gaining the most on him. That's where I plan to pass on the next turn.

Most races are won in the turns. And a combination of ability, determination, and nerves is what wins the turns. I win a lot of races because of my corner speeds.

If I'm trying to pass a car that's as fast as mine, I try to do it in Turn Two or Turn Four. I follow him through One and Three and through the short chutes, because there isn't time to get by there. Even if I was right beside him in the straightaway, there probably wouldn't be room to get past him by the next corner without getting pinched off. So I float back there and wait until I get into Two or Four, where I can really run hard and where I have long straights as I come out. Then I blow him off.

If I'm trying to get past someone who is running fast, right in the middle of the groove, I have to be able to run right through the middle of the turn and then tuck in just beneath him as I come off the corner. Or, at times, I wait and pick up the slight draft (the airstream) from his car and then pull out and pass him at the top of the straightaway.

I don't have time to think much about sensations. I try to look about 500 feet in front of my car at all times, so I've made up my mind what I'm going to do by the time I get there. It's always a matter of carrying out my plans.

It's sometimes hard to plan late in a race because you're so tired. And often it's very hot in the car: I've lost as much as fifteen pounds during a 500, just from the heat and the physical exertion. My arms get tired and my hands ache, and, a lot of times, when I'm going down the straightaway, I'm working my shoulders and flexing my fingers while I push down on the steering wheel with the butts of my hands. If there's nobody around me, I take one hand off the steering wheel and work it back and forth, and then the other. But I hardly ever notice any of these aches until something slows me down, like a caution light. Then, when I'm tooling around, waiting for them to get whatever it is cleared up, I hurt like hell.

I am ready for the unexpected at all times. If I feel the back end get loose in a corner, I know I have some control, but if I ever know the car is going completely around—say, somebody has spun in front of me, and I've had to turn hard and it goes—the first thing I try to do is determine if it's going 180 or 360 degrees. That gives me some idea how much room I'm going to need. If there's room, I try to let it spin 360 without touching the brakes and then try to "catch" it when it gets all the way back around. I try to steer and get back on the accelerator at just the right time. If I do, the car straightens out and I'm back in the race. You don't always have that much room. If I see I'm not going to make it without hitting something, I lock up the brakes and hope. That's all I can do.

If the back end jumps out on me and it's sliding along sideways, I sit there and correct with the steering wheel, hoping to gather it up. I do everything I can to keep it from getting too far sideways, because if that happens, there is always the chance that with the wheel corrected right and the car slowing down from the slide, the rear tires might get traction and cause the car to hook. Once that happens, it's too late. You're going to spin and hit the opposite wall. There's no stopping it.

I just don't spin as much as most other race drivers, but when I have spun, you may have noticed that I'm sitting in there turning the steering wheel back straight from time to time. I'm trying to get a feel of when it might stop sliding. And I'm trying to keep it from hooking.

The best way to avoid a spin is to pay attention. Don't get in over your head, and keep your eyes way out front so you can see trouble coming up. I try to do that so I can avoid it. There might be a place to drive to avoid it, miss the other cars, although I try to keep from getting down in the grass, because once you're down there, you have no control *and* no traction. So if I see that I'm going to have to go for the infield, I try to get the car going as straight as I can before I leave the track.

I avoid a lot of trouble because I know what my car is doing all the time. It gets a kind of rhythm to it, vibrations that tell me everything is all right. I can tell if there is even the slightest change in this rhythm, and I start looking at the gauges and trying to listen closely. At times I get a change in vibrations because of traffic. If I've been running by myself and another car pulls up behind me, it changes things, but I'm usually ready for that because I watch every car in my mirror. When another car comes up close behind, everything seems louder and it's almost like I'm in a vacuum.

I get used to the way the suspension feels, too. It's got a sort of pulse that I can feel in my fingertips, and I can tell the instant anything changes.

This is why you usually see me in the pits before something breaks, and not upside a wall *after* it breaks. It's also why I was able to tell Goodyear a lot about their tires. We didn't spend a lot of time patching up my race car or trying to figure out *why* it was spinning.

When I do spin, it's sometimes a dandy. I take down the fence and everything around. I think it's because I'm usually going so fast when it happens. There are a lot of drivers who can spin and get right back out there and go just like nothing had happened. They don't even know why they spun in the first place. I guess they're professional spinners. My friend Johnny Rutherford can loop that race car of his and get right back in the race. He does it all the time. I used to kid him about being the best spinner at Indianapolis.

But a driver like Rutherford is tough to beat when he's having a good day. Some days he's not.

All the driving skill in the world couldn't get the extra mile an hour I needed out of the Goodyear tires to get them in the show at Indy in 1964. I tried every combination. I changed weight around on the car. We changed everything. The Goodyears were a mile an hour slower than the Firestones. That might not sound like a lot, but one mile an hour could win just about any 500 if it's coming under the wheels of a top-running car.

I went to Jim Loulan. "Jim, you've got a tire in Akron that will get Goodyear in the race. Win it, in fact," I said.

"We've been through this before, A.J.," he said. "My engineers say it isn't the tire for Indy. They're afraid of it."

"Listen, Jim," I said, "I'm the one who was out there on it, not the goddamn engineers. It's a safe tire, and it's at least as fast as Firestone. And one more thing: If you don't use it, you're not gonna make the race."

Jim went back to his engineers, but it didn't do a bit of good. "They say it's just too loose, A.J. You're the only driver who can handle it, and they're afraid some of the other guys will demand it and they'll get out there and bust their asses."

"They can handle it, believe me," I said.

It was no use. They had a tire that was exactly the right compound and tread pattern, and they wouldn't release it. It had set an unofficial track record in testing. Firestone *expected* them to run it. They would have run it if they had had it.

The night before the first qualifying session, I called Goodyear's president, Vic Holt, at home. "Vic, you gotta tell those guys to let me use that tire," I said. "It's the only chance we've got, and we've all worked too damn hard to blow it now."

Vic said that he'd have to go by what his development people said. "They're experts," he said.

"Well, they may be experts about building tires," I said, "but they're sure as hell not experts about driving them. That's my job. And I know that tire's safe. I'll tell you what: Let me use the tire and I'll sign an affidavit taking full responsibility. It's my judgment against my ass."

Vic said, "No, A.J., it's our corporate policy to listen to our engineers."

I said, "Okay, there's no other choice. I'm running Firestones."

There *was* no other choice. It didn't have a thing to do with loyalty. The name of the game is *winning*, and I couldn't win on the Goodyears they had decided to offer to the Indy drivers. I was giving up a hell of a lot as it was, just trying to run against Jimmy Clark and the Lotus Ford and several of the rear-engine cars. I hated to admit it—in fact, Parnelli and Jim Hurtubise and I were the *last* to admit it—but the rear-engine cars *were* the cars of the future. They handled better and were faster. It was just sheer driving skill and determination that kept the three of us in contention inside our dinosaurs, as people had started to call them already. It pissed me off. I felt they were the *symbol* of the Indianapolis Speedway. I was going to stay with them.

But I couldn't stay with Goodyear. A dozen drivers had been practicing on Goodyears, and when we rolled my car out for qualifying the next day with Firestones on it, it started a stampede. All of them switched over to Firestone, because they figured that I was the one person who should know, having been Goodyear's chief tester.

The Goodyears they were using bounced the front wheel real bad, but a lot of drivers, particularly the newer ones, had stayed with them because I was using them. To them, that meant something significant.

Even with the Firestones, I still couldn't run with Clark, who got the pole. I qualified fifth, behind Bobby Marshman, Rodger Ward, and Parnelli Jones. All but Parnelli had rear-engine cars. And there wasn't a single car that even attempted to run the Goodyears.

The following day, Goodyear released the tire. But it was too late. You can't stampede drivers twice. Once they made the switch, they stayed with Firestone. There were still two weeks left before the race, and it looked like it was going to be the longest two weeks in history for the Goodyear people. But they stayed right there and did their public-relations thing, in spite of the fact that they didn't have a car in the race.

I told Goodyear what I felt, and they weren't used to it. Most of the other test drivers told them exactly what they wanted to hear, and that, in the long run, didn't do a thing for the tire-testing program. If half a dozen other drivers had stood up with me, they might have listened. But it shouldn't have taken that. I wanted to be honest with them, in telling them that the tire they were running wasn't worth a shit. Just like I would have wanted them to be honest with me. If they didn't think I was getting the job done, they should have told me.

Before the race, Parnelli said to me, "We might just have to run over a car or two, if we expect to win."

"Well, buddy boy," I said, "we'll just stand on it, and *vroom*, if those guys in their funny cars can't keep ahead, we might just have to do that."

Sachs had switched to a rear-engine car. He was starting in the middle of the sixth row. He was right behind Dave MacDonald, who was driving one of the Mickey Thompson cars—the lowest and widest car in the field. MacDonald had said he was concerned because the car didn't feel right. But we didn't pay too much attention, because he was a sports-car driver, and they're not used to Indy cars in the first place. "But if you get in trouble here," MacDonald said, "there's no place to go. All these walls, you know."

I needled Sachs. "That's the guy you're followin' out there today, Eddie."

Parnelli and I watched them line up all the rear-engine cars. "Looks like we're about to see the end of the dinosaur, huh?" I said. He nodded.

I was on the inside of the second row; Parnelli was right beside me. Gurney filled out the row. Four of the six cars in the first two rows were rear-engined.

One other thing: I wore my Goodyear driving suit. It wasn't as finely embroidered as the Firestone suits. They had had them made for all the drivers who were using their tires in practice, and the local company that made them didn't have much more experience than Goodyear. The winged foot between the "Good" and the "Year" looked more like a carrot than a winged foot. But I wore it.

When they dropped the green flag, Parnelli and I shot past Ward and closed the door on Gurney, who had started to move up on the outside. Clark took the lead going into One and Marshman tucked in behind him. Parnelli and I were single file behind them. Two Fords and two Offys. We stayed that way for the first lap: a freight train, with two new diesel engines and two old steam locomotives right behind them.

I didn't see it start. I saw it later on television and saw the horrible pictures everywhere, so I know what happened.

MacDonald came out of Four and hit the bump. The car got sideways and spun right across the track and into the concrete retaining wall on the inside of the track. It bounced off the wall and the gas tanks broke open, spreading gasoline all over the track. It exploded. It was right in Sachs's path when he came into the straightaway. Eddie T-boned him.

There had been an ad in that morning's Indianapolis *Star*, a full-page ad, showing Eddie sitting in his car. The caption read "Eddie Sachs starts today's Indianapolis 500 completely surrounded by Marathon gasoline."

The gas tanks broke open with the tremendous impact of the crash. When I came out of Two, I saw a wall of flame shoot up in the air. It looked like an atomic bomb had been dropped. Oh, shit, I thought. As I came down the back stretch, I could see cars over there, spinning everywhere. Ronnie Duman drove through the flames and his car caught fire, but he got it down into the infield and jumped out and rolled in the grass to put out the fire on his driving suit. Johnny Rutherford's car went right through the fire and sailed over what was left of MacDonald's car. And it landed on all four wheels on the other side. He kept going.

The red light came on, which is something that has happened only one other time at Indianapolis, and then it was because of rain. It means *stop*, right where you are. It also means that something really bad has happened and that the track is totally blocked.

We got out of the cars and stood in Turn Three, talking. Nobody really had much to say. One of the USAC observers told us that MacDonald's and Sachs's cars were in the middle of it. I walked away. I didn't want to know right then. There would be a time to know, but right at that moment, I really didn't want anybody to confirm what I already knew, just from looking at the flames.

The flames were stopped, but there was still a cloud of black smoke from the burning tires and the paint and fiberglass. I thought of the ad again, and I was glad my car had alcohol in it.

There were still 199 laps to go.

I tried to dial all of it out of my mind. I thought about how I was going to drive the race, now that I knew Clark's car was that fast. Marshman had been faster than I expected, although he had qualified well. But you can't tell anything from one lap. I knew that Parnelli would be tough to get past because he was as determined as I was to beat the rear-engine cars. The race was stopped for more than an hour and a half, and my mind kept drifting back to Sachs. You can only dial something out for so long.

Eddie had told me one time that he had had the same experience on his first trip to Indy that I did. They wouldn't let him in, even though he was a race driver. He wasn't an Indy driver. So he came back the next year with a ride, but he flunked his driver's test. He stayed around and worked in a pit crew during the day and washed dishes in a restaurant at night, just so he could be around the Speedway for the month of May.

He had been in the hospital fifteen times from crashes, and people were always trying to get him to quit racing. "I'll quit the day I win Indy," he told them.

"But you're goin' to kill yourself," they told him.

"Well, quitting would be like dying to me, so . . ."

He told me after I beat him in 1961, "I try not to think about it too much. It just screws me up. That's how much I want to win. I think of Indianapolis every day of the year, every hour of the day. When I'm sleeping, I dream about winning it."

There were seven cars missing from the field when they restarted the race. Marshman led for a while, but he went down too low in One and bottomed out the low rear-engine car. He tore off a transmission plug and was out of the race. It was the twenty-ninth straight loss for poor old Lindsey Hopkins, who owned the car. Clark took over again, but he didn't stay in the lead long. His car owner, Colin Chapman, had made a deal with Dunlop, a British company, to supply tires for the British car. It turned out to be a bad move. Clark's tires started coming apart in big chunks. This set up such a vibration in the car that it completely destroyed the delicate suspension, causing the car to spin. Gurney, whose car also had Dunlops, was having problems, too, so Chapman called him in.

It was Parnelli and me. In the dinosaurs. We were both running as hard as our Offys would go, and we were pulling away from the Fords that were left in the race. Nobody seemed able to run with us. When Parnelli's car caught fire in the pits, I no longer had any competition. I sailed on to win my second Indianapolis 500.

Victory lane is always a big celebration, but this time it was quiet. They helicopter a copy of the Indianapolis *News* into the track with the name of the winner in a banner headline on Page One. The winner always holds it up, and everybody thinks it's a neat thing. It is, but I found out how they do it. At about the halfway point, they call down to the newspaper, where they've got a press ready, and they print a paper with the name of every driver who still has a chance. One front-page headline for every driver. Then they fly them all out to the track. When the race is over, they dig down and get the one that fits the outcome of the race.

There was a big smile on my face when they handed it to me. Then I read it:

FOYT WINNER IN 500;
SACHS, MACDONALD DIE

It took a lot away from my second victory.

But the ceremonies went on. Raymond Firestone presented me with a check for $7,500 for winning the race on Firestone tires. The television cameras and the still photographers shot away.

I gave the check back to him.

Would you believe that after I showed them that the Offy could do it, Bignotti told a bunch of reporters that we would probably have a rear-engine car the next year? "They're just too fast for us," he said.

It made me madder than hell. But I knew he was right.

Johnny White and I got to feuding on the sprint-car circuit. I went to go past him at Terre Haute and he drove me up into the fence. After the race I said, "Next time I come up there on the outside, I don't want you to put me in the goddamn fence no more. This is bullshit." So we got to Williams Grove, and on the last lap, I started to go around him, and he put me into the fence again.

I got it straightened out and ran second again. That was it. After the race I went straight to his car, and one thing led to another, and I had him by the throat of his uniform, almost pulled clear out of the car. Then Joe Pittman, who works for Parnelli, gave me some shit, so I threw him into the hurricane fence. Then everybody was giving me a hard time, so I just said, "To hell with all of you," and I left. But I felt like I was in the right.

I didn't think anything else about it until I got to San Angelo, Texas, where Goodyear's test track is. I went down there with my Indy car to break the world's closed-circuit speed record.

Everything was ready when I got there. The race car was there; Goodyear had brought the press in for the occasion. And one other thing: A telegram from USAC, telling me I had been suspended for punching Johnny White.

It wasn't the first time I had been suspended. I got suspended once because I threatened to punch out Tom Marchese, who was the track promoter at Milwaukee, but that was a bunch of crap, because Marchese was a friend of Henry Banks of USAC. I was used to USAC's suspensions, so I went on with my plans.

The record was 183 miles an hour and had been set a couple of years before on Chrysler's test track in Michigan. Like all records, I knew it could be broken, so I wanted to get it over with. Bignotti got the car ready and I took it out on the five-mile, circular track. Well, the track is dished out—"parabolic," the Goodyear guys said, which is a fancy term for "dished out." The car felt a little funny, but I could tell it was because the solid rear axle was having a little trouble with the odd-shaped track. I had never been on a track like that, but I could keep it under control, so I nailed it.

I went 184 the first lap. A new record. Then I went 194, and finally 200.4 miles an hour. Before I went out, they had said, "Try to get it up to two hundred, A.J.," so I did it. And I stopped the car about three miles from the little pit area they had set up, where all the press was waiting. I waited out there. I waited for one of the Goodyear guys to come. It was Bill Neely who showed up. He skidded to a stop right beside the car. I was sitting on the left-rear tire.

"Want me to bring it in?" I asked him. And I pointed to the tire. There wasn't a bit of tread rubber on it. The heat buildup had been so great on the outside edge of the tire, because it was the only part that was touching the track, that finally the tread had started to come off in chunks about the size of your hand. But they wanted a 200-mile-an-hour record, so I had stayed on it until I broke it.

"Hell, no," he said. "Wait right here. I'll go get you another tire and wheel and we'll change it right here."

"Whattaya gonna tell your press buddies?" I said.

"I don't know," he said. "I'll tell 'em you got lost."

In a minute he was back with another tire. He had one of the tire busters sneak it in the trunk while he told them all I had run out of gas. They made a big deal out of loading up a fuel can. "No, not in the trunk," he had told them. "Up there in the front seat, so I can watch it."

Until now, there weren't too many people who knew that story. Outside of Goodyear.

I took Roger McCluskey to the USAC hearing with me. He was driving in the race where I had had the problem with Johnny White. Roger was my character witness, I guess you could say.

"I didn't *hit* him," I told them. "Oh, I had him around the *head* pretty good and I was *holding* him all right. But I didn't *hit* him."

McCluskey supplied the clincher.

"A.J. didn't hit White," he testified. "If he had of, he would have tore his head off."

Case dismissed.

A lot of people asked me after the hearing if I really did hit him or not, and I always said I didn't, but, you know, when I look back on it, I'm not really sure. I do get pretty mad, and there are times when things happen, and, well, you know how it is.

But Johnny was a charger, like me. And the next race at Terre Haute, I broke the track record, and when I came in, Johnny was waiting to go out. He gave me a thumbs up. I nodded and smiled. You didn't hold grudges in those days.

Johnny went out to try to break my record and he flipped it over the wall. He was paralyzed from the crash, and I always felt bad about it, because I think we had built up a big rivalry and he was maybe trying too hard. He lived for a few years after that, and they always wheeled him around to my pits to see me. Damn, I hated to see him like that. I thought to myself, if anything like that ever happens to me, I just hope I *buy* it. I want it ended. I think that's probably why he died. I don't think he had the will to live.

We all took more chances in those days. A lot of drivers drove hard, and a lot of them got killed. When I think back at some of the chances I took, I can't believe I made it.

* * *

I had *conquered* Indianapolis. In the history of the race, only six drivers had won it more than once: Tommy Milton, Louis Meyer, Wilbur Shaw, Mauri Rose, Bill Vukovich, and Rodger Ward. The next step, I told myself, was to the three-time-winner plateau. That would eliminate half of the six.

I won a record ten Championship races that year, which ran my grand total to twenty-eight, an all-time record. I did it in only five years. Ralph DePalma had won twenty-six, which took him twenty years to do, and Rodger Ward had won twenty-five, which took thirteen years.

I felt it was time to take on the best in stock-car racing: NAS-CAR, the National Association for Stock Car Auto Racing. What it really means is balls-out racing from wire to wire in a big American sedan that they call a *stock* car, which is, of course, about as far from stock as I am from a chess champion.

The guys who drive NASCAR are legends, too. Many of them got their start running moonshine on some back Southern road at night, with a carload of cops chasing them flat out. NASCAR racing is done mostly in the South, because that's where all the wild drivers come from—from the hills of the Virginias and the Carolinas. They always sounded like my kind of race drivers, so what better way to celebrate the Fourth of July than to race against them?

When I got to Daytona, which is the Indianapolis of stock-car racing, I found out that everything I had heard was true. They were harder charging than most of the Indianapolis drivers. More than that, they raced every weekend, and that's tough. They all knew each other's driving style like they knew their own. I didn't. But I knew my own. That had to be a good start.

Another thing I noticed about those guys is that they played as hard as they drove. I mean, they went out and drank and raised hell all night and then got in the race car the next day and went like crazy. I couldn't understand how they could even stand to *listen* to a race car with a hangover, let alone drive one.

There was a place called Robinson's, where all the race crowd went to drink. Two of the top NASCAR drivers, Curtis Turner and Joe Weatherly, had an apartment across the street that they rented at race time. One night somebody asked Curtis why they stayed over there. "It isn't exactly the best apartment in Daytona, you know," the guy said.

"I know that," Curtis said, "but I figure the worst thing that can happen to me when I get ready to go home at night is that somebody might step on my fingers."

Curtis had an airplane. He flew the plane about like he drove his race car, flat out all the time. Curtis and a friend were up flying one day—flying and drinking, I might add—and they ran out of bourbon, so Curtis said, "Don't worry 'bout it, pal; that's Gaffney, South Carolina, down there and I've got a friend that runs a bootleg business out of the back of his restaurant. We'll just fly down there, land this little ol' plane, and get us another jug. Hell, we'll be back in the air before anybody sees us."

Sounded logical to the other guy. But what they didn't know was that there was a Little League baseball game being played right next to his friend's restaurant. And Curtis's plane wasn't exactly a "little ol' plane." It was a twin-engine Aero Commander. They had to fly under a power line to land. Just as they were ready to touch down, Curtis noticed the line of traffic coming from the ball game. He pulled it back up and got out of there, but he knew somebody had to get the numbers on the underside of his wing.

They flew all the way back to Charlotte about fifty feet off the ground, so radar wouldn't pick them up. And instead of going into the Charlotte airport, they went into a little strip at Concord, a few miles away. When Curtis radioed in to the man in the one-man tower, he garbled his numbers; you know, "This is N-*murf-mrf, grumf, murrf*, requesting landing instructions." He didn't want them to find him because he knew he would lose his pilot's license.

The voice at the other end said, "It's no use, Curtis. They're lookin' for you all over the South."

These were the guys I would be racing against in NASCAR. And I was eager to watch some of them run, like Richard Petty and David Pearson, and drivers who had been making the kind of name for themselves in stock-car racing that I had at Indy. I wanted to beat them. I had taken on all the old-timers at Indy— and the newcomers—and I had beaten them. And I liked the view from the top.

It was supposed to be a big Mopar year. "Mopar" stands for Chrysler products—Dodge and Plymouth. They were strong because of their hemi engine, which was a whole lot better than anything else around stock-car circles because of its special combustion chamber, which gave it its name.

I had a Ray Nichels–prepared Dodge, so I knew the car was competitive. But I knew it was going to be tough competing against the Southern drivers who raced every week. They knew the tracks and they knew each other. And they weren't the slightest bit impressed with the fact that I was a two-time Indianapolis winner and USAC champion. Their champion was Richard Petty, and they had had USAC drivers come down before to take over. It hadn't worked.

But we gained a mutual respect for one another. They had the right idea about racing; I'll say that. They were loose and relaxed, but when they got in a race car, they were flat serious. "The bullshit stops when the green flag drops" was their motto.

Joe Weatherly came up with the best line I ever heard about spinning a race car. He came out of the fourth turn and got a little sideways. He gathered it up some, but the car started to slide the other way, then back to the way it started. It went back and forth down the straightaway, first one way and then the other, but by the time he got to the first turn, he didn't have it gathered up all the way, and he hit the wall. He was walking back to the pits and a reporter asked him what happened—there's always someone around to ask dumb-ass questions like that. "I got a little behind on my steering," Joe said.

But it was Fireball Roberts who put one of the reporters in his place. Same situation, probably the same reporter.

"What happened out there, Fireball?" he asked.

"I crashed; that's what happened out there. It is possible to *crash*, you know," he said.

They talked a lot about cheating in NASCAR, like the time Cotton Owens showed up at Atlanta with a Grand National stock car—those are the fast ones. Well, it turned out that the car he had built was faster than anybody else's. Much faster. NASCAR officials went over the car with a fine-tooth comb. They weighed it. They were under it, over it, inside it. They took the engine apart, but they couldn't figure out why it was so much faster. There were restrictions, but the car seemed to meet every one of them. David Pearson as a driver helped, but not that much.

Finally somebody remembered the templates. They use exact-scale metal brackets, patterned from showroom cars. They slip the templates over the cars, just to make sure the drivers haven't lowered them. That's the only reason: just a guard against lowering the cars. They put it over Cotton's car, and everybody looked on in amazement. What they were looking at was a perfect seven-eighths-scale race car. Cotton had *built* the body. A size smaller. Because of that, the car had less frontal area, and less wind resistance. It went faster. But the work that went into the project must have been something like building the pyramids. It almost worked.

Another time, Smokey Yunick showed up at Daytona with one of his creations, which Curtis Turner was going to qualify. NASCAR rules say that you *can* cut out the fender openings to accommodate the larger tires. But Smokey hadn't cut them out. The rest of the drivers raised hell. "You have to cut them out," they claimed.

"Nope," Smokey said. "The book says you *can* cut them out."

Curtis went out and turned the first 150-mile-an-hour lap at Daytona. The smaller wheel openings probably helped in the wind-resistance department.

Then he cut out the wheel openings. More hell-raising. "You can't do that," they all said.

"Sure you can," Smokey said. "It says you can cut them out, but it doesn't say *when*."

When Smokey announced that the engine Curtis had set the track record with was just his backup engine, everybody almost fainted. "Wait'll y'all see the *race* engine." He didn't have a race engine any stronger than that one, but he had them all completely psyched out. And that's part of the game.

But some of Smokey's cars were flat suspicious. Once, they accused him of having an extra fuel supply somewhere in the car. Again they went over every inch, but they couldn't find a thing. They told him to take his car on back to the track. Curtis got in it and drove away. Later he came back when nobody was looking and got the gas tank they had forgotten to put back on.

"How'd that sumbitch run without the gas tank, Smokey?" Curtis asked in the garage area.

"Just gas in the carburetor, Curtis. That's all," he said.

Everybody but the NASCAR officials knew better. "Funny, but poor sportsmanship," the newspapers said.

Writers are constantly writing about sportsmanship in racing. They say I'm the worst loser who ever lived. They're probably right. But I didn't start in this sport to *lose*. And I didn't become the first four-time USAC champion by being a loser. I did it by being a winner. And I went on to win more championships. None of them by losing.

Racing is not a profession for sportsmen. I mean, there are guys who will run *over* you to win. If they try, you have to run them off the track before they run you off. I drive hard, but I drive clean. And I can give as much as I can take. More, in fact.

Cheating doesn't fall into the same category. I think any race driver worth his salt will cheat if he can. And, you know, I think "cheating" is a poor choice of words. We just bend the rules as far as they will possibly bend. If there's a loophole, we will sneak through it. Al Unser said, "A.J. showed us all how. He wrote the book on bending rules and running hard. The guys in racing are tough, but Foyt is tougher. I mean, he won't hurt you to win, but he will risk hurting himself. We just practice what A.J. preaches."

I think that says it pretty well.

NASCAR drivers pride themselves on their "cheating." They think they *invented* it. They didn't, of course, but they sure worked it out to an art. It was more of a necessity for them than it was at Indianapolis. Indy cars are race cars from the first bolt to the last, but stock cars actually start out as true *stock* cars, right-off-the-showroom-floor passenger cars.

The first NASCAR race was in something like 1948, and a bunch of guys, including Richard Petty's father, Lee, got together at a dirt track in Charlotte and raced whatever cars they could come up with. The run-what-you-brung days. The rules were that the cars had to be late model and had to be completely stock, which is about as dangerous for racing as anything could be.

Even today's cars—hell, *particularly* today's cars—would be totally unsafe on a racetrack. The shock absorbers and the springs are designed to give a good, soft ride, and that's not what you want for racing. You need a stiff suspension so the car won't lean and bounce all over the racetrack. And the unit-body frames, or whatever the particular manufacturer wants to call them, aren't strong enough to withstand the average 50-mile-an-hour crash, let alone a high-speed crash. A passenger car is not even close to being a race car. The only similarity between the Dodge I drove at Daytona and one you might see in the parking lot at the Speedway is the appearance.

But those first stock cars were just what the name said. Lee Petty had borrowed a friend's Buick Roadmaster for the first race, because it was heavy and fairly fast for a street machine. He was leading the race, but the car got to bouncing so bad that he flipped it. Totaled it. After the race, they washed off the number and towed it out to the highway and pushed it in a ditch, so the guy who owned the car could collect on his insurance.

It was right after that first race that they started to cheat. First came stiffer shocks. When everybody started using them,

NASCAR threw up its hands and made them legal. Then other suspension parts. Legal again. Then wheels and exhaust systems. And on and on until the stock car was a fast, safe machine.

This is where I came in.

The track record at Indy was 158 miles an hour. In 1965 Darel Dieringer sat on the pole at Daytona with a speed of 172. Man, that's motoring!

Dieringer's Mercury was the only Ford product that had a chance. I had been racing Fords, but I switched just before I went to Daytona. The Dodge was a faster race car.

Dieringer got an early lead, but he couldn't hold off the Mopars. Petty took over at about the fortieth lap, and Bobby Isaac and I were right behind him. I had a little trouble getting past Richard the first time, because he drives the same kind of groove I do—up high. But they do a thing in NASCAR called "drafting," and that helped me.

Drafting is simple. You just pull right up behind a guy at full speed and you follow him. And I mean *right* up behind, a few inches away from his rear bumper. What it does is stretch out the air foil that flows over the car at high speed. Instead of two separate foils, it makes one long one, which is more streamlined. Both cars go faster and they give better gas mileage. We did it at Indy some, but it works better on the bigger stock cars. Also, the Daytona track is much better for it, because you hardly have to lift for the turns. The track has much-higher-banked turns—31 degrees, compared to 12 degrees at Indy—so you can get on a guy's bumper and stay there for as long as you want. Then, when you're ready to break away and try to pass him, you just pull down out of the draft and there's a sort of slingshot effect from coming out of the partial vacuum you've been running in. It's only a couple of miles an hour, but if your car is about as powerful as the one you've been following, there's no way he can keep you back there.

The NASCAR drivers would rather be running second, in somebody's draft. They usually wait until the last turn of the last lap to break the draft, and then they sail right on by to win. Unless, of course, they're much faster to begin with. Then they're just like any other race drivers. They pour it on and build up as big a lead as they can.

The battle between Isaac and Petty and me went on for lap after lap, until Richard blew his engine. After that it was back and forth, Isaac one lap and me the next. Until there was only one lap left.

Isaac was leading and I was right on him. *Right* on him. A couple of times I was so close you couldn't tell if I was tapping his bumper or not. The papers said I was, but I really wasn't. You try not to hit somebody at 200 miles an hour, and we were running pretty close to that in the straightaways. Isaac *expected* the sling-shot. As I said, there's not much the front car can do about it. He can't keep you from passing, so the only thing he can do is use up the best part of the track, so that passing can be so dangerous that you won't try it.

That's exactly where Isaac was—right in the middle of the groove. He expected me to pass coming out of Four, but as we came out of Two, headed for the back straightaway, I made my move—earlier than most of them would have done it, because they figured that would give the guy a chance to slingshot *them* out of Four. If I got by in Two, I could hold him off. I knew it.

I drove up high on the bank and started past Isaac on the out-side. The force of breaking the draft, plus the speed from coming down off the high bank, shot me right square in the path of Isaac's front bumper. I felt my car get a little light, like it was up on its tiptoes, but I kept my foot to the floor. Isaac had two choices: Hit me square in the side, which would have meant crashing both cars at 175 miles an hour, or back off. He drove down low on the apron and backed off.

He had to drive down so low that he had no chance of getting set up to slingshot me in Four. I won Daytona. No driver had ever won both Indianapolis and Daytona before. And I did it in the same year.

*   *   *

It was a six-car Mopar sweep. Ford had used the slogan "Total Performance" the year before, because they had totally dominated racing, so after the Daytona race, Dick Williford, Plymouth's PR man, passed out badges that read "Total *What?*" Everybody was wearing them that night at the party at Robinson's.

At Salem, Indiana, they offered a $1,000 bonus to the first driver who could break the 100-mile-an-hour mark on the half-mile track in a sprint car. Nobody had ever done it. I went out and turned a 100.1 on the first lap.

Next I went to Sebring, Florida, for the twelve-hour sports-car race. Very European. Well, it wouldn't be the first time I had handled European types. It was a sporty-car crowd, though, and a lot of them said that just because a driver had won Indianapolis and Daytona didn't for one minute mean that he could come down there and just walk away with everything.

There were a lot of people with tweed on. And sports caps. They brought along fancy baskets of food and they sat around their cars, with little, checkered tablecloths on card tables, drinking wine and allowing as how their own kind would win this race.

That was enough right there.

The thing that I hated most was the Le Mans start they used in the race. You know, where they line up all the cars on one side of the track and the drivers on the other, and then they shoot a gun and you're supposed to run like hell and jump in your car, start it, and roar off. Shit. That's stupid.

Everything that could possibly go wrong did. Even with the snooty sporty-car drivers. There were two identical Austin-Healeys—a team—parked side by side. Both drivers ran over and tried to jump in the same car. Man, they were fighting each other over whose car it was. They were dead serious. I thought it was funny as hell.

Another driver jumped in his Ferrari roadster and his entire leg went down through the spokes in the steering wheel. He almost killed himself getting it out. Me? I didn't get a much better start. For one thing, the special Corvette that John Mecom had built wouldn't start. The goddamn car wouldn't *start.* The field went roaring away without me. The people in tweed snickered. I could see them over by the fence and on the bridge that went over the track. When I finally got it fired up and I nailed it, the car left in a cloud of burning rubber. I had to catch the field, and I had to show a few bastards what a real racer could do.

It was a twisting, turning road course. You had to be right on in the corners. There were tight turns—even a hairpin—and a long straightaway where you could really motor.

By the time I got back to the start/finish line, where the stuck-up sporty-car spectators were, I had passed fifty-one cars. I shrugged as I went past.

I had the race won, hands down, but the car went sour. Still before I dropped out, there were a lot of believers in the crowd.

By the time I got back to Daytona in 1965, I had a following in NASCAR.

I had switched back to Ford, because there had been a lot of changes in the year since the last race. For one thing, Mopar cars were gone. They had won so many races that it got boring—boring to everybody, that is, except the Chrysler people. Ford complained bitterly. They designed their own sophisticated engine and took the plans to Bill France, who ruled NASCAR with an iron hand. France took one look at the engine, which probably cost $20,000 a copy, and said, "Whoa!"

"Listen, if I let you guys use this engine," he said, "Chrysler will be in here next week with something even more exotic, and it will become the biggest pissing contest in the history of racing."

They had secret meetings over the whole thing. Very few people knew what was going on, but I got inside information from my friends at Ford. I've never before told anybody about my conversations with Ford.

In a desperate attempt to keep the thing from getting any more out of hand, Bill France made a decision. It was based on his fear that NASCAR racing was rapidly approaching the Indianapolis status, where it was so expensive to build a race car that the little guy didn't have a chance. France had started NASCAR because he *wanted* the little guy to have a chance. If the engine war got any worse, there would only be a handful of drivers who could afford to put cars on the track that were competitive.

France didn't allow Ford to bring in their new engine. He outlawed the Chrysler hemi. Chrysler was so pissed off that they pulled out of racing completely, leaving a lot of their drivers high and dry. And out of racing.

Lucky I had an official Ford ride.

There really wasn't much of a race to it. I got out front and built up a lead so big that it didn't look like anybody could catch me. A whole bunch of top Ford executives, including Henry Ford II, had come down from Detroit to watch their cars get back in the winner's circle. They leaned back in their expensive seats and counted the laps until the checkered flag, when they could go out and needle the Chrysler people. It was the old Goodyear-Firestone thing again—the thing most big companies get into racing for in the first place. They only tell their stockholders that it's for their image.

They were content in their paddock seats, but I was bored with being so far out front. By then we had two-way radios, and I had been talking to the guys in my crew. The radios are usually reserved for vital information, but at that point I was so far ahead that the only vital information I asked for was the phone number of a really good-looking brunette who was standing at the hurricane fence behind my pit. The pit stop before, I had asked one of the guys if he had gotten her phone number. I mean, that's how silly the pit stops were that day.

I radioed again: "Did you guys get that phone number?"

"No, we'll go get it, A.J.," a guy said. "Now, will you go on and race. We're tryin' to take a nap in here."

They were lounging all over the stacks of tires and generally just soaking up the Florida sunshine. It was time to shake them up. Without saying a word on the radio, I brought the car down low coming out of Three. I was down on the apron and around through Four and coming into the pits before any of them even noticed that I wasn't out there on the track anymore. All hell broke loose. They fell over the tires and ran into each other trying to get to the pit wall. Up in the paddock seats, the Ford executives dropped their drinks. Although Buddy Baker was *way* back in second place, he could win. And he was driving a Plymouth.

I came sliding to a stop in front of my pit. They were all there, wide-eyed and in a state of panic. They didn't have any tires ready or any gas. They were just standing there.

"What the hell's wrong?" they all screamed at the same time.

"Did you get that sweetie's phone number?" I asked.

"*What?*" they said. Again all at the same time.

"Did you get her *phone* number?" I asked again.

"We got the goddamn phone number. We *got* it. Now get the hell out of here."

I dumped it in first and stood on it. The car got a little sideways as I roared out of the pits. Nobody ever knew why I came in. But up in the stands, the Ford executives collapsed in their seats. I was out in plenty of time to beat Buddy Baker to the checkered flag. But my pit crew was still in a state of shock.

And they didn't get that phone number at all.

After the race the guys had their annual party at Robinson's. Of course, they have one the night before the race and the night before that and every night at Daytona. I didn't go. Bill Neely and I were out racing our rental Fords on the beach. It was a good race. I got him on the ocean side—his mistake—and I guess he figured the beach went straight up to New Jersey or someplace. It doesn't. At the big turn in the beach—a left-hander—I got it crossed up in front of him and he had to either T-bone me or drive into the ocean. He drove into the ocean. At an indicated

100 miles an hour. You'd be surprised how fast a car stops in the water. We left his car and called Avis and told them somebody stole his racer.

Meanwhile, back at the party, it got pretty wild. Darel Dieringer left in another rental car, and somewhere between Robinson's and Ormond Beach, he flipped it, at about 100 miles an hour. A cop was parked beside the road and saw the whole thing. He rushed over, just as Darel was pulling himself out of the driver's window. "Howdy, Officer," he slurred.

"Why, you're *drunk*," the cop said.

"Of course I'm drunk," Darel said. "You think I'm a stunt driver or something?"

⑦
... and the Bad

I made the switch to a rear-engine car. As much as I would have loved to have upheld the tradition of Indianapolis and kept driving Offy roadsters forever, it became apparent that they weren't competitive anymore. Now, don't get me wrong; that's not to say that a really good driver can't take any car and be competitive by sheer determination alone. He can. I did just that at Milwaukee in a Championship-car race.

Everybody there—at least the guys who had a chance of winning—had rear-engine cars. I did, too, except mine wasn't ready for the race. When it wasn't ready at qualifying time, I told the guys to unload the dirt car. Keep in mind, a dirt car is not only front-engined; it's set up for just what the name says: dirt. It handles completely different from even a front-engine *pavement* car.

To even try one on a surface other than dirt was insanity. At least, that's what everybody said.

A lot of drivers—particularly some of these mama's boys we have today—would have *watched* the race. But I went there to *race*, and I was going to, no matter what. We had the dirt car because I had raced and won with it the day before at a track in Illinois.

The dirt car looked strange, sitting there among all the Lotus Fords. A Championship dirt car is like a sprint car, just bigger. The driver sits up high in the cockpit. Dirt cars have solid axles and stiff suspensions, to make up for rough dirt tracks. A Lotus Ford is what they call a *sophisticated* race car. It's low and trim-looking and has independent rear suspension. You lie down in it. One other thing: It's a hell of a lot faster than a dirt car. And it handles maybe twice as good on an asphalt track like, say, the one at the Wisconsin State Fair Grounds in West Allis, where we were.

You can imagine the snickers when I took the car out. They snickered, that is, until I put it on the pole. The snickers turned to cheers when I led the race for the first lap, and a lot of laps after that. There was no way that old dirt car should have run with the Lotus Fords, but I *made* it run with them. Determination again. And, as I've already said, and I'll probably say it a dozen times more, I just don't race if I don't think I am going to win. I don't care what the odds are.

I threw the car into the turns and used up so much of the track that they couldn't get around me. And I led the race until tire problems ruined me. The tires weren't designed for a dirt car, and we blistered so many of them by dirt-tracking it (sliding through turns) that Daddy and the rest of the pit crew got burned hands from changing the hot tires. Gordon Johncock beat me in the end, but there wasn't a snicker when the race ended.

It again proved my point: A man can do whatever he wants to do. If he wants to do it bad enough. You have to push to the limit, and then some. If it took putting the front wheels on the back, that's exactly what I did. At DuQuoin, I ran Goodyears on the front and Firestones on the rear. Nobody had ever considered such a thing, but it worked for me, because I won the race. Instead of making both companies happy, it pissed them both off. Neither one could claim a victory.

At one race, I ran a Goodyear Stock Car Special on the right rear and Goodyear Speedway Specials on the other three corners. I set a track record. It gave the car what I called "stagger," and, after that, we tried it often in tire tests if all else failed. We tried everything in tire tests.

Both tire companies were into racing right up to their armpits. I know Goodyear spent $50,000,000 *one year* in racing; that included tests and salaries and development and expenses. And paying drivers to run their tires. Firestone did the same thing, just not quite as big.

And the tests didn't always produce good results. Billy Wade and Jimmy Pardue and Bobby Marshman all were killed in tire tests. There seemed to be no stopping it. Both companies fought tooth and nail to find more miles an hour, and speeds went up at all tracks.

The Goodyear-Firestone tire wars brought other companies into racing because there was so much publicity and so much advertising. Newspaper and magazine ads suddenly featured race cars instead of passenger-car tires. It all started to resemble the gold rush, with everybody trying to outspend everybody else. If anything, it created an even bigger gap between the good drivers and the mediocre ones. The rich were getting richer and the poor were getting poorer. It spoiled a lot of good drivers who would have become great drivers if they had been a little hungrier.

There was money everywhere. In addition to the purses I won, I had endorsements and advertisements. From tire tests alone, I made enough money to buy a thousand-acre ranch at Hockley, Texas, just outside of Houston. I invested the rest. American racing was getting worldwide attention.

*   *   *

I guess you could say I'm a flag waver—strictly American. I won't even drive foreign cars. Hell, I won't even wear a shirt with French cuffs. It was only natural that when I got to Indianapolis in 1965 and saw all the fast European cars there, it pissed me off. And the European drivers. I made up my mind right there that I was going to sit on the pole.

First off, Mario Andretti—who was born in *Italy*—set a new track record of 158.849. There were 100,000 people there—just for the *qualifying*—and they went wild. They always do when somebody breaks a record. Or breaks his ass.

I was next in line, but I told USAC officials that I had a problem with my injectors. I *said* that, but actually I was stalling. I wanted to see how Jimmy Clark was going to qualify, so we pushed my car back to the garage area. That automatically moved me to the end of the qualifying order, right behind Clark.

Clark pushed the record up over 160 miles an hour. I'll have to admit—he was pretty good. The place was a madhouse. They were still screaming when we pushed my car back to the pit area. In fact, when they saw me coming, they let out a roar you could hear all the way to East St. Louis, Illinois.

It was five minutes till six—five minutes till the track closed for qualifying. By the time the starter was in place in the nose of the car, it was fifty seconds till six. But all you have to do is get the car on the track before six; then you can stay until you qualify. The engine started. Then it sputtered and died. It started again, and died. The third time, it ran. They pushed me out of the pits and I was on the track with five seconds to spare. I hadn't intended to cut it that close.

The entire crowd was on its feet. My first lap was 159.665. The second was over 160. The crowd had stopped screaming. They *all* were holding their breath. I was, too, because my car wasn't anywhere near as fast as Clark's. I've never admitted it, but I was hanging it out so far that I was right on the edge of disaster in every corner. I was *over* the edge. But I'd be damned if I was going to let Clark beat me.

I had five miles to go—two laps—and I needed to find half a mile an hour. The third lap was over 161—a *whole* mile an hour faster. My fourth lap was also over 161. When the announcement was made that I had a new track record of 161.233, everybody exhaled at the same time. They tore up programs and threw hats and just about tore down the Speedway. When the announcer stuck the microphone in my face as I pulled into the pits, I was ready to talk. A lot of times I'm not, but that day I had something to say.

"It's good to bring the record back to the United States," I said. Andretti didn't like it. Clark thought it was funny.

Unfortunately, that was my moment in the sun at Indy that year. The car broke about halfway through the race. Some days you eat the bear, and some days the bear eats you.

My bad luck followed me away from Indianapolis.

I went to Riverside to run a Holman and Moody Ford on the road course. The course wasn't built for stock cars, but, then, the stock cars weren't built for a road course, so I figured that about evened things out. It was the kind of challenge that made it interesting.

When you're running well, everything seems to fly by; a race is over in no time, it seems. But if your car isn't running well and you're hanging back there in the middle of the pack, the day seems like an eternity. That day at Riverside had turned into the longest day of my career. I started out like a house on fire, but about halfway through the race, I lost my brakes. I mean, they were *gone*. It's an eleven-turn course, and I was charging so hard in that big old sled that I just wore the brakes out. But I was following Junior Johnson and Marvin Panch, and I had confidence in their ability, so I was running as hard as they were. But the guy in front of *them* got in trouble and they had to brake. All three of us braked, in fact. Two of us slowed down. I kept pumping, but nothing happened. You always keep hoping. Hell, I've been upside down and still pounding on the brakes.

When Dean Moon saw the "Moon eyes" painted inside the

double-zero number on the car before the race, he said, "Looks like a double-O omen to me, A.J." I remembered that.

Now I had two choices: Hit Junior full bore and probably hurt him bad or swing right and drive off the course. There was about a thirty-foot drop off the track to the right, so that didn't make that alternative too attractive, but it was the one I chose. When the car left the track, at about 150 miles an hour, the wheel dropped down into a hole in the dirt and the right-front part of the bumper dug in; it catapulted the car about fifty feet in the air. It felt like I had been shot out of a cannon.

A lot of drivers have said that when they crash, it all happens so fast they don't remember anything. They sort of blank out. Well, maybe they want to blank out, because I remember every second of it. And it all seems to take a long time. While I'm waiting to hit, I always anticipate the pain. It always hurts, even if you don't break anything. It hurts in every joint. Hell, it even hurts your fingernails. That day it seemed like the car was sailing along through the air for ten minutes. Finally I felt it start down, and I braced myself as hard as I could. I knew it would hurt; I just didn't know how hard I was going to hit, and how much it was going to hurt.

The car came down right square on its top. Everything got real quiet. The only thing I could hear was a strange wheezing. Then I realized it was me, gasping for air. That's all I remember until I woke up in the hospital the next day.

I had a broken back and a fractured heel and several other broken bones and a punctured lung. It was the first time I had really been hurt bad in a race car. I had been bruised and banged up before, but nothing like this. You're always bruised. You can see black-and-blue areas where the shoulder harness was, and you ache all over. But this time I couldn't even breathe without pain running all over my body.

The first thing I remembered when I came to was something odd I had done before I left Houston. I had called Lucy from the airport and told her exactly where I had parked the car, and reminded her where the extra key was hidden. I had never done that before.

Then I thought of Mother. She had a bad heart, and I got worried about her hearing all this on the radio.

"Get me a phone," I mumbled.

They must have thought I was delirious, because nobody moved. "Get me a goddamn phone," I said. They got me a phone.

"I'm all right," I said when Mother answered. "Everything's fine. Now, don't you worry. I'll be home soon." Then I passed out for another day.

The newspaper articles said I would probably never race again. They quoted one of the doctors. "Well, that's a bunch of bull crap," I told the nurse. I demanded that they fly me back to a hospital in Houston. "I need to be with my family," I said. They agreed. The only thing was, when I went back to Houston, I went straight home and not to the hospital. The ambulance driver said, "But they told me to take you to Methodist Hospital."

"Well, I'm telling you to take me to my home," I said. "Now, get this son of a bitch moving."

I couldn't understand how I could be so healthy and strong one minute and a helpless cripple the next.

When I told Lucy I was going to Phoenix to watch the race, she said, "A.J., there's nothing I would like more than to get you out of here, but that's the craziest thing I've ever heard. It's only been three weeks and here you are talking about going to a race. Why, you can't even get out of your wheelchair. Next thing you know you'll be talking about racing again."

Lucy is a mind reader.

By the time I got to Phoenix, I had figured out how to walk without a cane or anything. I knew just how to move so the pain wouldn't make me flinch. I didn't want those guys to see me in a wheelchair, and I sure didn't want them to hear me scream. But, I'll tell you right now, there were a lot of times I wanted to.

When I got back into a race car a month later, I had almost

perfected my walking to the point where people couldn't see the limp. But every time I slid in through the window of the race car at the Atlanta track, I thought I was going to pass out. Before the race, some guy from the Atlanta *Journal* or one of the newspapers down there asked me why I was there. "I'm a race driver," I said. "Where else should I be?"

When I walked away, Freddie Lorenzen said, "Look at that guy. He hurts so bad he can't sleep at night, but he's gonna run the wheels off that race car."

And I did run it hard, although there were times when the pain caused my vision to blur. But it wasn't blurred vision that caused the trouble. I went past Marvin Panch and into Turn Three, and when I lifted, the car didn't slow down. The throttle was stuck wide open. I thought, "Oh, no, not Riverside again."

I went past Panch and spun the car toward the wall. It was better than hitting the concrete head on.

The pain shot through me like I had been hit by an elephant rifle when the car crashed sideways into the wall. And everything was quiet again. I could hear a race car go by from time to time, but I just wanted to sit there for a minute. When I pulled myself out the window of the car, I thought for sure I was going to pass out, but I told myself, "No way, buddy boy. You're not gonna pass out here in front of sixty thousand people."

I waved to the crowd before I got into the ambulance to go to the infield hospital for a checkup. I lay down inside. But I didn't pass out. In fact, I was back in the pits in time to see Panch come in, suffering from heat exhaustion. Leonard Wood ran up to me and grabbed me by the arm. "Can you take over, A.J.?" he asked.

I didn't have time to think about it. "Hell, yes," I said. And I got in the car.

Panch was in first place when he came in, and I kept the car there for the last third of the race. Later, in victory circle, I said, "If you can't beat 'em, join 'em."

And I walked back to the garage area, trying not to let the pain show. After all, the doctor at the track hospital had said I must sure be tough. "I've never examined anybody after a crash whose pulse was *normal*," he said.

The string of injuries carried over to the next year. I was roaring down the front straightaway at Milwaukee in the Championship car when the suspension broke. I knew I was going to crash. It was the third time in as many weeks that something had broken on the car. And I crashed every time.

As the car went into the long slide, I thought, God damn, I'd like to have my roadster back. Then the wall interrupted my daydreams. When I hit, I saw something go sailing over my head. I looked up and hunkered down at the same time. It was one of my wheels. The car immediately burst into flames. I ripped open my shoulder harness, but I couldn't get out. My feet were stuck. I slid back down in the seat and watched the firemen as they put their extinguishers into action. They were spraying the fire on the *track*. "Put out the *car*, goddammit," I screamed. "The fire in the *car*."

They didn't hear me.

The flames were all around me, but I had gotten my feet loose. I had to put my hands in the flames to push myself free, but I figured it was better to lose my hands than my life. It took three tries and I could see the skin bubbling on my hands.

More pain and more recovery time. It was starting to get monotonous. It also got me to thinking that my luck had run out.

I had never really thought too much about fear, but suddenly I had all kinds of time to think about a lot of things I hadn't thought about before. And I realized that there are some things I fear. I'll be honest about it. I fear water. I've been afraid of it since I was a kid and capsized a boat in the Gulf of Mexico; a high-school buddy drowned right before my eyes, and I ended up tying myself to a buoy and floating for ten hours before somebody found me. I think I've got a good reason for being afraid of water.

And I scare the dogshit out of myself a lot of times in a race car. In fact, I get scared almost every time I get in a race car.

And, if I'm not scaring myself, somebody else is doing it for me. I'm not like most of the other guys who say they've never been scared in a race car. Well, if they haven't been, they're just not driving as hard as they should be. Because if you drive a race car as hard as it will go, you're bound to scare yourself.

I get a thrill two or three times in every race. Sometimes more. And everybody who says he doesn't is lying either to himself or to the rest of the world. Or both.

Maybe it isn't a real fear, but it sure as hell is a good, sound *respect*. I'll tell you: I respect all cars. I've gotten thrills in sprint cars and midgets and Indy cars and stock cars. Even rental cars. The guys who say they haven't are full of bullshit. You get into a turn a little deeper than you should or you take a line through that doesn't quite work or somebody blows an engine in front of you at 200 miles an hour, and, I'll guarantee you, a man would be crazy not to get a thrill.

You *learn* respect when you learn what a race car can do to you. I've seen a lot of drivers get killed, and each accident has made an impression on me. I don't sit around and think about it all the time, and I don't mourn like a lot of people do. You see, I've got this big defense mechanism to keep me from getting too upset. I just put it out of my mind.

But death is something every race driver has to face. I tell myself it's not on my mind, but it really is. I don't think I have any death wish or a suicide complex; those are things some writer must have dreamed up to sell books. Hell, if I had a death wish, there are a lot of ways I could end it that would be easier than auto racing. If you have to work this hard at killing yourself, then you really don't want to do it that bad.

I don't dream about dying in a race car. In fact, the only dream I ever had about dying was about a highway accident, and then all I saw was my body lying beside the road, all covered up. There was a wrecked car in the background. An orange car.

Race drivers know it's a dangerous occupation, but they keep telling themselves that it's going to happen to somebody else and not to them. I think there are a lot, too, who drive race cars just so they can tell other people what heroes they are. I've heard many of them in bars telling some broad, "Sweetie, I could get killed out there tomorrow." To me that's asinine. If I thought I was going to get killed, I wouldn't be out there the next day.

There's nothing *wrong* with having respect for the sport, but as for being afraid of it, well, if that's the case, then a person should get out. There's a big difference between *scaring* yourself and flat being afraid. The scare goes away. But the thing that comes right after being afraid is *overcaution*, followed closely by a mistake. Racing is not the kind of sport you make too many mistakes in. I mean, if you make a mistake in football, the worst thing that can happen is the other team might score on you. But a mistake in auto racing could be your last one.

A baseball can travel at 100 miles an hour, but a race car can go twice that fast. And you're strapped to it. And that baseball goes wherever you point it; so does a race car, but you go with it.

With fear and respect in their proper places, I had time to think about injuries—*bad* injuries, where you're crippled or your brains are scrambled. I told Lucy that if anything like that ever happened to me, I wanted somebody to put an end to it.

I think people are surprised that I've gotten this far, because they think I take chances. They say I'm braver than most drivers, but I don't think that is necessarily true. I don't think I'm any braver than the next guy. I just think I use a little more common sense than some. When you get right down to it, a lot of the bravery thing is just talk—a completely phony attitude. A good race driver can do a lot better with brains than he can with brave.

While I was in the hospital, recovering from my burns, I was mean as a bear. I wanted out of there. Worse than that, I couldn't do anything for myself, because my hands were wrapped in bandages. I mean, *anything*; like peeing, for example. I used to wait for Lucy to come and take me to the bathroom. Hell, I couldn't go if the nurse took it out for me. And I got madder than hell if she was late, because a lot of times I really had to go. I would yell at her. "What would you do if the only person in the world who could help you pee didn't show up? I mean, damn, it's been all *night.*"

It was one of the few times I actually had to wait as long as the doctors said to get back to driving, because I couldn't hold the steering wheel with my hands bandaged. So I went to the races and helped wherever I could. Like with practical jokes.

Bobby Unser and I put a firecracker in his brother Al's salad one day at Howard Johnson's. There was lettuce all over the dining room.

And Dan Gurney and I discovered that if you take mashed potatoes and stick an M-80 firecracker to a motel-room doorknob, it will blow the knob clear off.

I learned a lot of useful information like that.

⑧
You Gotta Get Back on the Horse

The start of the 1967 season was the worst of any for me. I've never said it before, but I *made* myself come back. I could have retired at that point and lived very comfortably for the rest of my life. I was in a good enough financial position to do it.

But I wanted to race. The only thing was that I was scared shitless every time I got in the car. So I made myself drive harder than I really wanted to. I made myself get back on the horse that threw me. You see, I still had mixed emotions. I wanted to win, but I wasn't sure it all was worth it. By pushing myself even harder than I had before, I did start winning again; and that's the greatest therapy in the world. The fear started to go away with the victories. It was at about this point that I realized that I was as much afraid of losing as I was of getting hurt.

By the time I got to Indianapolis, I was riding high again. For one thing, I had two cars entered. The Sheraton-Thompson racing team had expanded. Joe Leonard was driving my second car, and that provided us with a shot at first *and* second. By now I was not even content with winning the race for the third time. I wanted second place as well.

Leonard, who had been a great motorcycle-racing champion, had come to Indy two years before to drive for the Gurney team. And he had immediately caught the spirit of the whole show. At the time, Gurney and his crew were staying out at the Howard Johnson Motel near the Speedway. Gurney was the Yamaha motorcycle distributor for the West Coast, so all of his team had Yamaha bikes to ride back and forth to the track. His other driver, Jerry Grant, decided on Leonard's first day in Indianapolis that he would lend a helping hand. They were all ready to go to the track, and Grant proceeded to tell Leonard how to ride the Yamaha bike. Keep in mind, Grant didn't know about Leonard's skill with a bike. Leonard just said, "Oh, I see, this lever here," and, "You mean, push this pedal?" and things like that.

When Grant thought Joey had it down well enough to try it, he jumped on his bike and said, "Let's go to the track," and he took off. Leonard waited until he was a block or so away and then he fired up his bike. By the time he got to Grant, he was up on the rear wheel. He went by him not only doing a wheelie but doing donuts around him.

At this point, Grant was screaming at him, "You son of a bitch!"

Leonard was about as superstitious as most race drivers, and he wouldn't even *talk* about death. Well, my old Heights buddy Bobby Waltrip was an undertaker. He had a chain of funeral homes, and Leonard didn't even like to have him *around*. "Whattaya have that undertaker around here for, anyway?" he asked once. Bobby and I made it worse by talking about funerals. Then Bobby sized him up and said, "You think Joey would fit in a number seven, A.J.?"

"What's a goddamn number seven?" he asked.

Then Bobby told him it was one of his best caskets. It drove Joey right up the wall. We kept going.

"Joey," I said, "Bobby and I've been talking and we decided that this is your day."

"You mean the day I'm gonna win?"

"No, Joey," Bobby said, "the day you're gonna buy it. You know, get *killed*."

"Ah, for chrissakes, knock it off," Joey said.

"No, really," I said. "We want to do everything we can, and Bobby here is gonna just embalm you right here and have your body flown back so your widow won't have to go through all that at home."

Leonard sat down. We went on. "I mean, both Bobby and I had this dream, and, you know, Bobby's never been wrong about dreams like that." That was all we had to say. Joey was so upset he had to go take a sedative.

Andy Granatelli had called before the season started and asked me if I wanted to drive the STP Turbocar. I told him, "Hell, no, turbines are for airplanes." After watching Parnelli put in on the pole at Indy, I wondered if I had made a mistake. But I figured the car would break and we wouldn't have to worry. I was hiding my head in the sand, because it was clearly faster than anything out there, including my two cars. It didn't matter; I felt that Granatelli had brought along a circus atmosphere to Indianapolis, and I didn't want to be a part of it.

When the Turbocar was still running strong at the halfway point, I *was* worried. I figured the only thing I could do was keep pressure on Parnelli, forcing him to drive as hard as he could go. The constant high speed might make the car break. I took the lead briefly at about lap 130 when Parnelli went in for fuel. He took it back when I pitted, and this time, when I went by the STP pits, I gave Granatelli the finger.

I followed Parnelli lap after lap, driving harder than I had ever driven. With four laps to go I felt it was all over, but I kept pushing Parnelli. I can never say if that was the reason or not—the car may have broken anyway—but on the next lap Parnelli slowed down. By the time I went past him, he was coasting. I was about to move into a very select circle of three-time Indianapolis winners. Joey Leonard was third in my other car. Happy as a lark. But happier just to be alive.

I was counting the money on the white-flag lap. I stormed into Turn One, drove down across the corner and through Two, and flew down the back straightaway. I was lined up perfectly through Three and Four. Suddenly it was "Oh, shit" time again. All I had was the main straightaway to go and the race was mine. But Bobby Grim spun coming out of Four and hit the wall in the main straight. Chuck Hulse spun into Carl Williams, and there were cars spinning everywhere. There was smoke all over and I couldn't see where to go. I went down low and there wasn't any hole there, so I brought it back up high, all the time braking as easily as I could—just enough to slow the car down, but not enough to spin it. I dodged three cars and took it back to the center of the groove. I dumped it into second gear and stood on it. I didn't know what else to do. I figured that whatever I hit I was going to take to the finish line with me. I wasn't going to be denied that victory.

When I came out of the smoke and saw a clear racetrack, I couldn't believe it. I had missed everything. Pat Vidan waved the checkered flag as I drove past him, and then he brought out the red flag to stop the race. I was the only car to finish the full 200 laps, because the track was completely blocked. Al Unser was second, two laps back, and Joey was right behind him.

Two weeks after my third Indianapolis victory I was in France, ready to run the granddaddy of all sports-car races, the Twenty-four Hours of Le Mans.

Ford had put together a really professional racing team. Their Mark II cars were as sleek-looking as any Ferrari ever made, and they would probably blow the doors off anything in the world. It was a hell of a first-time effort, but they had the bucks to spend, just like they had in developing a fine Indy engine.

But with all the money and all the sophistication of the cars, they still almost missed the boat. They had been testing the car at Daytona and it didn't handle worth a damn, so, in desperation, they called me to come over and see if I could get it straightened out for them. All their high-powered engineers couldn't tell what was wrong. I flew to Daytona.

The cars were beautiful. I was impressed. But they said they were "darting," which is something some passenger cars do on the highway, though few drivers even notice it. The car moves over quickly in, say, lane-change maneuvers, sort of jumps.

I climbed into the car, buckled up, and took off. I got 250 feet down the pit road and stopped. That was all I needed. When I backed up to the pits, they said, "What's wrong? Why don't you go on out and try it?"

"I don't have to," I told them. "You've got two different-size tires on the rear. That's your problem."

The Ford engineers said, "No way. Look here: They're both marked the same."

The Goodyear engineers said, "That's right. The same."

"Measure them," I said. "You'll see. They're not the same size."

They measured the tires, and in spite of the fact that they were both designated the same size, there was almost a three-inch difference in the circumference. When you backed off, it gave the car a ratchet effect; that let it run one way. When you picked up the throttle, it ran the other way. They had already changed the rear end two or three times. They had changed everything they could think of.

When they got the proper-size tires on, they said, "Okay, go ahead and try it now."

"It's okay now," I said. "Let McLaren try it."

Bruce McLaren was the test driver, and he got in it and took off. After ten laps, he came back in and said, "You won't believe it, boys, but it's perfect."

McLaren was smart. He would prove that in later years with his Indy cars, but he had never run up against anything like this. But when I backed off to shift gears going down the pit road, the car darted, and I knew immediately what it was. It's hard to build tires the same size, and at 200 miles an hour, you can really tell it, if you know what you're looking for. We had purposely put stagger in some of the dirt cars we had, so I knew all about it. And I knew if you didn't want stagger, then you had to measure the tires carefully.

You have to know how the chassis works and how the tires work. You have to know everything if you are going to run a car at its limit. The exceptions are few. There haven't been many drivers like Eddie Sachs, who had talent enough to put an ill-handling car up front. He was the exception. There are more drivers like Johnny Rutherford, who don't know that much about the car, and there are a lot of them who think they know it all, and it gets them in a lot of trouble.

The early drivers knew more about their cars because they couldn't afford mechanics; they had to learn it all themselves. Today most drivers—and a lot of mechanics, for that matter—only know "R&R"—remove and replace.

And there were drivers like Sammy Sessions, who insisted when he was driving my second car that it felt like it wanted to spin. It was at Pocono, and he said, "It feels just like it wants to knock the fence down."

"It won't do it," I said. "It's set up right. Just stay on it and try to knock the fence down. Try it."

He did, and picked up four miles an hour. It's possible to work yourself into a rut, and you either stay there or you start going backwards. Sammy had done that, and the Ford engineers and McLaren had done it.

By the time they got the cars to Le Mans, they were right.

I had heard talk of Le Mans all my life. It was supposed to be the "Indianapolis of sports-car racing." Well, there were a lot of spectators there, almost like Indy, and the course—even though it was a road course—looked a little tough, but it sure as hell wasn't Indianapolis. For one thing, some of the drivers I watched wouldn't have gotten through the first turn at Indy.

The course was more than eight miles long. Dan Gurney was my copilot, and he had been there before, so I listened to him as he explained it to me. You have to have a copilot because nobody could drive the entire twenty-four hours at speed and make it. "Physically impossible," they said.

"Well, it might be real tough, but nothing's impossible," I told them.

I took the Ford out on the course. I thought it was just a little old country road, so I told them I was ready to qualify. I had driven roads like that all my life.

The race wasn't that difficult. I got the car out front in my four-hour turn at the wheel. Gurney kept it there in his. When I got back in the car for my second shift, it had gotten dark, and everything took on a different look. I was glad, because it had started to get a little boring, in spite of the fact that we were breaking every record in the book.

Here's what the course consisted of:

Just outside town, along old RN158, the main drag from Alençon to Tours, the road widens up a bit and becomes a dead straightaway for about three and a half miles. Once every year they chase all the hay shakers off there—the horse-drawn wagons and old Citroëns and the old men pedaling bicycles loaded up with bunches of tied twigs—and it becomes the Mulsanne Straight, then and now the fastest stretch of road ever built into a closed circuit.

There are trees up close along both sides, and down toward the end of the straight you have to be hitting 200 or 210 miles an hour or you might as well park it. And as if you haven't got enough to do just hanging on, they've got this row of signs off to one side that tell you something—if you could read the things at that speed. Well, the signs are counting down kilometers, because at the end of the straight, just after this little 200-mile-an-hour soft right-hand dogleg, they've got this 35-mile-an-hour corner where you've got to suck everything up tight. Suddenly you're going in the other direction. Back off a bit and hit the brakes, really mash down, then drag it down to first gear and breathe the brakes. Then hammer her back up to somewhere around 180 mph; gear down to 40 mph for a right-hander; gear down again for that slow left-right; punch it back to 160. Stand on it some more and crank it around the White House Corner, and you had better plan to be hitting 180 and climbing as you go past the pits or everybody will think you're a *tourist*. Over the hill and into the S's, where, usually, you are suddenly right up to your ass in little Alfas buzzing along in their own little race. You do all this 350 times in 24 hours, driving through night and day, and half the time it is raining down at one end of the track and sunny at the other, and most of the time they've got this crosswind that huffs up and blows you over one whole lane.

I was driving the two-to-six-A.M. shift, and I was really getting tired. I kept looking at the lighted timer on the dash, and I was counting the minutes until I could get out of the car. My back ached, and, to make matters worse, it was starting to get foggy. But I kept telling myself, "Just a few more laps." Finally it was time to come in, so I brought the Mark II roaring into the pits and got out of the car. The crew had one side up in the air and new rubber on quickly. I started to walk away, but the boss of the Ford team, Jacque Passino, said, "Uh, A.J., don't run off."

"Whattaya mean, don't run off?" I said. "I'm gonna take a nap."

"Well, I don't know how to tell you this," he said—and I knew it was going to be a bitch— "but we can't find Gurney."

"Whattaya mean, you can't *find* Gurney?" I said in disbelief.

"We don't know where he is," he said. "I'm afraid you'll have to go back out there."

I could have cried. My butt was dragging, but I got back in the car and drove another four-hour shift. And, do you know, I found out later that Gurney did it on purpose. I told him, "Thanks a lot, buddy." But he knew all about road racing, and he knew the early-morning shift is the worst, with the fog and later with the sun in your eyes. It's the time at Le Mans when they wreck all the cars. The drivers are tired and the cars start to reach the breaking point. And there is a lot of smoke hanging over the track from the campfires. It's like a blanket, particularly around the end of the Mulsanne Straight. There are some little bridges there, and they're completely covered with smoke and fog. You drop down and zing through, and it's like going through a tunnel. Sort of like driving a big slot car. You can feel the suspension working on the rough road, and the wind whistles between the car and the cement bridges.

I kept the car in first place. In fact, my lap times were faster than Gurney's. We won everything. We covered 3,249 miles in the 24 hours, for an average speed of 135.48 miles an hour, which not only broke the record but broke it by the widest margin in history. And I became the only driver ever to win Indy and Le Mans. It was just like Indy and Daytona: I won them in the same year. It definitely was the year I ate the bear.

Late in the season, I was so far ahead on points that I went out to run the Phoenix race knowing damn well that I was going to win the championship. There was no way I could lose it. Well, there was *one* way. If Andretti won. But, like I said, there was no way I was ever going to lose that sumbitch. I mean, from the minute we rolled the orange race car out of the truck, I had it won. I know, you've heard it a million times; you've heard football players say it about the Super Bowl and you've heard boxers say it about the championship—Ali was good at that—but, damn it, there are times when you *do* know it. Phoenix was one of those times.

All I had to do was finish the race—just *finish*—and I had it. If I didn't finish, Andretti had a mathematical chance. A lot of people—like, everybody I talked to—though I should just stroke it. "Now, A.J." was the way every conversation started. And it ended "I know you're a charger, but for chrissakes, today take it easy. I mean, Jesus, all you have to do is *finish*."

"Yeah, I know," I told them all. "Just finish."

Well, bullshit. The day I go out on a racetrack and "just finish" is the day they'll all be going by and saying "Look how natural he looks."

So I went out there and I nailed it. I was not only going to win the championship; I was going to win the *race*. I wish to hell somebody had told Jerry Grant this. There was a spin, and to avoid it I must have run half a mile out in the boondocks, knocking over Joshua trees and those goddamn cactuses that are the state tree of Arizona, whatever they're called. Well, I finally got it stopped, and I looked around and saw a cloud of dust coming at me. It looked like that goddamn roadrunner in the cartoons. It was Grant, sliding sideways, and I'll be a son of a bitch if he didn't hit me. I mean, here I was, all by myself out in the desert, and I got T-boned.

I jumped out of the car and ran back into the pits and flagged Roger McCluskey in. "Gimme your car, Roger. I gotta finish this race." Roger didn't even ask any questions. He got out of the car and did a sort of bow, leaning over to one side and holding an arm outstretched toward the car with the palm of his hand up. Roger McCluskey is a classy sumbitch.

So I finished the race and I won the championship.

Later Andretti said to a bunch of media guys, "That goddamn Foyt will do anything to win."

Not too many people realize that. Andretti's pretty sharp.

The STP Turbocar had run so well at Indy that turbo fever hit everybody. Just like with the rear-engine cars, I felt it was too radical. For one thing, it was too *quiet*. They called Parnelli's car the Whooshmobile because that's the sound it made when it came by. The roar of the race car was gone, and, to me at least, that took a lot away from the feeling of a race. An entire race with Whooshmobiles would be like watching thirty-three Electroluxes run.

USAC felt pretty much the same way, so they put restrictions on it. The air intake on a turbine car is called the "annulus." The size of that had been restricted to 23 square inches in 1967; in 1968 they tightened it to 15. It was a little like strangling somebody. But the car had been so much faster than the other cars that they had to try to keep the race competitive. I don't always agree with USAC, but this time I did.

Most people gave up on it. Most people. Some continued with plans, because if there ever was an opportunity to cheat, the Turbocar was it. Goodyear got involved in a Turbocar project *before* the restriction. In fact, they wound up spending nearly a million dollars on a Carroll Shelby Turbocar that was built by Ken Wallis, who was a former RAF fighter pilot. He had built the STP turbine car.

When the new rules came out, there were secret meetings between Shelby and Goodyear and some of the people building the car. They met in garages and motels and everywhere. The whole thing was a typical Shelby big deal. When they found out about the restrictions, somebody went back to the drawing board and created an annulus that was 15 inches when the car was sitting in the pits, but when you wound it up, the annulus started to open, like the aperture on a camera. Whatever made them think they could get by with it I'll never know. Just imagine: a car whooshing along with the pack and all of a sudden there's a burst of speed and it's gone. Like Superman. An idiot could have figured out why. I could have told them they couldn't trust a Limey.

Goodyear found out about it and said, "No way. Lock the car up." They padlocked the car in the garage at gasoline alley. And the night before the committee was supposed to inspect it, it disappeared. I don't know where they took it, but I'll bet that today, somewhere, it's the world's only million-dollar planter.

*   *   *

George Bignotti and I decided to part company. For the last time, it turned out. Neither of our nervous systems could stand it. There were a lot of victories and a lot of happy moments, but there was also so much fighting that it wasn't worth it. We parted friends. And I moved Daddy into George's spot. From then on, we built our own cars. We painted them "Foyt Orange," which actually was a 1965 Ford Mustang color called Poppy Red, but I always liked it. Besides, after I started winning so many races and so many championships, a lot of race drivers began to paint their cars pearl white, like mine had been. The orange was a pleasant change. And I settled on a number: 14. I was number 1 most years—when I was the defending champion—but there were a few times when I had to take number 2, and that didn't set well with me. As far as I was concerned, there wasn't a number 2. First is first, and second is nowhere. Number 14 had been a lucky number at the Speedway. Bill Vukovich had used it, and Tony Bettenhausen and Wilbur Shaw and Louie Meyer. It had a good history.

Number 14 and I rode along on the crest of a big wave. But with celebrity status there were also some problems. Lucy and I couldn't go where we wanted all the time. I mean, it was tough to go to a restaurant without being spotted. Now, don't get me wrong; I appreciated being asked for autographs and having my picture taken with the "little woman," but I also appreciated my privacy. I've always been a private person, and now I was in the spotlight all the time. So we found quiet little restaurants where we could be left alone, or we stayed home.

And Lucy insisted that the kids' pictures never appear in the paper. Any magazine stories or television footage on our family life always avoided any mention of the kids. Still, there was one kidnap threat on Terry, so somebody had to take her to school every day and walk her right to her homeroom. I wasn't sure at times if it was worth it to be a celebrity.

But it had its moments. I got stopped for speeding one day and the cop said, "Okay, who do you think you are, A. J. Foyt?"

The celebrity bit put a wedge between a lot of the drivers and me. There was so much written about A. J. Foyt—"Super Tex," "Tough Tony," and so on—that a lot of them became jealous. And I couldn't blame them a whole lot. But I didn't *ask* for it; it came with the territory. I had won more races than anybody—in more kinds of cars. Nobody had done what I had. Everybody expected me to reach some kind of plateau, someplace where I would level off for a while and then start down the other side. But I don't think a driver reaches a *plateau*. Some get *satisfied* with what they're doing, and that starts them down the other side. But not me. I could win every race of the season and lose the last one, and I would feel like I'd been a loser all my life.

There were periods when I didn't win. It happens to every athlete; I don't care what sport it is. The slumps great baseball players have are a good example. I got in a slump in 1968 in stock cars, and it wound up causing a rift between Goodyear and me.

Goodyear had bounced Tony Webner out as director of racing. I never did understand it, but Bob Lane, who was a PR vice-president, got the idea that Tony was partying more than he was directing, so he brought in a guy from the sales staff named Larry Truesdale to run the racing show. Truesdale had never even been to a race before, but the whole thing was just to shuffle Tony out. Truesdale and I never did hit it off as well as Tony and I had, so when he accused me of not running hard enough, I hit the ceiling. Well, we went round and round, and Truesdale ended up firing me as a Goodyear driver. In those days being a "Goodyear driver" meant that you got a certain number of tire tests and a lot of free tires—most of them stuffed with money—and assorted expensive gifts. In exchange, you drove on Goodyear tires and said nice things about the company to the news media. You were instructed to always mention the company name when you were interviewed on network TV after the race. You know: "Aw, the car was okay, but it was the Goodyear tires that really did it." You've heard it.

The whole thing came to a head at Indianapolis. The tires that

Goodyear had for the NASCAR circuit at that point just weren't as good as Firestone's. I was driving a Ralph Moody Ford on the road course at Indianapolis Raceway Park. Truesdale and the engineers had been giving me a hard time because in the previous races I had sat on the pole and then got beat in the race. They blamed me, and I kept telling them that the compound was changing in the tires when they got super hot. It was getting slippery as hell.

They said, "You're looking for excuses."

I said, "Your tires aren't worth a shit."

Well, the day I got fired, I was in a bad mood when I arrived at the track. I guess what people say about me is true: I *am* moody, and there are a lot of times when I want to be left alone. It's one of the reasons I haven't hit it off too well with the press. They have been too insistent at times, and, well, if you must know, I've roughed a few of them up.

This is the mood I was in when I got to the track. The landing gear had collapsed on my airplane when I landed at Roscoe Turner's airport, and I had crashed. That would have done it right there, but Truesdale nailed me when I got to the track, and I told him to stuff his tires—and I didn't mean with money. So he fired me.

"Suits me fine, buddy boy," I said. "We'll put Firestones on and run your ass right off the track."

I not only sat on the pole; I lapped the entire field. In fact, I won by so big a margin that it pissed off the other drivers. But I had a point to prove. After the race, I went over to the Goodyear tire truck and said, "Okay, now whatta you bastards have to say? You think it's still me?"

Getting fired cost me a lot of money, but I wasn't going to take the blame for their lives. I proved they were wrong. Truesdale couldn't stand that. He even canceled a deal I had with Goodyear to build a service store on a piece of property of mine in Houston. I could have said, "Yes, sir, Mr. Truesdale; you and your engineers are exactly right," but I wasn't about to. I wasn't going to let them call me a complete idiot. Nobody's going to back me into a corner. If I'm wrong, I'll go to the corner myself. But nobody's going to send me there.

I've always worked that way with a sponsor. If they give me a winning product, I'll use it. But if it's not right, I won't use it for *any* price. It's why you've never seen my name on a bunch of products in ads. I won't endorse anything I don't believe in.

And, in the long run, I came out on top. They finally admitted the tires were wrong. As for Truesdale, he resigned later. There was a lot of talk about payola and under-the-table deals. But none of the deals was with me.

When Goodyear moved Leo Mehl into the top racing spot, we got things patched up between us.

Definitely the wildest thing about racing in those days was going back and forth to the track. There was one rental-car race after another, and a lot of drivers wore out their welcome with the rental-car companies. Bobby Unser had to have somebody else rent his cars for him for a while because he destroyed so many. The word was out on him.

We were racing at Ontario, once, and a couple of Firestone engineers asked me in the lobby of the Holiday Inn one morning if they could ride to the track with me. "Sure," I said, "if you've got your brave pills with you."

"Listen, Tex, there's no use trying to scare us," one of them said. "We've been through it all. We don't scare."

I told Jimmy Greer to ride to the track with Daddy.

When I picked up the two guys in front of the motel, I had the passenger door locked. "Door's stuck," I said. "Hop in the back." I got the car on the freeway and got it going as fast as it would go—about 100—and I jumped in the back seat with them. It scared the dogshit out of them. There was nothing but asses and elbows from them trying to get to the steering wheel. One held the wheel as they both tried to get in the front seat at the same time. The car was all over the road, but they finally got it stopped. When we got to the track, one was driving and I was sitting in the back seat by myself. They both were still white as a sheet.

But the fun with Firestone came to an end. After the mid-'70s, Firestone wasn't around anymore. It was hard for me to believe that they had pulled out of racing. Within ten years, Goodyear had run them off the racetrack. They came to the Speedway loaded for bear and they flat got run out. And it wasn't all just dollars. Sure, Goodyear spent millions; but they had better engineers and better products. There had been problems in the early days. Tires chunked under full fuel loads and tires got slippery and there were crashes when tires blew, but Goodyear stayed right there, and they corrected the problems.

When I heard the news that Firestone was pulling out, I remembered two things. The first was how cocky they had been when I brought Goodyear to the Speedway, and the other was the time that Lloyd Ruby blew a Firestone at Indy. There had been several blown tires on both sides, and Firestone had asked their drivers—told them, in fact—not to mention a *blown* tire anymore when they were being interviewed. "Say a suspension part broke or something like that," they said. "But don't say you blew a tire." Well, Ruby *did* blow a tire, so when Jim Wilson from WISH-TV was interviewing him after the crash, Jim said, "What happened out there, Lloyd?"

"Well, Jim," he said, "I blew a wheel."

Racing wasn't going to be the same without Firestone. Who would there be to beat?

Most of the time you *make* your own luck in racing. So-called hard-luck drivers either aren't paying attention or have been too hard on the equipment. Racing is a sport that takes 100 percent concentration, 100 percent of the time.

In the 1973 Indy 500, we had another first-lap destruction derby. But this time I was ready for it. Jack Starnes, my engine man, told me on the two-way radio that Pat Vidan had the green flag in his hand. Information like that is handy, because it gives you a chance to get a little jump on the field. I had started pretty far back because of qualifying problems, so I needed to get a jump. When I came out of Four, I punched it, just as Pat raised the flag. I got past several cars before the flag was dropped, but I was so far back nobody noticed. As it turned out, it was a good thing. Salt Walther is a race driver who knows one thing: speed. He doesn't have any skill or anything else. He just goes fast. The only problem is he can't control the car at speed. Well, he lost it and started an eleven-car chain-reaction crash. Because I was going faster than anybody else coming down the front straight, I was able to drive right under the accident. If I hadn't cheated a little on the start, I would have been right in the middle of it.

Who says crime doesn't pay?

George Snider was driving my other car, and he went right *through* the mess. To show you how busy a driver is when something like that happens, I saw him get completely sideways. Later he was parked in the infield with all four tires cut down, and I asked him how the hell he got through. He said, "I just drove *straight* through." He had been so busy trying to get it straight and miss everything that he didn't even realize he had been sideways. He was busy concentrating on saving it.

Concentration is everything. I remember one night at Ascot Park in California when some kid in a sprint car was determined to pass me—just because I was A. J. Foyt, I guess. He went into the turn so fast and so high that I backed off—because I knew he was going to spin, not because I was afraid to run in there with him. If anybody has the nerve to try to outdrive me in a corner, I'll go right in with him. His ass busts the same way as mine. But I knew what was going to happen on this one. The rear end of his car slid out and he spun right in front of me. I picked my spot and aimed right *at* his spinning race car. I figured he was going to be past that point when I got there. I punched it, and as I went by, his car *had* slid out of the way. I missed him by inches. He hit the wall. But he panicked and I stayed cool. He got in over his head and he hit his brakes, and it was all over then.

I made my luck better in 1973 by teaming up with Jim Gilmore to form the best team I ever had. I had Daddy on one side and Jim, who is like a brother, on the other.

There are other times when your luck is made for you. I was running the sprinter at DuQuoin, and I came in for a routine fuel stop under yellow. I needed only five or six gallons, but we didn't have the regular dump can, because we really didn't expect to fuel the car. It's just that I thought it would be a little edge. Security. They were dumping in the fuel from a regular oil can, and I let the clutch slip a little, enough for the car to move. The guy spilled about half a gallon of fuel down the back of my uniform. I didn't even know it, but when I accelerated out of the pits, all the nitro (nitromethane) we had put in the fuel caused it to pop, and it ignited the back of the car. In a second I was completely on fire. It was burning down inside my uniform. I ripped off my harness and rolled out of the car. I still hadn't felt the pain from the fire, but I sure felt the pain as my own race car ran over my ankle. It's a strange sensation, hearing your own bones break. You can actually *hear* it inside your head.

The car ran into the guardrail, and I was rolling on the ground. I jumped up and ran right into the fence because I couldn't run right. Daddy was right there with a fire extinguisher to put me out. As I lay there, patting out the little wisps of smoke on my uniform, I looked down at my foot. It was pointed in completely the wrong direction.

And there are times when you just get *screwed*. Luck can come in many different forms. I have had big leads in races and they've brought out the yellow flag for no good reason, except that the race is on national television and they want to get the cars closer together so it will look more interesting to the viewers. NASCAR is worse about that than USAC.

And in the 1976 Indy race it was a combination of USAC and Mother Nature. It's tradition to cheat on yellow. Drivers have always done it. You're not allowed to improve your position when the yellow is out, but all the drivers do if they can get away with it, usually over in the back straight somewhere. In '76 I had been outrunning Johnny Rutherford all day. I could have beaten

him, but just after the halfway point, there was a yellow flag.
Rutherford ran full bore for 23 seconds after the yellow came out.
The reason I know it was 23 seconds is that they talked about it on
television. It was that obvious. He ran through all the yellow
lights and wound up in first place. And I'll be damned if it didn't
rain and the race was called. Since it was in the middle of lap
103, they reverted back to lap 102, and if a race is over half run,
it's official.

But I didn't cry about it, like a lot of drivers would. I let them
know in no uncertain terms that I thought it was shitty, and I
stomped back to gasoline alley.

Most of the time, drivers holler because they flat got outsmarted and it embarrasses them. But I figure if somebody out-
smarts me, it's my own fault.

I've been accused of practically everything. Some of it is true,
but a lot isn't. Bignotti accused me one time of carrying an extra
five gallons of fuel in the canister of my fire extinguisher at Ontario. Hell, that would be unsafe. You can't put out a fire with
methanol. It was a ridiculous charge. Besides, it was more like
three gallons.

And there have been all kinds of charges that I was running
nitrous oxide in the engine. They took me off the pole and
moved me clear to the back of the field at Daytona one year for
that. You see, if you inject nitrous oxide (laughing gas, just like
the dentist uses), it gives you a burst of speed and probably 150
extra horsepower. But you have to use it sparingly, because the
officials tend to get suspicious if your car takes off and flies over
the pack. You use just a little bit of it coming out of a corner,
when you would normally be accelerating anyway. Then hardly
nobody notices. Except, of course, the driver you've just blown
off.

But that time at Daytona I really didn't know the guys had put
it in there. But it sure did make the car run good. I would like to
point out, though, that there were a lot of other guys caught, too.
So my boys were just trying to keep me competitive.

They accused Wally Dallenbach of using nitrous at Indy in

1975, and I'd be willing to bet that he did. Just by the way the car sounded and by the fact that he ran away from everybody so easy. Until he burned a piston. Nitrous does that if you use it too long.

One year at Daytona I was accused of using more fuel, but that time it was completely legal. There's always a lot of fuel that goes out the vent tube when you accelerate out of the pits. The cars leave a trail of gasoline, but it evaporates right away, and it's no hazard. Well, I put in an extra little tank to catch this. The tank drained it back into the main tank and I saved maybe half a gallon on each pit stop. They checked the rules until they were blue in the face, but they couldn't find anything wrong with it. I just outsmarted them. It was like Smokey Yunick and his fender-cutting bit.

Linda Vaughan has been around auto racing about as long as I have. She started as Miss Atlanta Raceway; then she was Miss Firebird, and finally Miss Hurst Golden Shifter. Linda is Mother Earth to the race drivers. She also has the biggest tits in the world. Everybody in racing would give half his purse to see them.

Linda was riding from the track into town with me one night when I got stopped for speeding. I mean, I was really moving and it was about the fifth time I had been stopped that week, so I was afraid I was going to lose my license. I said to Linda, "You just do what I say when that cop comes up here."

"Sure, Sweetie Pie," Linda said. Linda cooperates like that.

The cop came up and said, "Where the hell do you think you're going at that speed, fella?"

"Well, Officer, this girl just made me an offer I didn't *want* to refuse, so I was in a hurry to get to the motel. You know what I mean." And I winked at him. "I mean, did you ever see tits like that?" I whispered to him. And I motioned for Linda to take one out.

She did.

"Gawd . . . damn," the cop said. "Hey, you mind if I show my buddy back there in the cruiser?"

I didn't get a ticket.

It was a time of wacky events.

Curtis Turner was going to fly a bunch of us down to Charlotte after the first qualifying weekend. He had so many people in the plane that I had to get out and lift the tail off the ground, just to get it back up on the tricycle landing gear. But somehow we made it.

After Indy in 1976, Bobby Waltrip and I went to New York for a presentation, and we met some guy named Sam who wanted to take us out to what he called a "cabaret theater." "It's a hell of a show," he said. "Just like *Hair*. You know, all these nude girls running around onstage and everything."

Well, the nude girls sold me. Sam took along an Oriental girl who called herself the "Japanese Princess" but who was actually just a hooker. I had already pissed her off by telling her that, so she wasn't saying much to me.

It turned out that the play was so damn goofy—one of those Greenwich Village things—that Bobby and I weren't even watching. The place was so seedy that I wouldn't drink anything unless it was in a bottle, so I had been drinking beer. About the middle of the play, I leaned over and whispered to Bobby, "Hey, I gotta pee."

"Hell, A.J.," he said, "you can't get out from back there. There's half a dozen tables jammed in here. And the john's way over there."

"I can't help it," I said. "I gotta pee. Now!"

"Damn," he said. "Here, take this." He gave me a plastic drinking glass. I really did have to go, so I unzipped and filled the glass under the table. The only problem was, I really had to go. I mean a lot.

"Gimme another one," I whispered. He gave me another one. I filled it.

"Gimme another one," I said.

"Jesus Christ, A.J., we don't *have* any more," he said.

"Well, I can't stop," I said.

By this time it was hitting the concrete floor and splashing all over everything. Nobody was watching the stage anymore. Even the actors had stopped acting, and they were watching. Sam jumped up and said, "Aw, come on, A.J., you're gettin' it on our shoes."

Everybody in the place gave me a standing ovation. Even the actors applauded.

⑨
There's Never Been a Four-Time Winner—Before

Everybody always assumed I would retire if I ever won Indy four times. After all, people must have figured, there's never been a four-time winner before, and Foyt is forty-two years old, so . . .

Late in the 1977 race, when I was out front, what people had been saying went through my mind. They were right, of course; it *was* time to quit. I had been to the winner's circle three times already, and here I was headed there for a record fourth time. I would have liked to have found the guard who wouldn't let me into the garage area in 1956 and '57. A lot of things like that went through my head.

It had been one of those races where I felt I was going to win from the start. I mean, *really* felt it. There are days like that. I felt it with my steak and eggs that morning and I felt it as my challengers fell off, one by one.

By the time they waved the checkered flag at me, I had completely changed my mind. It was a very short retirement. The sight of the black and white waving just for me was something that I wasn't anyways near ready to walk away from. Or the cheering crowd. I wouldn't have quit for anything. There were a lot of surprised people in the winner's circle when I said, "See you next year."

There had been the usual close calls during the race, but that certainly wasn't any reason for quitting; definitely my age wasn't any reason. I could still run with drivers of any age. I always had been able to. To hell with predictions and to hell with close calls. I decided to stay around for Five.

Close calls don't bother me anyway. If you want to know, every car is involved in four or five near misses in every race. It doesn't matter if it's Indy or some little old dirt track; there are at least that many times when somebody almost hits you or you nearly lose it yourself. You screw up a lot of times that nobody knows about. Not even your mechanic. Hell, it may be as high as ten times each race. Multiply that by the number of cars and you have maybe 300 close ones that don't show up on TV or in the grandstands. You only see the ones that go totally out of control.

This is one reason rules should be even tougher. But, if anything, it's getting easier each year to get in the 500. Right now, anybody with the bucks can walk right in there and plop his ass down in a race car and say, "Look at me; I'm a big, brave race driver." Well, that's bullshit. It's the main reason a lot of us got together in 1979 to form CART (Championship Auto Racing Teams). As the name says, it was a bunch of race teams banded together for the good of racing—the drivers and car owners and not a lot of fat-cat USAC executives. All the bullshit was going to end. I thought.

My enthusiasm lasted about three races. Hell, CART was starting to do the same damn things USAC had been doing: nit-picking changes and bending the rules for the top drivers and car owners. I pulled out and I've remained neutral. USAC and CART are both pissing in the wind.

What Championship auto racing really needs is an organization like most other sports have. There should be a Pete Rozelle. The closest thing racing has to it is NASCAR. In fact, NASCAR is head and shoulders above any sanctioning body in auto racing. Bill France formed a strong group, and he's held it together for thirty-five years, simply beause he's a strong and talented man. He has run it with an iron hand, but that's what it takes. No matter who has fought him, he's come out on top; Chrysler tried it when he restricted their cars because they were winning everything. He just said, "Wait a minute, this isn't a fair. We gotta give Ford and General Motors a chance."

He was right; it had gotten flat boring to watch the Mopar cars win everything with their hemi engines. And then Ford fought him and lost; and even big, tough General Motors came out second best. He's a tough man. There's nobody in CART or USAC with balls like Bill France. But, you know, as tough as he is, he's always been fair. Like it or not, everybody gets the same treatment. He may not have been right every time, but he's been honest and he's been consistent.

In CART or USAC you get treatment according to who you are.

Another thing: Bill France put up a lot of his own money over the years to make NASCAR work. Sure, he's made a lot of money back from it. But why shouldn't he? He's put a lot of it back in. I'll bet Roger Penske and Pat Patrick, two of the major organizers of CART, have yet to put a damn dime of their own money into auto racing, at least for the sake of improving the sport. You will never see the day when they do put any money back. Take Penske, for example. He's a wealthy man today, and if it hadn't been for Championship auto racing and the big sponsors it brought him, he probably wouldn't have a nickel. He tried NASCAR, but his cars never did a thing down there. They were losers. Hell, I've been competitive no matter what I've run down there, so an outsider *can* do it. Considering that those guys are tough to begin with and they run together every weekend, nobody is going to waltz in there and win all the marbles every time. But I've been a lot more competitive than Penske has, and I've done it without the million-dollar sponsorship he had. But that's the difference in starting at the bottom like I did and starting at the top like he did. You don't get determination by being a big promoter and walking around with your hand out all the time. You have to get grease under your fingernails.

Most of these big-deal guys will cut each other's throats in a minute. I've never operated that way; I've never gone behind another guy's back to get a sponsor. But they will. They're vicious people. Now, this may sound strange, but, in spite of what I've said, I like Penske and Patrick. As people. I just don't want to deal with them. They're in racing for *status*. I'm in it to break every record in the book. Winning is still the most important thing in the world to me.

I don't really care about money for money's sake. I understand that it's a measure of a person's success, and I'll be the first to admit that it feels damn good to have as much money as I have, but I could care less to discuss the value of my ranch or a particular racehorse I own or a certain piece of property—even my Chevy dealership. Sure, I'm interested in how well I'm doing overall, but I leave that up to Jack Trotter, my good friend and financial consultant. I told him a long time ago, "Go ahead and invest it how you want, but if I ever see you in a big black Cadillac, smokin' a big black cigar while I'm alongside the road, diggin' a ditch, I'll know you've had me."

But I trust him. A lot of people in CART and USAC I don't

trust. Man, the minute you turned your back on a lot of them, they would reach up and bite you in the ass. That's a hell of a way to go racing. In fact, I've told the people at the Indianapolis Speedway that they don't even *need* a sanctioning body to run their race. They could get along well without either CART or USAC. Better, probably. It's the most important racing event in the world, and they can get all the drivers just by opening up the gates to gasoline alley. And they can get 300,000 fans to come and watch them. What do they need an outside organization for? They have been doing pretty well since 1911. And, if things keep going the way they are, I predict that someday you will see them running the whole show themselves.

But don't look at me to run things up there. There has been a lot of talk of me retiring and taking over the Speedway. Well, I'll tell you right now, they're rumors. I don't want to run the Speedway. I've always been very close to the Hulman family—I respected Tony as much as any man who ever lived—and they've always asked my advice a lot, but I want to keep it just that way. And why shouldn't they ask me about certain things? Nobody else has ever run twenty-five races there. Or won four. They *should* ask me.

But as for running the show, they've got people who can do it. They've always managed in the past. When Tony Hulman bought the Speedway after World War II, they were going to bulldoze it down. "Auto racing is dead," everybody said. "What we need here is a housing development." Well, Tony showed the world that auto racing wasn't dead, and the people up there can continue showing them. The Speedway should be a national landmark.

I hope they come up with somebody as president of the Speedway who will put CART and USAC in their place, just like Bill France has stood up to everybody, and like Tony Hulman did.

I would like to see one full international race committee, like FIA, which has some long French name. FIA regulates racing for the rest of the world now, but, if anything, it is more screwed up than CART and USAC, so maybe I'm hoping for too much. But it would be nice if you could join one organization and race anywhere in the world. Not that I want to race in Europe; I tried that, and I didn't care for it too much. I never felt an American driver got a fair shake in Europe. Maybe a one-organization situation would help. Sure, Andretti ran over there, and he won the world championship, but he was born over there. He's one of them. I was born and raised here, and that's where I intend to do my racing. I don't need to go over there. I've won their best race—Le Mans—and I've raced against their best drivers over here, and I never thought they were too tough. They just don't charge hard like our drivers.

There are two exceptions: Jimmy Clark and Jackie Stewart. They're as good as any drivers I've ever run against. I remember when Jimmy Clark first came to Indy in 1963, and nobody paid much attention to him until the race started. He took a car that wasn't that good to begin with and he ran the wheels off it. Graham Hill, who was world champion that year, didn't even make the show.

The next year, Clark overcame probably the worst-handling car and the worst tires I ever saw, and he was leading the race when the suspension went to hell and he crashed. Colin Chapman, the guy everybody gave credit to for starting the rear-engine revolution, never cared a damn thing for his driver's safety. I hate to say it now that he's dead, but in those days he didn't even have the parts of his cars X-rayed, like all the rest of us do. It's the only way you can tell if there are flaws in the metal—hairline cracks or whatever—and anybody who doesn't do it doesn't have his driver's interest in mind. Not to mention his ass.

Chapman signed a deal with Dunlop to use their tires. Well, Goodyear and Firestone spent millions of dollars in developing a safe, fast tire for Indy, and Dunlop didn't even test there. His tires showed it. They were absolutely unsafe.

But Clark took the car and put on a real show. He spent as much time going backwards as he did forwards, but he missed all the other cars, and that's a hell of a feat. It didn't say much for Chapman's cars, but it sure did for Clark.

Stewart was just as good. But they are definitely the exceptions. I mean, it seems like I'm talking about a lot of dead people, and I usually don't do that, but Graham Hill, the Englishman, *backed* into his victory at Indy in 1966. It was the year Billy Foster caused the big first-lap crash that took eleven cars out of the race—including mine. Andretti and Parnelli Jones and Hurtubise and Ward and McCluskey and Al Unser and Lloyd Ruby all broke their cars later in the race, so there wasn't anybody left at checkered-flag time to run with Hill. He must have been as surprised as everybody else when he won it.

The thing that really pisses me off about most of the European drivers is the way they drive. Not only don't they charge hard; they get upset if somebody else does. I've always had the philosophy that if I could get past somebody, I was going to go, whether it was in a turn or on the straightaway. Well, anytime I found a European driver out of the groove just enough that I could pass him, high or low, it didn't matter, I did it. I blew him right off. Hell, we do it at Indy all the time and nobody gets upset. But they said, "That's not the way we approach a turn, old sport." Well, "old sport" my ass. That's the way I approach a turn. And it's the way I'm going to continue approaching turns. When I stop is the day you see me *watching a race*.

And another thing—I might as well get the whole European thing off my chest—I've always felt Formula One racing was a stacked deck. Listen to this: If you have team drivers—say, two factory Renaults—and if one of them is number one in points, the other is told not to pass him. Can you imagine that? Tell that to Al Unser or Johnny Rutherford. After they stop laughing, they'll blow your doors off so bad you won't know what happened. And if I can pass someone, I'll do it; I don't care if he's in my other car or if he's Christ himself. When I'm in a race car, I've got one thing in mind: passing *everybody*.

A couple years ago the whole Formula One circuit was upset

with this guy Carlos Reutemann, from Argentina or somewhere down there. He kept passing his teammate, who was number one, and it pissed everybody off. Personally, I thought he was putting on the only good show in all of Formula One racing.

To me, their follow-the-leader stuff isn't racing. It's a show. I'm just not used to it. I'm used to balls-out running and wheel-to-wheel competition. Anything less than that doesn't interest me. Hell, people should see some real competition, not just *zoom, zoom, zoom* every once in a while. They need to see what a driver can really do.

Most of the time, the Indianapolis 500 is a perfect example of real automobile competition. The 1981 race was a perfect example of a racing organization completely screwing something up. If you remember, the 1981 Indianapolis 500 was the race that Bobby Unser won, and then the next day they took it away from him and gave it to Mario Andretti because they said Bobby broke the rules. Then, to make themselves look even more ridiculous, months later they changed their minds again and gave it back to Bobby. It made USAC look like complete jackasses.

Bobby did make a bad mistake. He was completely in the wrong, but I think they needed to settle it that day and not wait until the following day when everybody had gone home thinking Bobby had won. The mistake Bobby made was passing cars under yellow. It's the same thing Rutherford did to me in 1976, and they didn't do a thing about it then. It's the same thing drivers have been doing since the first race.

The whole thing was a little like Watergate. Bobby didn't *have* to do it. He outran everybody that day, and there was no way Mario could run with him. But Bobby is a racer, too, and he's going to take every advantage he can get. Penske, who owned the Unser car, says he has film of Andretti doing the same thing, but he is wrong. I was right there, and I waved Andretti by. I was having trouble accelerating, so I told him to go ahead.

I think Bobby was wrong, but I also think he won the race, and fair and square as far as I'm concerned. But if USAC was going to take the race away from him, it shouldn't have been given back. Right is right, and if they felt he was wrong then he was wrong. Simple. The whole thing is like a year when nobody won the race.

It was a bad year for me, too. I started in the front row and steadily went downhill. The car got weaker and weaker. But, like I said, it was a bad year at Indy. I got things started by getting into another hassle with the press. Robin Miller of the Indianapolis *Star* wrote that over the years Goodyear had given me special tires and that everybody, in fact, had given me special equipment—things other drivers couldn't get. Well, that's so much bullshit. So I grabbed him and slammed him up against the wall. Then Dave Overpeck, another writer, said I should apologize, and I told them all that it would be a cold day in hell before I apologized for reacting to something that was a goddamn lie.

For some reason, the press people think that I owe them something. But I'll tell you right now: If they walk up to me when I'm busy or even just when I don't feel like talking to them, they can kiss my ass, because I don't owe them a damn thing. I don't need the press. One year, for example, I was having trouble with my car and some guy wanted an interview. I said, "Maybe later, but not now." Well, that wasn't good enough. He kept following me around and kept sticking the microphone in my face. "Get that goddamn mike out of my face," I told him. But he didn't do it, so I grabbed it away from him and dragged him across the garage, and I was about to deck him when a bunch of people pulled me away. He yelled, "But I'm from CBS and you *owe* me an interview."

"Listen, buddy boy," I said. "I don't owe you a goddamn thing. Just because you have a camera doesn't entitle you to a thing in this garage."

I sued *Sports Illustrated* a few years ago because they quoted me as saying, after I had won a NASCAR race, "Now I've beaten these hillbillies, I'm gonna take on those European fags." Well, to begin with, I've got more respect for the NASCAR drivers than anybody, and I wouldn't say that about them. And, as for the "European fags" remark, I don't feel that way at all. Oh, I think they're maybe a little different, and I've already told you how I feel about their driving. As for what they do off the racetrack, I couldn't care less.

We settled with *Sports Illustrated* for a couple hundred thousand dollars, but that was all I wanted. Actually all I really wanted was to prove they were wrong.

I had everything together for the 1982 Indy 500. It was my Silver Anniversary race. Twenty-five years. Nobody else had even driven it twenty times. And I wanted to win that race. The car was really good. I was on the outside of the front row and ready to take the lead on the first lap. In fact, I was *going* to take the lead. I wanted to show everybody that A.J. was still the king, even after twenty-five years at Indy.

But let me set the stage for you: Rick Mears was on the pole; Kevin Cogan was in the middle of the front row; then me on the outside. I was a little concerned with Cogan being up there, so I planned to keep my eye on him. I didn't have to watch him for long. I can't even count the number of times races have been ruined even before the first lap. The 1982 race was another one.

It's up to the man on the pole to bring the field around for the start, and I thought Mears was bringing us around too slow. The biggest problem with the field going slow is that it forces most of the cars to run in low gears, and when the green flag is dropped and the drivers stand on them, the cars get all out of shape.

That's exactly what happened. They waved the green flag and we all accelerated. But I didn't even have a *chance* to take the lead into Turn One. Cogan got sideways and swung over to the right and hit me. Then he spun right across the track and Mario Andretti hit him broadside. I was so pissed off I could have torn Cogan's head off.

I got the car into the pits while we were waiting for the restart and found out that the front suspension was bent. We had to work like mad, changing parts and adjusting everything, but we got it done in time. Now, keep in mind, we spent days setting the suspension up just right. It was perfect. Now we had a few minutes in the pits to set it the same way. But I was right there on my hands and knees, working with Daddy and Jack Starnes and the rest of the crew, measuring as best we could to set it the same way. I checked every bolt and every adjustment time after time. We favored the toe in on the outside, because we thought if the wheel angle was to go either way, that would be best.

In the pits, I stayed away from Cogan for two reasons: One, I was too busy fixing the car; and two, I knew if I found him, they would probably throw me out of the race for what I did.

When they dropped the green flag the second time, I shot into the lead like I came from a cannon. I wanted to find out right then if our guesses were right. And I wanted to get out of the way. I took a big lead into One and I held it. The car felt perfect. A lot of people have said that it was one of the bravest things I have ever done—charging into One flat out, not knowing if the suspension was right or not—but I didn't look at it that way. I had complete confidence in the job we had done, and I also had confidence in myself. I felt that I could make it handle if it wasn't right. It all goes back to basic trainng.

The biggest controversy was over what caused Cogan to hit me in the first place. He and Penske, whose car it was, said a half shaft broke. Well, half shaft my ass. It may have broken, but if it did, it broke when Andretti hit him. Here's what happened: The Penske cars have five-speed gearboxes, and Cogan was running in lower gears, planning to outjump me and push me to the wall. He knew that if he got me out of the groove, I would be spinning my wheels up in the gray stuff along the fence—the rubber dust that blows up there. But Mears brought them down so slow, Cogan didn't know what to do, and when he saw the flag raised, he jumped on it before it was actually waved. Well, when he jumped on it, the boost from the turbocharger took hold, and the car got sideways and got away from him.

They can talk about half shafts until they're blue in the face, but the rest of us in that race know it is bullshit.

As for Mario hitting him, that couldn't have been avoided under the circumstances. Cogan was right there in front of him, sideways. But the old Mario—the Mario before he won the world championship, the hungrier Mario—might not have been there to *hit* Cogan. If he had that much speed—enough to hit him that hard—the old Mario might have beaten us all to the turn. He might have been gone.

The films don't tell much, because the new race tires don't smoke much when you light them up and get sideways. You used to be able to look at a film and tell from the tire smoke exactly where and why something had happened. But not anymore. You'll have to take my word for it; that's how it happened.

I thought about it for many laps, and it made me so mad that it caused me to drive even harder. I'll tell you, I had that race *won.* Until the car stuck in third gear. I got out of the car in the pits and started beating on it with a hammer. I was so damn mad, because I really wanted to win that one. It was my twenty-fifth year and all. But, more than that, I wanted to be the first five-time champion. I think that would put it out of reach of anybody. But I could have beat on that gearbox all day and not gotten it unstuck. After we got it back to the garage, Jack took the cover off and flicked it back in place with his finger.

As for the race, I think it was pretty poor. There was the Cogan thing, where he was flat to blame—and I'm not afraid to say it. It's more than he would do if the situation was reversed. Most of these new guys aren't even man enough to fight, let alone speak out. They wait until your back is turned and then they run to the press and let them do their talking for them. Hell, if I'm right, I stand up for my rights. I don't sit there and whine like the Cogans of racing.

The end of the race was about as bad as the start. They say how close it was—and it was close—but Johncock wasn't outrunning anybody; he was *outbraving* them. It was just a lucky shot. I mean, there is no way he should have beaten Mears. When a man can gain as much time as Mears did and still get beat, it's not a case of Johncock outrunning him. His car wasn't even close to Mears's car. Gordy's car had started pushing real bad—you could tell that—and Mears should have been able to drive right by him. But Gordy chopped him off. If it had been me in Mears's place, the third-place car would have won the race. But that's the difference between me and Mears. He took second, which might be fine for him. But not for me.

I don't blame Gordy; that was pretty brave, and he wanted to win. But I do blame him for his attitude since he won. He's become one of the biggest crybabies in racing. Just because he won the 500 he thinks he's super big now and everybody should do things his way. I got news for him: Winning the race alone doesn't make you that important. Johncock's name—or Mears's or Bobby Unser's or anybody's, for that matter—doesn't seem to have the power that mine does. They've all *backed* into about as many wins as they've gotten by actually outrunning somebody. Everybody likes a charger; I don't care if it's auto racing or baseball or football.

A lot of people don't like me, but every time I go out, they know that if they're not real careful, I'm going to win the race, and they know I'm not going to back up and let someone *take* it away from me.

It's just like at Michigan this year. Johncock said, "Aw, you're just here for the money. You'll make a big deal out of it and probably quit after ten laps."

I said, "Listen, buddy boy, you ain't never seen the day you can run with me, and I'll show you that tomorrow."

Johncock gets on his high horse and thinks everybody's like him. I guess he said that because my car really hadn't been running too well a few weeks earlier at Cleveland. It was all screwed up, in fact, and I just stopped instead of going on and probably wrecking it. But that's one thing I've learned from experience. I was running next to last and I was just tearing up the car trying to keep up. It was going to cost me a lot of money. You see, I own my own equipment. Most of those other guys don't, and they really don't care. They just go out there and destroy a lot of equipment and go home; they let the poor bastard who's paying the bills worry about it.

There's a time when it makes sense to abuse a race car, like when you're in front or you feel you've got the horses to get there; and there's a time when it doesn't pay, like when the car isn't worth a shit and you're making it worse. Cleveland was one of those days. So I pulled out. Later, when we tore the engine down, we found that the clutch had already gone. It had eaten through the fingers, and it wouldn't have run another ten laps anyway. You get to know those things. If you're smart.

Johncock is like most guys who win Indy: They change overnight. One of the USAC officials said to me the other day, "God damn, I can't believe it. Johnny Rutherford's *talking* to me again." Johnny hasn't done a thing for the past two years in racing, so he's back down to earth again.

I've tried hard over the years not to change—win or lose. Oh, there's no question, if I win, I'm happier, and a whole lot easier to get along with for, say, the first couple of hours after a race, but I don't think I try to act like Jesus Christ himself when I do win. If I do act like that, I hope somebody hits me in the head with a club. Take the day after Indy this year: I was back on the ranch, digging a septic tank with a shovel, while everybody else was in Indianapolis getting ready for the victory dinner. I told Eddie and Val Ray, two of the guys who work for me at the ranch, "Here I was yesterday, with hundreds of thousands of people cheering me like I was a hero, and today I'm digging in shit with a hand shovel." But that's the way I've always been. I'm not the banquet type. If I win, I have to be there, but if I lose, well, what's the sense of celebrating somebody else's victory? Leave the celebrating to them.

I've always stayed pretty much to myself. A hundred people have tried to get me to join country clubs and social organizations of all types, but I wouldn't be happy. I mean, I'm with people most of the time, thousands of people, and I sure as hell don't need to go out and find more on my own time. I'd rather be at the ranch alone, running the bulldozer or the tractor or anything. Just by myself.

It's why I don't hang out in bars like a lot of the other drivers. If I hadn't other interests, like the ranch and the Chevy dealership, I might have turned out to be a drunk like a lot of them have. I think the reason most of them drink and raise so much hell is because they don't have anything else to do. It's why a lot of sports figures go bad. There's always booze and broads and drugs thrown at you, and parties and dinners and nightclubs. I could get drunk and laid every day if I wanted to.

I've seen more freeloading phonies at country clubs than anywhere else. I take that back. I spent some time around unlimited hydroplane racing—the "thunder boats," they call them—and there are more phonies there than at country clubs. But not many more.

I get more kick out of baling hay and building fence. It's damn hard work, but it's rewarding to know that you've done it all yourself. I painted all the white fence on my ranch, and there are miles of it. In fact, I painted it when I was healing from the big crash at Michigan last summer. My arm had just been taken out of a cast. I had lost about a pound of muscle. It was gone, ripped away. And the doctor told me I should come in every day for therapy. "Work that hand and build up the arm again," he said. Well, I'd be damned if I was going into some hospital to work out my arm. I painted about four miles of fence. You can look all around my ranch today and see the results of my personal therapy.

I don't like to sit on my ass when there's something to be done. I'm not like a lot of these guys who are unemployed today. Hell, they may have worked twenty years in some factory and that's all in this world they know how to do. At least, it's all they *will* do. Once that job's gone, they're through. I've tried to teach my kids this: Any day you can learn to do something that you couldn't do yesterday, you're that much better off. Most people sit back and let the government take care of them. I'm glad Reagan is tightening up on some of this welfare bullshit. I think he's doing a good job.

I've busted up my body and scarred myelf and gotten burned—I've got scars I'll carry to my grave—just to make some money. I've paid my taxes all along, and to think I'm paying for some of these freeloading bastards—well, it really bugs me. It's wrong, and I hope Reagan takes it all away, except for those who really can't work—the old and the crippled, people like that. The rest of them can work if they really want to.

Racing isn't much different from our welfare program: It needs some belt-tightening. For one thing, I would like to see the crybabies eliminated. I just wouldn't know which end to start at—the new ones or the old ones—because I don't know which are worse, the crybaby new kids or the crybaby old kids. One thing: The olds, at least, are safer to have on the track. It just gets on your nerves to hear them bellyaching. It can be downright dangerous to have some of the new ones around.

Take Hector Rebaque at Michigan in 1982. He came right up and ran into me full bore. Hell, you ought to have enough depth perception to be able to tell when somebody has slowed down. Spike Gehlhausen's car had hung in second gear and I'd had to slow down, so here came Rebaque, charging like mad—in spite of the fact that he was way back in the field—and he crashed into me. At Cleveland, he almost ran into the back of the crash truck. A guy like that should be sent down to the minors. And maybe kept there.

But CART and USAC are so busy arguing about everything that they will take anybody, just to get cars. They got two drivers killed who didn't have any experience in Indianapolis cars. And it's lucky Rebaque didn't get me killed.

In the old days, I knew exactly what each driver was going to do. I knew that if I tried to go under Tony Bettenhausen, for instance, he would tighten up on me, so I was better off working him high. But I always kept him thinking I was going to stay low, and then I went by him on the outside. And I knew how they were going to work me. I knew drivers like Rodger Ward and Eddie Sachs—a lot of them, in fact—were going to get by *me* at times, no matter what I did. But, the point is, we knew each other and each knew what the others might do.

I should have known better, but I tried to work Kevin Cogan like I did the older guys. It was at Michigan in 1982. I had been working him high, where I was running better. I ran there for several laps, and then one lap he came through right there where I was running, up high, so I drove down under him, and I'll be damned if he didn't come down across me. I think he got too high and was trying to get back down in the groove he had been working in. The only problem was, I was already there.

His ass end got out—you can see it in the films—and he lost it. And he took me with him. Then he gets on television and says, "Well, I've set track records and I've been in the front row at Indianapolis. What do I have to do to prove myself?"

I'll tell him right now: All he has to do to prove himself is use his goddamn head. I mean, he's wrecked about six or seven cars. He may have sat on the pole, but he's also gone backwards, and most of the time he's just been in everybody's way trying to prove a point.

He may be all right on a road course, but an oval is different. When a guy gets under you on an oval, you don't try to come back across his front end. I guess he thought he would buffalo me. Well, I got news for his young ass: I've been hurt before, and there was no way I was going to let him get by with it. It cost me another $150,000 race car and another broken arm, but there was no way I was going to let him come down through there.

I hate to put the mouth on him, but the kid's nothing but a big fake. I jumped out of the car and ran over there and grabbed him by the front of the helmet—I didn't even know my arm was broken, I was so mad. I don't know why I didn't hit him. But I just shoved him back in the car and walked away.

When Mario Andretti was coming up, he and I went through a stage of running into each other, because he was chopping me off. But, one thing: He won't do it today. He went through that stage, and he realized he couldn't do it, so we will run wheel to wheel today, and we respect each other as drivers. But that's a case of a guy learning something. Andretti became a fine race driver. Some of these new kids like Cogan and Garza and Rebaque will never learn anything.

I heard one day that Tom Sneva and Cogan were water-skiing and Sneva dunked him or something. Well, Cogan left. He said, "You got my hair wet."

Wet hair. Goddamn. What would they say if they had to sleep in the backs of cars or eat beans? Things I did, and Parnelli and Hurtubise and drivers like that did, too.

You used to be able to tell if a driver was having a bad day. You could tell if his car wasn't working or if he was having trouble with this or that. Or if he didn't feel right. You could watch him for a couple of laps and you could tell. And there were days when he went sailing by you, and you knew he was having a great day. Today you have no idea. Some of the drivers are down here one time and way up there another. And if everything isn't perfect, they can't compete. At times, it has to be better than perfect. There's a whole breed of race drivers coming up who think they're so smart, but they really can't get out there and compete without some big advantage. Sure, we had advantages at times, and we cheated at times, but we also raced hard. And we could have won—any number of us—*without* cheating. But just try to tell one of these new hotshots that the only reason he won was because he outcheated you. He gets madder than hell because he thinks he *outsmarted* you. Most of them don't know what smart is.

Today it's just "follow the leader": Wait and see what some guy is doing and then do the same thing. Everybody tries to drive whatever kind of car is winning. They all use the same equipment. Nobody even tries to develop anything on his own, like, say, George Bignotti and I used to do. Or A. J. Watson or Frank Kurtis. I could go on and on. It's "Monkey see, monkey do" now.

Sure, the Penske cars are good. But some of the teams are just lucky. I think the Patrick cars have been lucky. They haven't been the fastest cars in the races they've won; they've just been the *luckiest* cars. Cars, in general, are much better than they used to be. There's no question. But why shouldn't they be? They're designed by teams of engineers with computers and fat corporate checkbooks, not by race drivers and race mechanics with a big toolbox and a ton of experience. Where it used to take a whole lot of driver skill to be a winner, I think today it takes a lot of car and a lot more luck—75 percent car and 25 percent driver.

If we have all these poor-to-mediocre drivers, who are the good ones? I personally feel that Al Unser is the most underrated driver around today. He's smart and he's got a lot of ability. A lot of race drivers feel this way, but the outside world doesn't know how good he is. I think he's one of the best to come along in my time. Bobby Unser, who is retired now, was a hard charger, but I think Al is a smarter race driver. Mario Andretti is good, and Johnny Rutherford is good, but Johnny's kind of off and on. When he's got his act together, Johnny is a hard driver to beat. Gordon Johncock is a lot like that. Aside from these few, I don't think there are that many really good drivers.

There were several good drivers that never got proper recognition because they didn't win Indianapolis. They came close many times but didn't win it. Drivers like Lloyd Ruby and Jim Hurtubise were every bit as good as some of the guys who won Indy, and it's a damn shame that their names can't go down in the record books somehow. Then there's my friend Ralph Ligouri, who tried about twenty times and never even made the show at Indy.

You have to give some of those guys credit for staying in there. Today's playboy set of drivers sure wouldn't keep trying like that, particularly if they didn't have Daddy to put up the money. I think of Eddie Sachs, the day he got killed. Here was this good guy who wanted to win Indy so bad, and somebody else's mistake did him in.

I can't really remember any other drivers who stood out that much. There were some pretty good ones, but none who stood out like Rodger Ward or Andretti or Al. I just sort of got it all hooked together early in my career and got it going good, and I've been going that way ever since. Oh, I remember seeing some of the early guys race, and I've heard a lot of tales about drivers like Frank Lockhart and Wilbur Shaw and Bill Vukovich, and they must have been good, but I never raced against them, so I can't really say for sure. But, to be truthful, I haven't really had to worry about too many other race drivers since the day I started racing, and that goes all the way back to the Houston dirt-track days.

I know I've never been intimidated by *any* race driver. I've always felt that I could give them all they wanted. If they wanted to be brave, I could be just as brave, and if they wanted to play dirty, I could play just as dirty as they could. Just because I hated to have a driver like Rodger Ward on my tail didn't by any stretch of the imagination mean that he was intimidating me. He was a threat to my winning, and *that* intimidates me. Anybody who tries to take the checkered flag away from me will always be a threat. But that threat is also why I have enjoyed racing so much.

There is nothing as boring or just as flat uninteresting as being a lap or two ahead of everybody. There's no magic to it. But when you're racing somebody wheel to wheel—when he leads one time around and you lead the next, and you come by the third time side by side—hell, man, that's what it's all about. It's what keeps me going. If it's adrenaline, then it's my natural high. It's what I thrive on. I've never needed anything else.

There have always been some drivers I have watched very closely, but that's because of the mistakes they might make. I would spin a car on purpose before I would follow some drivers through a hole. There are some others I wouldn't think twice about before following. If, for instance, I'm following Al Unser and there is a godawful wreck in front of him and he starts through the only tiny hole in the spinning cars there is, I'll go right with him. We both may crash when we get there, but I've got enough faith in him as a race driver to know that there wasn't another damn place to go.

There are some drivers, like some of the new ones, that I wouldn't follow into the men's room. Particularly the men's room. If they don't know any more about what they're doing in there than they do on the racetrack, a man could get wet.

Not wanting to follow them on the track isn't a case of being afraid. There's no fear involved; it's just good common sense. You don't play Russian roulette if you're smart, and you don't rely on inexperienced, immature race drivers. I didn't get through thirty years of racing by being stupid.

Somebody started comparing Rick Mears's first four years in Championship-car racing with my first four years.

Well, let me surprise a lot of people: Rick Mears has a good head on his shoulders and he's a good race driver. A very good race driver. That's coming from A. J. Foyt, not some ragged-ass newspaper reporter who has never been on a racetrack. Rick won a lot more money in his first four years than I did, but let's be fair about it: There is a lot more money around today than there was when I started. I won just as many races, but I won them in average-at-best cars. He started in absolute top equipment. There just isn't better equipment around today than Penske's. Rick has outqualified me at times, but when it's come down to actual racing—wheel-to-wheel racing—he's never outrun me.

Without sounding like I'm protesting too much, let me say this: If you're going to compare apples, compare apples. Compare Rick Mears with his brother, Roger. They've come up through the same background. I came up through dirt tracks where everybody had the same equipment, and the purses were smaller than what they pay for a driver's suit today. But Roger used to outrun Rick everywhere they ran. So what has made Rick appear to be a better driver today? Simple: equipment. It's not that Rick is that much better; he isn't. It's just that poor old Roger has gone out there in some poor race cars and he's wrecked a lot. He's been upside down because something has broken or fallen off the car. And I don't care if I had been driving some of that stuff; I probably couldn't have gone any faster than Roger did.

I just wish people would stop comparing me to some of these kids coming up. For one thing, it's a different ball game today. Driver ability isn't that important anymore. It's like Danny Ongais. He has some bad habits—and one of them may be running out of brains. He lacks concentration, really.

I would like to see any of them run a race like the Hoosier Hundred. On dirt. Like Mario and Johnny Rutherford and a lot of the rest of us "old-timers" did.

Epilogue

I'm fortunate to still be on top after nearly thirty years. I don't drive as many races now as I used to, but I still feel like I'm a potential winner every time I get in a race car. I've always said that the day I don't want to be up front is the day I'll walk away from racing. If I hadn't felt that way in every race, I wouldn't have run one more lap. I would have brought it into the pits, taken off my helmet, and walked away from it.

Fortunately, everybody in my family has let me do things exactly the way I wanted to. Lucy suggested that I might want to consider quitting after I won Indy in 1961. I asked her right then not to make me decide between her and racing, because I loved both and could handle both. She knew which way I would have gone, so she went about raising the kids, and she did a beautiful job. She never again suggested that I retire.

Nobody gave our marriage a chance, because we came from different sides of the tracks, and, as I said, neither of us ever expected my racing to make me as much money as it has. Why, I've paid as much for a single racehorse as I ever expected to *have* in my entire life.

I never expected to become a celebrity. I mean, who would have thought that the son of the president of the United States would be a guest in my suite on race day at Indianapolis? I never even expected to *have* a suite there. But Mike Reagan was there last year. Secret Service agents and all.

So if I die in the next race, I'll be one of the few men who has made a good living doing exactly what he wanted to do. Oh, I've had headaches with some cars and there have been some seasons that haven't been as good as others, but for the most part I've got more headaches with the business part of my life right now than I ever had with racing, even in the days when I was running some ragged cars.

I've always been able to stay close to my family, even though racing has kept me away on a lot of holidays. I always called my mother on Mother's Day, if I wasn't home, and my father on Father's Day, if he wasn't with me. And, I'll admit it, I miss my mother. When she died, a big part of me died with her. I used to worry a lot about what the newspapers said about me; there were always rumors about me being wild and having all these broads and everything, and even though they didn't bother Lucy, they bothered me, and it worried me mostly because I didn't feel that Mother would understand like Lucy did. Now that she's gone, I don't give a shit what they say.

I dream about my mother all the time. I dreamed the other night that she was dying again. I could see all those tubes in her, and Daddy was there and Marlene and Lucy, and I woke up about three in the morning just scared to death.

Daddy's sick now. I learned it while I was writing this book, and the doctors say he's got cancer. I really don't know how to handle it. I've never been in auto racing without Daddy. I haven't got to the point yet where I can be philosophical about it. It's bothering me so much, I don't want to talk about it.

A lot of people think I'm going to retire, but I don't know. I don't have time to think about retiring right now. After all, I won the 24 Hours of Daytona in 1983. I mean, hell, it was the first time I had been in a sports car in sixteen years, and I'm proud of that victory. I'm not slowing down; I want to get that straight. I still have excellent vision—20/15—and I think that's the single most important thing for a race driver: his eyes. Once they go, you might as well forget it. But I won the Pocono 500 last year, and there are a lot of race drivers who will never even do that, at any age.

If I do quit, it will be because of all the infighting and the squabbles and the lawsuits; it won't be because I don't feel competitive anymore. I am concerned that it's getting like a rush-hour expressway out there. I mean, with all the wild kids coming up. Anybody would be concerned. If you put a whole bunch of people in high-performance cars—Ferraris or something like that—and let them go out on the expressway and drive as fast as they wanted to, and these people didn't know the first thing about driving those cars, you'd quit driving on the expressway. Hell, you'd start riding the bus. Well, that's sort of the way driving Indy cars has become.

And I'm tired of all the jealousy. Everybody has always been jealous of me, but it seems to be getting worse. I'm not the least bit jealous of anybody. I'm getting to be an oddity at Indy.

As far as retirement is concerned, I'll say this: I'll *tell* everybody when I want to retire. Nobody will tell me. It won't be because I'm hurt; that just makes me more determined.

There's no question: I used to heal faster. I heal a little slower after every crash. I always take my own casts off—long before the doctor says I should—and the last time, I actually had to go back in and have it put on again.

After the last crash at Michigan I was sick at my stomach for a long time. That's never happened before. And I got headaches often; the doctors said that was from the inner brain being jammed against the outer brain. I still refuse to lie around in a hospital. But it's getting harder to come back from each crash. I'm tired of hurting. Maybe if the press would stop telling everybody that I will probably retire after "this one," I might.

Maybe I am ready. Maybe next year will be my last.

I've been into horseracing for the past few years, and I seem to be getting in a whole lot deeper. At first it was real scary because I didn't know much about it. I mean, you can pay fifty grand for a horse and not even know if he can run or not. That's scary. But I'm going about it exactly the same way I did with car racing: I pay as I go, and I do it in cash.

The only thing is, if a car doesn't run, I can fix it. With a horse, well, hell, everything you do is a chance. I bought a horse called Barbizon's Flower, who ran second in the Debutante Stakes, and, do you know, I bought her sister and she can't run a lick.

Me and my son, Tony, who helps me keep the operation going, are learning horseracing the same as I learned car racing, by making mistakes and learning from them. And with people like my friend J. T. Lundy of Calumet Farm to help me, I'm really starting to pick up a lot of good information. Bill Rudy, who handles PR for Churchill Downs, told some people recently that he expects me to be a real "threat" to the sport in a few years. I hope he's right.

I know one thing: I spend a lot of time on my ranch and I'm proud not only of the horses but of the whole thing. I mean, I took a bulldozer and I carved a really nice ranch out of a real thicket. It's a showplace—a lot like some of the Kentucky horse farms—and I did most of it myself, the miles and miles of white board fence and all.

And another thing, the horses are a good escape for me. Nobody gives a damn if I've just won Indy or if I even ran it or not. They look on me as "A. J. Foyt, the horse owner." And I like that. I think it adds a lot to my image.

Here's my plan for horseracing: I've started at the bottom and I've already worked up *toward* the top. I plan to run twenty or twenty-five horses at a time and keep trying every angle I can until I win the Kentucky Derby. That's my goal, and if anybody doubts me, just remember, there were a lot of people who didn't think I would ever win Indy. Once.

I'll keep buying and training and trading until I find that one horse—that Alydar—that will make me famous in *horse* racing. For now, *I'm* the boss hoss.

It's the same at my Chevrolet dealership. I know, a lot of celebrities own car agencies and they never even show up, but I do more than lend my name to it. I want to be in on everything that is going on. Sure, I've got a good general manager in Merle Davidson, but that's just like it is with Jack Starnes as my engine builder. I mean, I trust both of these guys, but I want to see for myself. That's the way I am. There are a lot of people around me who have been here for many years, but I just never turn anything over to anybody and forget about it. I follow it through personally. It drives Cherie Stamps, my secretary, crazy trying to keep up with me, but she's been with me long enough that she's used to it by now.

We've got the Chevy dealership up to about five thousand new-car sales a year, and we're making money. I want to keep it that way, so I always spend as much time there as possible. I make sure that everything is running right—from the new cars being delivered, right down to the restaurant. That's right, we've even got a restaurant there.

I'm on the boards of directors of the Greenway Bank and SCI (Service Corporation International), the biggest funeral service outfit in the country. And I own a piece of the Houston Astros baseball team. I've got enough that I don't have to *depend* on auto racing anymore. Jim Gilmore and I are going to hit the races we want to race. Big or small. Whatever sounds like fun.

That is part of my future. I'm planning for it. I think I plan ahead a little more than most people because, well, I know that there's always a chance that something *might* happen. But I don't plan on getting killed. I do look at the worst that could possibly happen. I try to make sure that everything is paid for and that all is in order so my family won't have to worry about anything. I think it's why I've tried to invest my money well and haven't gone hog-wild in spending. I've always wanted my family to have the best, and, whether I'm gone or not, they will. I live well, but I don't drive a Rolls-Royce, like Reggie Jackson. I don't even have a mink coat. But I drive a current-model Cadillac, and we live in a fine home in a fine section of Houston. And I wear a gold Rolex watch, so I don't do too bad, either.

As for planning for my old age—I get a lot of stupid questions like that these days—I'm not *planning* for it. I don't even want to think of old age. You want to know the truth? I don't want to *get* old—I mean, toddling, slobbering, soup-spilling old. A few gray hairs wouldn't be bad. In fact, a few hairs, period, wouldn't be bad. But, I'll tell you right now, I'd really just rather be gone than be too old. Besides, I'm not the type who will grow old gracefully.

People who are close to me say that I dwell a lot on dying, but that's simply not true. I have a lot of plans for my children and my grandchildren and Lucy and my family, and some of them aren't carried out yet, so if I have somebody I know I can trust, I often ask him to make sure so-and-so is taken care of in case I'm killed. It's not that I'm preoccupied with dying; it's just that my family means so much to me, and I want to make sure they're provided for.

But, as for death, I feel that when it's my time, I'll be ready to go.

I don't think any real race driver wants to die. It's just something that makes good reading. If they did want to die, you wouldn't see them fighting so hard to correct a spin or to avoid a crash, or you wouldn't see them fighting so hard to get out of a car that's on fire; they would just stay in there until they were well done.

For right now, I'm going to do everything I can to enjoy what I've already got. And what I've done. When a person gets to his late forties, it's difficult for him not to look back and sort of take stock of his life. And I'm pretty pleased with how everything has turned out. It doesn't really bother me that I didn't graduate from high school. I feel like I've got common sense. I don't think that automatically comes with a diploma. I mean, I'm comfortable with what I know, and, I'll tell you, I don't know all that many people who *have* common sense, no matter how much education they have. I know people with college degrees who can't even start a lawn mower.

There's no question: A college degree might have made it easier for me, particularly if it had been in mechanical engineering. But my degree from the college of hard knocks has gotten me to the same place. It's just that people like George Bignotti and me can't put it all down in graphs and tell it in high-falutin' terms like some of the college engineers. But we get the job done, and I'll bet we know as much engineering as the next guy. I've felt a little uneasy at times around people with college degrees, but I've learned to live with it, and if I were reborn tomorrow, and I had a chance to replan my life, I don't think I would do things much different.

My parents could probably have sent me to college if I had wanted to go—we weren't that poor. But I knew what I wanted to do, so I figured I might as well get at it. And learning to drive a race car at sixteen is better than learning to drive one even four years later. Besides, I was happy doing what I was doing, and most of the college graduates I knew were miserable in their lives.

I've had my ups and downs, but I've had a lot of fun in life, and I've made a good living doing something I love to do. I really couldn't have had a better life, but it's mostly because I've *made* it happen. I've worked hard at being number one. And, no matter what it was I wanted, I got it—cars, clothes, victories, anything. I told my family years ago, "You should never settle for second, that's wrong."

I've never learned to settle for second. It's a little late to change now.

APPENDIX

MAJOR EVENTS WON BY A. J. FOYT

Date	Sanctioning Body	Car Type	Location	Length/Surface*	Distance
1957					
May 12th	USAC	Midget	Kansas City, Mo.	1/4 D	100 laps
Sept. 11th	USAC	Midget	Xenia, Ohio	1/4 P	50 laps
1958					
None					
1959					
Sept. 13th	USAC	Sprint	Salem, Ind.	1/2 P	100 laps
Oct. 11th	USAC	Sprint	Houston, Texas	1/2 P	50 laps
Nov. 21st	USAC	Midget	Corpus Christi, Texas	1/4 P	50 laps
1960					
Feb. 7th	USAC	Midget	Los Angeles, Calif.	1/2 D	100 laps
Apr. 17th	USAC	Sprint	Reading, Pa.	1/2 D	30 laps
Apr. 24th	USAC	Sprint	Langhorne, Pa.	1 D	50 laps
June 10th	USAC	Midget	Anderson, Ind.	1/4 P	50 laps
Sept. 5th	USAC	Champ	DuQuoin, Ill.	1 D	100 miles
Sept. 17th	USAC	Champ	Indpls. Fairgrounds, Ind.	1 D	100 miles
Oct. 9th	USAC	Sprint	Williams Grove, Pa.	1/2 D	50 laps
Oct. 30th	USAC	Champ	Sacramento, Calif.	1 D	100 miles
Nov. 20th	USAC	Champ	Phoenix, Ariz.	1 D	100 miles
Nov. 24th	USAC	Midget	Los Angeles, Calif.	1/2 D	122* laps
1961					
Mar. 19th	USAC	Midget	San Bernardino, Calif.	1/4 D	50 laps
Mar. 26th	USAC	Sprint	Reading, Pa.	1/2 D	30 laps
Apr. 15th	USAC	Midget	Los Angeles, Calif.	1/2 D	50 laps
Apr. 30th	USAC	Sprint	Salem, Ind.	1/2 P	30 laps
May 28th	USAC	Sprint	Indpls. Raceway Park, Ind.	5/8 D	30 laps

*D: Dirt
P: Pavement
RC: Road course

May 30th	USAC	Champ	Indianapolis, Ind.	2-1/2 P	500 miles
June 18th	USAC	Champ	Langhorne, Pa.	1 D*	100 miles
June 30th	USAC	Midget	Anderson, Ind.	1/4 P	50 laps
July 29th	USAC	Midget	San Bernardino, Calif.	1/4 D	50 laps
Aug. 4th	USAC	Midget	Lawrenceberg, Ind.	1/4 D	40 laps
Aug. 6th	USAC	Sprint	Salem, Ind.	1/2 P	30 laps
Sept. 4th	USAC	Champ	DuQuoin, Ill.	1 D	100 miles
Sept. 8th	USAC	Sprint	Lancaster, N.Y.	1/2 D	30 laps
Sept. 16th	USAC	Champ	Indpls. Fairgrounds, Ind.	1 D	100 miles
Sept. 17th	USAC	Sprint	Reading, Pa.	1/2 D	30 laps
Oct. 1st	USAC	Midget	Terre Haute, Ind.	1/2 D	75 laps
Oct. 21st	USAC	Midget	Los Angeles, Calif.	1/2 D	40 laps
Nov. 4th	USAC	Midget	San Bernardino, Calif.	1/4 D	50 laps
Nov. 23rd	USAC	Midget	Los Angeles, Calif.	1/2 D	150 laps

1962

Feb. 25th	USAC	Stock	Los Angeles, Calif.	1/2 D	100 laps
Apr. 8th	USAC	Champ	Trenton, N.J.	1 P	100 miles
May 27th	USAC	Sprint	Indpls. Raceway Park, Ind.	5/8 P	50 laps
June 10th	USAC	Champ	Milwaukee, Wisc.	1 P	100 miles
July 1st	USAC	Champ	Langhorne, Pa.	1 D	100 miles
Sept. 30th	USAC	Sprint	Salem, Ind.	1/2 P	100 laps
Oct. 7th	USAC	Stock	Detroit, Mich.	1 D	150 laps
Oct. 20th	USAC	Midget	Los Angeles, Calif.	1/2 D	40 laps
Oct. 28th	USAC	Champ	Sacramento, Calif.	1 D	100 miles

1963

Mar. 24th	USAC	Sprint	Reading, Pa.	1/2 D	30 laps
Apr. 7th	USAC	Sprint	Williams Grove, Pa.	1/2 D	100 laps
Apr. 21st	USAC	Champ	Trenton, N.J.	1 P	100 miles
Apr. 28th	USAC	Stock	Indpls. Raceway Park, Ind.	2-1/2 P-RC	300 miles
May 5th	USAC	Stock	Langhorne, Pa.	1 D	150 laps
June 23rd	USAC	Champ	Langhorne, Pa.	1 D	100 miles
July 7th	USAC	Stock	Indpls. Raceway Park, Ind.	5/8 P	250 laps
July 28th	USAC	Champ	Trenton, N.J.	1 P	150 miles
Aug. 31st	USAC	Sprint	DuQuoin, Ill.	1 D	25 laps
Sept. 2nd	USAC	Champ	DuQuoin, Ill.	1 D	100 miles
Sept. 4th	USAC	Stock	Indpls. Fairgrounds, Ind.	1 D	100 miles
Sept. 22nd	USAC	Champ	Trenton, N.J.	1 P	200 miles
Oct. 5th	USAC	Sprint	Williams Grove, Pa.	1/2 D	30 laps
Nov. 2nd	USAC	Sprint	Gardena, Calif.	1/2 D	30 laps
Dec. 6th	SCCA	Sports	Nassau, Bahamas	4-1/2 P-RC	25 laps
Dec. 8th	SCCA	Sports	Nassau, Bahamas	4-1/2 P-RC	56 laps

1964

Date	Org.	Type	Location		Distance
Jan. 26th	USAC	Sprint	Phoenix, Ariz.	1 D	50 laps
Mar. 22nd	USAC	Champ	Phoenix, Ariz.	1 P	100 miles
Mar. 29th	USAC	Sprint	Reading, Pa.	1/2 D	30 laps
Apr. 12th	USAC	Sprint	Williams Grove, Pa.	1/2 D	30 laps
Apr. 19th	USAC	Champ	Trenton, N.J.	1 P	100 miles
May 30th	USAC	Champ	Indianapolis, Ind.	2-1/2 P	500 miles
June 7th	USAC	Champ	Milwaukee, Wisc.	1 P	100 miles
June 14th	USAC	Sprint	Terre Haute, Ind.	1/2 D	30 laps
June 21st	USAC	Champ	Langhorne, Pa.	1 D	100 miles
July 4th	NASCAR	Stock	Daytona, Fla.	2-1/2 P	400 miles
July 18th	USAC	Sprint	Mechanicsburg, Pa.	1/2 D	30 laps
July 19th	USAC	Champ	Trenton, N.J.	1 P	150 miles
Aug. 22nd	USAC	Champ	Springfield, Ill.	1 D	100 miles
Sept. 7th	USAC	Champ	DuQuoin, Ill.	1 D	100 miles
Sept. 9th	USAC	Stock	Indpls. Fairgrounds, Ind.	1 D	100 miles
Sept. 13th	USAC	Stock	Langhorne, Pa.	1 D	250 miles
Sept. 26th	USAC	Champ	Indpls. Fairgrounds, Ind.	1 D	100 miles
Oct. 25th	USAC	Champ	Sacramento, Calif.	1 D	100 miles
Nov. 29th	USAC	Stock	Hanford, Calif.	1-1/2 P	200 miles

1965

Date	Org.	Type	Location		Distance
July 4th	NASCAR	Stock	Daytona, Fla.	2-1/2 P	400 miles
July 18th	USAC	Champ	Trenton, N.J.	1 P	150 miles
Aug. 21st	USAC	Champ	Springfield, Ill.	1 D	100 miles
Sept. 7th	USAC	Stock	Indpls. Fairgrounds, Ind.	1 D	100 miles
Sept. 18th	USAC	Champ	Indpls. Fairgrounds, Ind.	1 D	100 miles
Sept. 26th	USAC	Champ	Trenton, N.J.	1 P	200 miles
Oct. 10th	USAC	Midget	Terre Haute, Ind.	1/2 D	100 laps
Nov. 13th	USAC	Sprint	Gardena, Calif.	1/2 D	30 laps
Nov. 20th	USAC	Midget	Phoenix, Ariz.	1/2 D	50 laps
Nov. 21st	USAC	Champ	Phoenix, Ariz.	1 P	200 miles

1966

Date	Org.	Type	Location		Distance
Apr. 9th	USAC	Midget	Gardena, Calif.	1/2 D	50 laps
Nov. 13th	USAC	Sprint	Altamont, Calif.	1/2 P	30 laps

1967

Date	Org.	Type	Location		Distance
May 30th	USAC	Champ	Indianapolis, Ind.	2-1/2 P	500 miles
June 11th	FIA	Sports	Le Mans, France	8.35 P-RC	24 hrs.**
Aug. 19th	USAC	Champ	Springfield, Ill.	1 D	100 miles
Sept. 4th	USAC	Champ	DuQuoin, Ill.	1 D	100 miles
Sept. 17th	USAC	Stock	Milwaukee, Wisc.	1 P	250 miles

*Co-driven with Dan Gurney

Sept. 24th	USAC	Champ	Trenton, N.J.	1 P	200 miles
Oct. 1st	USAC	Champ	Sacramento, Calif.	1 D	100 miles
Oct. 11th	USAC	Sprint	Gardena, Calif.	1/2 D	30 laps

1968

May 5th	USAC	Stock	Indpls. Raceway Park, Ind.	2-1/2 P-RC	250 miles
July 7th	USAC	Champ	Castle Rock, Colo.	2.66 P-RC	150 miles
July 14th	USAC	Stock	Milwaukee, Wisc.	1 P	200 miles
Aug. 23rd	USAC	Stock	Indpls. Fairgrounds, Ind.	1 D	100 miles
Sept. 7th	USAC	Champ	Indpls. Fairgrounds, Ind.	1 D	100 miles
Sept. 13th	USAC	Stock	Cincinnati, Ohio	1/2 P	50 miles
Sept. 29th	USAC	Champ	Sacramento, Calif.	1 D	100 miles
Nov. 3rd	USAC	Champ	Hanford, Calif.	1.5 P	250 miles

1969

June 21st	USAC	Stock	Indpls. Fairgrounds, Ind.	1 D	100 miles
Aug. 3rd	USAC	Stock	Dover, Del.	1 P	200 miles
Aug. 31st	USAC	Stock	DuQuoin, Ill.	1 D	100 miles
Sept. 6th	USAC	Champ	Indpls. Fairgrounds, Ind.	1 D	100 miles
Sept. 20th	USAC	Stock	Nazareth, Pa.	1-1/8	100 miles
Oct. 5th	USAC	Stock	New Bremen, Ohio	1/2 P	100 miles
Oct. 11th	USAC	Stock	Sedalia, Mo.	1 D	100 miles
Oct. 25th	USAC	Stock	Memphis, Tenn.	1.7 P	200 miles

1970

Jan. 18th	NASCAR	Stock	Riverside, Calif.	2.6 RC	500 miles
Mar. 14th	USAC	Midget	Houston, Texas	1/5 D	100 laps
Apr. 18th	USAC	Stock	Phoenix, Ariz.	1 P	200 miles
May 3rd	USAC	Stock	Clermont, Ind.	2.5 RC	250 miles
July 4th	USAC	Stock	Cambridge Jct., Mich.	2 P	200 miles
July 19th	USAC	Stock	Dover, Del.	1 P	200 miles
Aug. 20th	USAC	Stock	Milwaukee, Wisc.	1 P	

1971

Feb. 28th	NASCAR	Stock	Ontario, Calif.	2.5 P	500 miles
Apr. 4th	NASCAR	Stock	Atlanta, Ga.	1.5 P	500 miles
Aug. 19th	USAC	Stock	Milwaukee, Wisc.	1 P	150 miles
Aug. 22nd	USAC	Dirt	Springfield, Ill.	1 D	100 miles
Oct. 23rd	USAC	Champ	Phoenix, Ariz.	1 P	150 miles

1972

Feb. 20th	NASCAR	Stock	Daytona, Fla.	2.5 P	500 miles
Mar. 5th	NASCAR	Stock	Ontario, Calif.	2.5 P	500 miles
Sept. 4th	USAC	Dirt	DuQuoin, Ill.	1 D	100 miles

1973					
Apr. 15th	USAC	Champ	Trenton, N.J.	1.5 P	150 miles
July 1st	USAC	Champ	Pocono, Pa.	2.5 P	500 miles
July 15th	USAC	Stock	Cambridge Jct., Mich.	2 P	200 miles
1974					
Mar. 3rd	USAC	Champ	Ontario, Calif.	2.5 P	100 miles
May 24th	USAC	Sprint	Indpls. Fairgrounds, Ind.	1 D	50 miles
July 21st	USAC	Stock	Cambridge Jct., Mich.	2 P	200 miles
Sept. 22nd	USAC	Champ	Trenton, N.J.	1.5 P	150 miles
Oct. 20th	USAC	Sprint	World Series of Auto Racing		50 laps
1975					
Jan. 12th		Midget	Liverpool, Australia	1/4 P	14 laps
Jan. 14th		Midget	Christchurch, N.Z.	1/4 P	8 laps
Mar. 2nd	USAC	Champ	Ontario, Calif.	2.5 P	100 miles
Mar. 9th	USAC	Champ	Ontario, Calif.	2.5 P	500 miles
Apr. 6th	USAC	Champ	Trenton, N.J.	1.5 P	200 miles
Apr. 27th	USAC	Stock	Trenton, N.J.	1.5 P	150 miles
June 8th	USAC	Champ	Milwaukee, Wisc.	1 P	150 miles
June 29th	USAC	Champ	Pocono, Pa.	2.5 P	500 miles
July 20th	USAC	Champ	Brooklyn, Mich.	2 P	200 miles
Nov. 9th	USAC	Champ	Phoenix, Ariz.	1 P	150 miles
1976					
June 6th	USAC	Stock	College Station, Texas	2 P	500 miles
July 18th	USAC	Stock	Brooklyn, Mich.	2 P	200 miles
Aug. 1st	USAC	Stock	College Station, Texas	2 P	150 miles
Aug. 1st	USAC	Champ	College Station, Texas	2 P	150 miles
Sept. 18th	USAC	Champ	Brooklyn, Mich.	2 P	150 miles
1977					
Mar. 6th	USAC	Champ	Ontario, Calif.	2-1/2 P	200 miles
May 29th	USAC	Champ	Indianapolis, Ind.	2-1/2 P	500 miles
July 3rd	USAC	Champ	Mosport, Ontario	2.459 PRC	300 km
1978					
Feb. 16th	NASCAR	Stock	Daytona, Fla.	2-1/2 P	125 miles
Mar. 12th	USAC	Stock	College Station, Texas	2 P	250 miles
Mar. 25th	USAC	Stock	Ontario, Calif.	2-1/2 P	200 miles
June 10th	USAC	Stock	Mosport, Canada	2.459 PRC	125 miles
Aug. 13th	USAC	Stock	Milwaukee, Wisc.	1 P	200 miles
Nov. 12th	USAC	Stock	College Station, Texas	2 P	250 miles

1979

Mar. 11th	USAC	Stock	College Station, Texas	2 P	250 miles
Mar. 25th	USAC	Stock	Ontario, Calif.	2.5 P	200 miles
Mar. 25th	USAC	Champ*	Ontario, Calif.	2.5P	200 miles
Apr. 8th	USAC	Champ	College Station, Texas	2 P	200 miles
June 10th	USAC	Champ	Milwaukee, Wisc.	1 P	150 miles
June 24th	USAC	Champ	Pocono, Pa.	2.5 P	500 miles
July 29th	USAC	Champ	College Station, Texas	2 P	200 miles
Aug. 18th	USAC	Stock	Milwaukee, Wisc.	1 P	200 miles
Aug. 19th	USAC	Stock	Springfield, Ill.	1 D	100 miles

1981

June 21st	USAC	Champ	Pocono, Pa.	2.5 P	500 miles

1983

Feb. 5-6th	FIA	Sports	Daytona, Fla.	3.8 P-RC	24 hrs.